Katherine Anne Porter's *Ship of Fools*

Katherine Anne Porter's *Ship of Fools*

New Interpretations and Transatlantic Contexts

EDITED BY

Thomas Austenfeld

UNT PRESS

Denton, Texas

Printed in the United States of America

10 9 8 7 6 5 4 3 2 1

Permissions:

University of North Texas Press
1155 Union Circle #311336
Denton, TX 76203-5017

The paper used in this book meets the minimum requirements of the American National Standard for Permanence of Paper for Printed Library Materials, z39.48.1984. Binding materials have been chosen for durability.

Library of Congress Cataloging-in-Publication Data

Katherine Anne Porter's Ship of fools : new interpretations and transatlantic contexts / edited by Thomas Austenfeld. -- First edition.

pages cm

Includes bibliographical references and index.

ISBN 978-1-57441-593-3 (cloth : alk. paper)

1. Porter, Katherine Anne, 1890-1980--Criticism and interpretation.
2. Porter, Katherine Anne, 1890-1980. Ship of fools. 3. Ship of fools (Motion picture)--History and criticism. I. Austenfeld, Thomas, 1960- editor.

PS3531.O752S535 2015

813'.54--dc23

2014045433

ebook: 978-1-57441-606-0

The electronic edition of this book was made possible by the support of the Vick Family Foundation.

Table of Contents

List of Images vii

List of Figures ix

List of Tables xi

Acknowledgments xiii

Introduction: New Contexts for Katherine Anne Porter's *Ship of Fools*
Thomas Austenfeld 1

Fools and Folly in Erasmus and Porter
Jewel Spears Brooker 17

"After All, What Is This Life Itself?": Humanist Contexts of Death and Immortality in Katherine Anne Porter's *Ship of Fools*
Dimiter Daphinoff 31

Paratexts and the Rhetorical Factor in Literature: Sebastian Brant and Katherine Anne Porter
Joachim Knape 49

"Before the Voyage Ended": An Examination of the Serial Publication of *Ship of Fools,* 1944–1959
Beth Alvarez 85

"Mad with Virtue and Piety": Faulkner's Ike McCaslin and Porter's Dr. Schumann
Robert H. Brinkmeyer, Jr. 113

Ship of Fools the Film: In Context
Christine Hait 127

Transnationalizing Porter's Germans in Stanley Kramer's *Ship of Fools* (1965): West and East German Responses
Anne-Marie Scholz 149

Ship of Fools: A Severe Blow to Faith
Alexandra Subramanian 169

The Weimar Moment in Katherine Anne Porter's *Ship of Fools*
Joseph Kuhn 187

Katherine Anne Porter's *Ship of Fools*: Failed Novel, Classic Satire, or Private Joke?
Darlene Harbour Unrue 213

Notes on Contributors 237

Index 239

List of Images

Image 1: Hieronymus Bosch: *The Allegory of Intemperance*, c. 1495-1500 32

Image 2: *The Ship of Fools*, p. 331 36

Image 3: *The Ship of Fools*, p. 278 37

List of Figures

Figure 1: Title page of Locher's *Stultifera Navis* (Basel 1497) 67

Figure 2: Title page of Barclay's *The Ship of Fools*, ed. Jamieson (1874) 68

Figure 3: Second title page of Brant's *Narrenschiff* (Basel 1494) 69

Figure 4: Title page of Porter's *Ship of Fools* (1962), iii 70

Figure 5: Brant's *Narrenschiff* preface (Basel 1494) 71

Figure 6: Last page of Brant's *Narrenschiff* (Basel 1494) 72

Figure 7: Spine of Porter's *Ship of Fools* (1962) and sidebar of Brant's *Narrenschiff* chapter 5 (Basel 1494) 73

Figure 8: First page of Brant's *Narrenschiff* chapter 5 (Basel 1494) 74

Figure 9: Porter's publications listed in her *Ship of Fools* (1962), ii 75

Figure 10: Dedication to Barbara Wescott in her *Ship of Fools* (1962), v 75

Figure 11: Preface of Porter's *Ship of Fools* (1962), vii 76

Figure 12: Porter's *Characters* in her *Ship of Fools* (1962), xi 77

Figure 13: Last page of Porter's *Ship of Fools* (1962), 497 78

Figure 14: The outcasts aboard the *Vera*, the dwarf Karl Glocken (Michael Dunn) and the Jewish-German salesman Julius Löwenthal (Heinz Rühmann) converse about the meaning of "Germanness" in Stanley Kramer's *Ship of Fools* (1965) 156

List of Tables

Table 1a: Serially Published Excerpts of *Ship of Fools* in Chronological Order 104

Table 1b: Serially Published Excerpts in Chronological Order, continued 105

Table 2a: Excerpts in Numerical Page Order 106

Table 2b: Excerpts in Numerical Page Order, continued 107

Table 2c: Excerpts in Numerical Page Order, continued 108

Table 2d: Excerpts in Numerical Page Order, continued 109

Acknowledgments

This volume originates with an academic conference held at the University of Fribourg (Switzerland) in May of 2012. Entitled *Narrenschiff / Ship of Fools: A Transatlantic Encounter,* the conference brought together European and American scholars in a joint, comparative endeavor. The Swiss State Secretariat for Education, Research and Innovation (SERI) provided major funding; Dr. Benedikt Hauser successfully shepherded the application. The Rectorate of the University of Fribourg, notably Rector Guido Vergauwen, provided additional funding, spectacular meeting places, and logistical support. Subsequent to the conference, outstanding papers were chosen for publication, supplemented by other essays about *Ship of Fools* on which scholars were working at the time. Karen DeVinney at the University of North Texas Press offered sound advice as the volume was being readied for publication. The readers for the Press deserve thanks for their careful comments which helped improve the text. I would like to thank all the contributors for their patience and diligence. Beth Alvarez, friend and curator *extraordinaire*, has been unfailing in her support from start to finish. My assistants Emmanuelle Bourguet and Ola Madhour provided help with the conference. In addition, I would like to thank Dr. Albert Debrunner for his expert guidance through the significant sites of Basel's humanistic heritage ranging from manuscripts to monuments.

As always, I thank Anne Marie: our conversation about Katherine Anne Porter began thirty years ago and has continued to this day.

Fribourg, February 2015

Thomas Austenfeld

Katherine Anne Porter's *Ship of Fools*

Introduction

New Contexts for Katherine Anne Porter's *Ship of Fools*

Thomas Austenfeld

Between November 1920 and October 1923, Katherine Anne Porter spent approximately seventeen months in Mexico distributed across three extended visits. Before taking her third trip, she felt sufficiently confident to proclaim that Mexico was her "familiar country" ("Why" 869). There is no question that Porter's Mexican stories and essays eventually provided her with the literary breakthrough that made her a bona-fide member of the modernist generation. In "Why I Write about Mexico," she acknowledged her hemispheric rootedness when she confessed, "[l]iterally speaking, I have never been out of America" (870). By contrast, when she left the American continent for the first time, she began an intellectual journey that resulted in a text—the novel *Ship of Fools*—which exceeds in length all of her Mexican stories and essays put together. Looking back at her arrival in Europe twenty-five years later, in 1956, she referred both to her imagined cultural innocence and political prescience when writing to her editor, "I felt the very earth of Europe shake under my feet when I stepped ashore . . . I already knew about Mussolini, and a little but not enough about Hitler" (Porter to Seymour Lawrence, May 2, 1956, *Letters* 504).[1] In retrospect, the approximately thirty-five years from 1931 to 1965, beginning with Porter's departure from Mexico and concluding with the screening of the film *Ship of Fools*, were above all a period of maturation. Porter traveled from Veracruz to Bremerhaven in 1931 without setting foot on United States territory. Beginning with the now famous log-letter to Caroline Gordon recording her initial observations aboard the ship (*Letters* 46–60), continuing with the eventual publication of the novel *Ship of Fools* in 1962, and coming to a close in 1965 with the film *Ship of Fools*, directed by Stanley Kramer, Porter's mind matured even as her novel took shape. Put differently: the education of Katherine Anne Porter during the second half of her life was always accompanied by the growth of the novel. This key period in Porter's life—roughly from her fortieth to her seventy-fifth birthday—turned out to be a period of incremental darkening of her vision in the face of political developments. These thirty-five years, however, did not induce Porter to explain "Why I write about Europe." By 1965, such an essay was no longer necessary. *Ship of Fools* had taken its place. The answers were there, but it would take another generation to untangle them.

The critical reception of *Ship of Fools* in 1962 was predictably foreshortening, in part because of the enormous anticipation that Porter and her publishers had built up over the long years of its coming to completion. Rarely had a novel by a living writer been announced and anticipated more feverishly. Yet *Ship of Fools* did not stand up well to the scrutiny brought to bear upon it by critics such as Theodore Solotaroff and Wayne Booth. After the initial excitement, a foreseeable cooling of literary emotions ensued, and critics united in voicing their sense that, in writing a large and unwieldy novel, Porter had strayed from the territory of her perfection, the finely chiseled short story.[2] The 1965 film brought her the lucrative reward she had waited for, and the remaining years of her literary life were filled with prizes and awards and some of the troubles of old age. But the commercial blandishments seemed only to add to the critical questions that had been raised. Critics expressed disappointment at the lack of accomplishment they detected in the novel, they compared it unfavorably to Porter's stories, they focused on the commercial success of the movie, or they simply could not stomach the procession of despicable characters displayed in the novel. In sum, readers and critics alike had expected *Ship of Fools* to be both the summation and the pinnacle of Porter's earlier work. It turned out not to be that at all, but rather a somewhat unwieldy text that baffled its readers.

For the thirty-year period following the film, Porter's novel has rarely received sustained attention, but since the turn of the millennium, a variety of scholars have attempted to grapple with the text in new ways. In singling out two articles and two books, I hope to show that a satisfying interpretation of the novel still eludes us, notwithstanding a variety of enlightening approaches. In 2009, Lisa Roney turned to *Ship of Fools* to build a convincing argument about received notions of health and eugenics in the modernist era, both in Nazi Germany and in the larger world. In the context of Porter's own history of chronic illness, including her battle with "the socially stigmatized tuberculosis of the early twentieth century" (104), Roney examines parallels between life in a sanatorium and aboard a ship and shows how Porter sets up dualisms and parallels that largely reflect racial, economic, and sanitary prejudices of the time. In 2007, Robert Brinkmeyer took a fresh look at the transformation of the novel's plotline into film. After chronicling Porter's many attempts at completing the text during a composition history covering nearly thirty years and linking its structural weaknesses to the author's increasing obsession with fascism in all its real and imagined forms, Brinkmeyer asks himself what attracted director Stanley Kramer to this text. Clearly, Porter's allegorical ambitions would not have appealed to him. Abby Mann, writer of the screenplay, interprets the novel more realistically than it reads in the original. Brinkmeyer concludes that nothing beyond "the most general outlines of character and plot" (76) survived into the film.

In a balanced judgment, Darlene Unrue opines in her 2005 biography of Porter that "in more ways than one *Ship of Fools* encompasses Katherine Anne's life and art ... and it folds in her external and her internal life over the course of sixty years" (*Life 257*). Janis Stout's 2013 bio-historical study of Porter's relationship to her Texas roots takes a close look at the novel in two different frames of reference. In her chapter on World War II, Stout correctly observes that the political insights proffered by the characters in the novel, set in the historical moment of 1931, came across as less than profound in 1962 (see *South* 153), and she seeks to resolve the issue of the text's genre by offering to "reconceive *Ship of Fools* as a novel about prejudice" (155). In a harsher judgment in a later chapter, "Sexual Politics and *Ship of Fools*," Stout traces Porter's confusing relationship to 1960s feminism and faults her for failing to reproduce in the novel the kind of admirable women characters and complex thinking about gender she had limned in her story "Rope" and her essay "St. Augustine and the Bullfight" (193–201). Both biographies, Unrue's more general and Stout's more particular one, do what biographies are supposed to do; that is, they look at an artist in the context of her life. But in seeking to explain the novel's repetitive scenes of unpleasant sexuality and racism with reference to Porter's life experiences, Stout's reading of the novel does not reach back into the humanistic tradition of satire or fully account for the long shadow of Porter's historical experience and literary absorption not just of Germany but of Europe in general.

Remarkably, Porter never disowned her novel. In her literary efforts, between the publication of *Ship of Fools* and her death in 1980, Porter would cast another long glance back and return to a moment some time before her departure for Europe: to the time before and after the execution of Sacco and Vanzetti in 1927. In this particular retrospect, she looked back across a period that now measured almost fifty years. When she published *The Never-Ending Wrong* in 1977, a text in which she revisited the clash of the American justice system with people willing to die for their convictions, she indicted her own country nearly as mercilessly as she had her German characters aboard the *Vera* in *Ship of Fools*. By 1977, Porter's vision of the chances that people of principle stood in the world had turned deeply pessimistic, far beyond her indictments in *Ship of Fools*. In her afterword to *The Never-Ending Wrong*, referencing specifically Emma Goldman and Prince Kropotkin but including others as well, Porter writes that she has never lost sympathy "for the cause to which they devoted their lives—to ameliorate the anguish that human beings inflict on each other—the never-ending wrong, forever incurable" ("Never-ending" 866).

In looking at the political history of Europe in the first two thirds of the twentieth century, marked by world wars and dictatorships, by displacement and persecution, by the Holocaust and, later, the Iron Curtain, one could be forgiven for turning pessimistic. Yet Porter did not merely project an emotion and reflect it in her writing; rather, she engaged deeply with the minds and writings of the Western tradition—ranging from Augustine and Erasmus via Luther and Nietzsche—that she felt had contributed to setting the terms of the discussion which she joined by writing *Ship of Fools*.[3] As I have argued before elsewhere, *Ship of Fools* was probably never intended as a novel of incident. It is a novel of ideas we can investigate (see Austenfeld 147).

The present volume, *Katherine Anne Porter's* Ship of Fools*: New Interpretations and Transatlantic Contexts*, is therefore an attempt to enlarge the terms of discussion about the novel by explicitly invoking, above all, Sebastian Brant's late medieval allegory *Das Narrenschiff / Stultifera Navis* (German: 1494, Latin: 1497) to which Porter points her readers in the novel's preface. Our approach does not begin with Porter's own world, so ably described and analyzed by her American biographers, although we arrive there in good time. This book begins instead with an inquiry into the world from which *Ship of Fools* arose and leads from there as far as the reception history of the film which it created. Our subtitle, *New Interpretations and Transatlantic Contexts,* points directly to the connections—hitherto unexplored—between Porter and Sebastian Brant, Porter's most important model among the many European minds she engaged in her thinking. Sebastian Brant's *Narrenschiff* has now been around for over 500 years; that is, ten times as long as Porter's novel. If Porter herself, in 1977, looked back fifty years to let 1927 come alive again, then this volume takes the occasion of the fiftieth anniversary of the publication of *Ship of Fools* to tackle once more the question of the novel's uncertain canonical status and to attempt a comparative reading with its Medieval and Renaissance forebears. Ships are no longer our most customary means of transportation but, as they recede into a kind of mythical past, they gain in symbolic importance. In April of 2012, half of the Western world commemorated the sinking of the *Titanic* in 1912, a ship whose story is now more than one hundred years old.

The ever-peripatetic Porter lived in Basel, Switzerland, from the first week in June to December 2, 1932, just eight months after her transatlantic crossing from Veracruz to Bremerhaven that is the kernel of the narrative constituting *Ship of Fools.* Basel, an ancient center of European humanism and of bookmaking, impressed Porter deeply. She reports that she discovered Brant's text while living in Basel. (The text was available to her in an English translation going back to an edition produced in 1509 by Alexander Barclay.) Porter's signals to her readers concerning the significance of Brant far exceed her adaptation of his title; she indicates her indebtedness to Brant especially through her brief preface, where she reports her experience of reading Brant, "I read [the text] in Basel in the summer of 1932 when I had still vividly in mind the impressions of my first voyage to Europe," and concludes with the cryptic sentence, "I am a passenger on that ship."

Seen together, these essays show Katherine Anne Porter in conversation with European minds and European politics as well as with large questions of human identity and morality, through the medium of *Ship of Fools,* apparent in ways that were perhaps not fully evident in 1962. The conversation that takes place in this book assumes its shape thanks to a half-century of critical distance. While Porter's reputation continues to rest firmly on her short stories first, her essays second, and finally on the well-established sense that she was deeply respected by her modernist (and sometime agrarian) fellow writers—among them Robert Penn Warren and Peter Taylor—for her stylistic accomplishments, this book expands and completes Porter's critical reputation significantly by placing renewed attention on the novel that troubled, agitated, fascinated, dogged, and exasperated her for the better part of thirty years.

This book enlarges our views of Porter in several significant ways. For the first time in Porter criticism, a group of scholars has taken the author's notice to readers—that she read Brant in 1932—seriously. Contributors to this volume set Porter's novel variously in current critical discourses, among them film studies, transatlantic studies, political philosophy, and interdisciplinary rhetoric. The essays resulting from these considerations expand our sense of Porter's intellectual scope considerably beyond her traditional Southern and Mexican contexts into her engagement with Europe and, through Europe, back to the ethical and moral questions that haunted her throughout her life. The collection demonstrates that *Ship of Fools* is an underrated novel: it challenges us even if, and as, we account for its acknowledged structural weaknesses. The need of readers and critics of the early sixties to see it as the culmination of Porter's work contributed to an early misunderstanding. Begun before the Nazis came to power in Germany, concluded seventeen years after the end of World War II, the novel partakes of so many historical discourses that only a multiplicity of views can come even close to doing justice to its complexity.

*

The first two essays in this collection take the reader into increasing depths of European intellectual history and the potential to read *Ship of Fools* through hitherto untried connections. Jewel Spears Brooker lays out the clear contrast between the uses of folly in Desiderius Erasmus and Katherine Anne Porter. Where Erasmus seeks to teach and to mend character by gentle satire, Porter caricatures her fools and ridicules her specific characters instead of just their faults. Brooker concedes that Porter knew and understood Erasmus well, but that her modernist mind was finally unable to share his humanist world view. Brooker then turns her critical eye to the two writers' portrayal of children: Erasmus was at bottom an educator who saw potential in the shaping of human minds, whereas Porter's twins Ric and Rac are already beyond shaping. Dimiter Daphinoff invites us into the intellectual universe around the year 1500 by considering Sebastian Brant, Thomas More, Desiderius Erasmus, and even Hieronymus Bosch with respect to the moral certainties from which they drew their authority. When humanists exposed the follies of their contemporaries and illustrated their abusive practices, whether in the realms of sexuality, gluttony, or pride, they felt free to let their literary or artistic subjects fail, go to hell, or otherwise flounder, because they were able to offer an alternative vision, be it Christian or humanist, as a remedy open to all. Porter's characters, by contrast, subject to identical sins, have no such hope. Their hopelessness makes their illusions all the more affecting, and their fear of death is correspondingly stronger in the absence of any assurance about an afterlife.

The next two essays focus on the material text itself and the manner in which it communicates to and with the reader. Joachim Knape, editor of the scholarly edition of Sebastian Brant's German text of the *Narrenschiff*, performs a rhetorical analysis on the paratexts of the first publication of *Ship of Fools* in 1962. He shows how the deliberate intertextual connections between Porter's work and Brant's *Narrenschiff* both direct and mislead the modern reader, especially so in the publisher's use of an adapted Medieval ornament for the spine of the book. When approached in this rhetorical and semiological manner, Porter's book again emerges as concerned primarily with *telling*, while Brant's priority was *arguing*. Knape continues to carefully delineate the differing and, in part, contradictory messages that both Porter and Brant communicate on the rhetorical and on the poetical levels of their texts. He demonstrates that Porter's efforts at verisimilitude can be fruitfully analyzed with the tools of rhetoric. Next, Beth Alvarez traces the complex publication history of *Ship of Fools* in the periodical publications of excerpts ranging from 1944 to 1959. She effectively reconstructs what Porter planned to do, how she adapted some of her characters and the various foci of the longer work, how and when she changed characters' names and hence their functions in the plot, and even the degree to which Porter already saw a film script as a distinct possibility as early as 1943, as her correspondence with a representative of Paramount Pictures reveals. The history of the serial publications documented by Alvarez may well help to reconcile today's readers with the episodic nature of *Ship of Fools.*

No matter how much Porter either knew, intuited, or eventually learned about Europe, she remained a child of the South. Robert H. Brinkmeyer's essay is therefore an important anchor in this collection. Southern modernists—and here Faulkner and Porter meet on common ground—struggled mightily with values and their corruption. In a largely secular universe, "values" need not denote an adherence to transcendental assurances, but the term certainly serves to suggest what kinds of principles of human behavior are embodied in the characters' actions. In this kind of investigation, the manner in which humanist and modernist texts, respectively, foreground values is of paramount importance. Ike McCaslin's noble principles about historical guilt and its expiation through the repudiation of ill-gotten property ultimately damage his humanity. Brinkmeyer carefully delineates the price of principled behavior in McCaslin so as to complicate our received image of Dr. Schumann, who is often uncritically considered the moral center of *Ship of Fools.* Dr. Schumann's principles so effectively remove him from human connections that he loses empathy and the fullness of potential humanity. As Brinkmeyer demonstrates, Dr. Schumann fails repeatedly when presented with opportunities for principled practice, such as a distasteful conversation about Jews at the captain's table and his half-willing amorous involvement with La Condesa. Porter does not condemn Dr. Schumann entirely, but she shows him to be as flawed, in many ways, as the other characters on the ship.

The general public knows *Ship of Fools* the film, not necessarily the novel. Two complementary essays trace the novel's afterlife in the film by the same name. From an American point of view, Christine Hait specifically addresses the cinematic contexts of Porter's writing life as she examines the 1965 film in its own historical moment. Stanley Kramer's career as director, his collaboration with screenwriter Abby Mann, the manner in which Americans in 1965 looked back at the Holocaust, and the degree to which Porter approved the plot changes from novel to film all emerge as important considerations. Competing directly with *The Sound of Music* and *The Pawnbroker*, *Ship of Fools*—in black and white—had to carve out a space in the crowded production scene of the mid-sixties. Hait makes the chorus of the film's contemporary American reviewers come to life again as the film develops its own aesthetic history in some ways apart from the novel that inspired it. Given filmic conventions, the star-crossed lovers—the doctor and La Condesa—inspire considerably more sympathy on the screen than in the text.

From a European point of view, Anne-Marie Scholz brings transnational theory to bear on the film and inquires into director Kramer's decisions concerning the transformations of Porter's characters. Given the seemingly permanent separation of East and West Germany from 1961 onwards, and in accordance with the increasing ideological differences between the two German states at the time, the reception of a film portraying Germany's Nazi past was quite different in the two Germanys. West German reviewers deplored the film's stereotypes, while East German critics tended to accept some of the characters as credible.

Alexandra Subramanian takes us into Porter's private thoughts. The "blow to faith" to which Subramanian refers in her title, indebted to a letter Porter wrote to Albert Erskine in 1941, is in reality the final stripping away of romantic conventions that so often kept writers from uncensored description. The unvarnished portrayal of sex, greed, prejudice, the mistreatment of Jews and the handicapped, in short, the inhuman behavior of the sorry lot of human beings on the upper deck of the *Vera*—excepting only its few decent passengers—nauseated not only Porter's readers but led to a crisis inside the publishing house of Little, Brown as well. Through a study of her letters to trusted friends and to her publisher Seymour Lawrence, Subramanian traces Porter's few, frank admissions about the vagaries of her own life from childhood through several marriages to the process of writing *Ship of Fools.* As Subramanian demonstrates, Porter is careful to show that the same passengers who inspire revulsion in the reader often reveal traumatic experiences in their own past, either in interior monologue or in unguarded admissions to fellow passengers. Cruelty, in *Ship of Fools*, is not graced with beauty but is shown in all its unvarnished reality. Porter's willingness to face humanity's shortcomings directly, Subramanian argues, reveals her devil-may-care honesty.

The two concluding essays of the volume recontextualize Porter's novel with respect to contemporary history and to genre. Joseph Kuhn urges us to reconsider the received historical interpretation of *Ship of Fools* as an all-too-obvious indictment of evil, German callousness, or Nazi aberrations. Beyond this, Kuhn argues, the action of the novel, set as it is in the late summer of 1931, prompts us to see it as a portrayal of late Weimar Germany. This premise lets the supposed allegorical character of the text recede into the background while bringing the characteristic features of a social or philosophical novel to the fore. The Weimar ship of state, then, according to Kuhn, is suggested in the figures of Captain Thiele and Dr. Schumann, illustrations of the hapless chancellors of disintegrating Weimar Germany. The intellectual conservatism and authoritarianism of prominent Weimar thinkers such as Carl Schmitt and Martin Heidegger, Kuhn reminds us, is different from straight National Socialist thought, though the one may lead to the other. A republic in crisis, then: this is how the *Vera* may be seen. Its proto-Nazis, Lizzi Spöckenkieker and Herr Rieber, Kuhn notes, are made ridiculous. The Weimar conservatives are trying to hold the center together—and they prove unable to preserve it.

Darlene Harbour Unrue's essay concludes the book by revealing biographical details of Porter's life to enlarge our possible answers to the question of the text's genre. Is it a novel, a satire, or a private joke? It is all three, of course, in ways that are richer than we previously imagined. As Unrue explains, Porter herself rejected "allegory" but favored "satire" as a mode that would explain the workings of her novel. In illustrative detail, Unrue explains Porter's choices of many of the key names for the novel's characters, choices with which she settles old scores—especially with former lovers or ex-husbands—even while underlining the missed opportunities of some characters for a nobler destiny. And Porter did not exclude herself from scorn, as the partial portrayals of herself in Jenny, Frau Rittersdorf, and La Condesa make clear.

In a recent conversation, Umberto Eco rephrased an observation that T. S. Eliot made at the beginning of the modernist movement in "Tradition and the Individual Talent": "A masterpiece isn't a masterpiece until it is well known and has absorbed all the interpretations to which it has given rise, which in turn make it what it is" (Eco 157). By this definition, *Ship of Fools* could not yet have been a "masterpiece" when it appeared in 1962. In our own time, however, it challenges us anew to look beyond its early dismissals. The essays in this volume are evidence of the complexity of contexts in which Katherine Anne Porter's only novel can live and have its being.

*

While the novel was thirty years in the making, readers can only truly begin tracing its history and literary impact since its publication. Before launching into the critical essays, then, it is worth recalling briefly the historical moment in 1962 into which the book was originally received. A glance at any encyclopedia will remind us of the truly dramatic political and social events that dominated the year: astronaut John Glenn was the first American to orbit the earth, James Meredith became the first black student at the University of Mississippi, Marilyn Monroe died, and Pope

John XXIII convened Vatican II. Literary culture was in transition: while John Steinbeck received the Nobel Prize for literature in 1962, the year also saw the publication—*inter alia*—of Betty Friedan's *The Feminine Mystique.* Among the contenders for the National Book award that year were Richard Yates's *Revolutionary Road,* Joseph Heller's *Catch-22* and Walker Percy's *The Moviegoer.* In the realm of nonfiction, Thomas S. Kuhn's *The Structure of Scientific Revolutions* along with Michael Harrington's *The Other America: Poverty in the United States* and Rachel Carson's *Silent Spring* challenged Americans to rethink their assumptions about scientific progress, the scourge of poverty, and the man-made destruction of the natural environment. Given this cornucopia of choices for prominent books published in 1962, it is all the more surprising to see what the creators of the highly popular TV series *Mad Men* did in their second season, which aired in 2008. *Mad Men* prides itself on its solid historical research even while heavily ironizing popular culture for entertainment purposes. In the episode "Six Month Leave,"[4] the character Betty Draper has just told her husband that he does not need to come home for a while, as their marital crisis is deepening. In this particular storyline, Marilyn Monroe has been found dead the same morning. Betty is at home, subdued, drinking alone and defrosting the fridge. Clearly, she is as unsettled as the environment around her. The sham suburban stability of the late fifties is crumbling into the social unrest of the early sixties. Betty listens to the radio briefly, but turns off the news and switches to classical music. As she sits on the sofa and opens a book, we recognize it as Katherine Anne Porter's *Ship of Fools.* In our day, then, popular culture has—with a wink—caught up with the significant legacy of Porter's novel. Isn't it time for scholarship to follow suit?

NOTES

1. *Letters of Katherine Anne* Porter, ed. Isabel Bayley. New York: Atlantic Monthly Press, 1990. 504
2. *Commentary* 35 (1963) reflects a complicated debate within the editorship of the journal itself, of which Solotaroff's review, "Ship of Fools and the Critics," *Commentary* 34 (1962): 277–86, is part. See also Booth, "Yes, but Are They Really Novels?" in *Yale Review* 51 (1962): 632–34. M. M. Liberman takes a larger historical view in "The Responsibility of the Novelist: The Critical Reception of *Ship of Fools*," *Criticism* 8 (1966): 377–88.
3. Augustine of Hippo, of course, was of North African origin, a region at that time under the rule of Rome. I am using "Western tradition" in an inclusive sense.
4. Season two, episode nine, Ch. 1 Title 6, 7:53 to 8:23

Works Cited

Austenfeld, Thomas. *American Women Writers and the Nazis: Ethics and Politics in Boyle, Porter, Stafford, and Hellman.* Charlottesville and London: University Press of Virginia, 2001.

Brinkmeyer, Robert H., Jr. "*Ship of Fools*: From Novel to Film." *Twentieth-Century American Fiction on Screen*, ed. R. Barton Palmer. Cambridge: Cambridge University Press, 2007. 65-77.

Eco, Umberto, and Jean-Claude Carrière. *This Is Not the End of the Book.* A conversation curated by Jean-Philippe de Tonnac, trans. Polly McLean. London: Vintage, 2012. Originally published as *N'espérez pas vous débarrasser des livres* (Paris: B. Grasset, 2009).

Mad Men, Seasons 1–4. Created by Matthew Weiner. Perf. Jon Hamm, Elisabeth Moss, January Jones. Lions Gate Home Entertainment UK, 2011. DVD.

Porter, Katherine Anne. *Collected Stories and Other Writings.* New York: Library of America, 2008.

———. *Letters of Katherine Anne Porter*, ed. Isabel Bayley. New York: Atlantic Monthly Press, 1990.

———. "The Never-Ending Wrong." *Collected Stories and Other Writings.* 830-866.

———. "Why I Write About Mexico." *Collected Stories and Other Writings.* 869-870.

Roney, Lisa. "Katherine Anne Porter's *Ship of Fools*: An Interrogation of Eugenics." *Papers on Language and Literature* 45, no. 1 (2009): 82–107.

Stout, Janis. *South by Southwest: Katherine Anne Porter and the Burden of Texas History.* Tuscaloosa: University of Alabama Press, 2013.

Unrue, Darlene. *Katherine Anne Porter: The Life of an Artist.* Jackson: University Press of Mississippi, 2005.

Fools and Folly in Erasmus and Porter

Jewel Spears Brooker

In the articulation of her literary ancestry, Katherine Anne Porter created a place of honor for Erasmus, and in her personal canon, she made room at the top for *The Praise of Folly.* She told her nephew that she had been formed by Erasmus "from her tenth year" (*Letters* 415). In 1932, she was reading him in Basel, and on June 19, 1941, she signed a contract with Doubleday to write his biography. After the publication of *Ship of Fools,* she reiterated her admiration, hinting that her representation of folly was inspired by his. Porter was drawn to Erasmus in large part because of his moral imagination. Both were keen observers of human nature and both considered folly to be endemic in the human condition. But they present strikingly different concepts of folly. For Erasmus, folly is foolishness, and although it is the butt of his satire, he generally finds it amusing. For Porter, on the other hand, folly is innate wickedness. When writing of ordinary human life in *The Praise of Folly,* he is tolerant and urbane; in contrast, in *Ship of Fools,* she is harsh and scornful. Unlike Porter, Erasmus actually likes his fools, and far more than she, he identifies with them in their folly.

My thesis is that although Porter was drawn to Erasmus because of his moral seriousness, she was unable to share his conclusions because she held an opposite view of human nature. The optimistic view of

Erasmus, explicit in his educational treatises and his debates with Luther, is that folly can be alleviated by education. He based his life's work on the idea that, though fallen, humankind retains the capacity for moral improvement. The darker view of Porter, evident in *Ship of Fools* and her appreciation of Augustine, is that folly is far more intractable. On July 14, 1947, she wrote to Andrew Lytle that "man . . . loves evil and cannot live without it." Porter's view is reflected in a remark by Frau Hutten in *Ship of Fools*: "there are many evil people in this world, many more evil than good . . . evil by nature, by choice, by deepest inclination, evil all through" (*SF* 294). Dr. Schumann, similarly, maintains that even the best people, in their hearts, sympathize "with the criminal because he really commits the deeds we only dream of doing" (*SF* 294). The contrasting views of Porter and Erasmus can be seen in their different approaches to characterization. In *The Praise of Folly*, Erasmus uses satire; in *Ship of Fools*, Porter uses caricature. In an excellent discussion of Porter's use of caricature, Thomas Walsh argues that although her occasional use of caricature in the short fiction is effective, it results in cardboard one-dimensional characters when extended to her long novel (212–13).

As a technique for criticizing character, caricature is often associated with satire, but they are not identical. Satire is normally directed towards intellectual or moral faults, or towards bad behavior. It points to things that can be corrected, and generally speaking, it is impersonal, directed at the sin, not the sinner, and directed at what is shared by many or most. The opposite is true of caricature. It is usually focused on physical characteristics, such as bow legs, a fat stomach, unruly hair, or a crooked nose. Caricature is directed towards the individual, emphasizing his difference, what makes him unique. These principles were noted by the dean of English satirists in "Verses on the Death of Dr. Swift," where he says of himself:

> Yet, Malice never was his Aim;
> He lash'd the vice, but spar'd the Name.
> No Individual could resent,
> Where Thousands equally were meant.

His Satyr points at no Defect,
But what all Mortals may correct; . . .
He spar'd a Hump or crooked Nose,
Whose owners set not up for Beaux. (ll. 459–468)

Satire, as Swift points out, is not malicious. The purpose is to correct, to educate, to encourage moral improvement; the purpose of caricature, on the other hand, is to dehumanize, to humiliate and mock. Satire is associated with redemption, but caricature with rejection. Caricature is best suited for short pieces in which the emphasis is on the surface. As Walsh points out, it is not suited for in-depth probing of character (212–14). Stout makes a similar point, arguing that, unlike the characters in Porter's short stories, the characters in *Ship of Fools* are static, displaying little or no growth (213). Porter's reliance on caricature, furthermore, undercuts her ability to deal with her announced theme of human depravity, for caricature by definition strips characters of complexity. By reducing her characters to cartoonish versions of themselves, she greatly diminishes the possibility of probing the mystery of evil.

There can be no doubt that Porter understood the distinction between satire and caricature. In *Ship of Fools*, Jenny Brown, a character modeled on Porter herself, is an artist, and one of her specialties is caricature. She enjoys sketching her lover, David, in portraits that double not only his age, but also the size of his chin and stomach. As she adds "a roll of fat across the base of his skull," she exults in her handiwork, referring to her drawing as "the execution of a little murder." As she lingers over David's symbolic corpse, she wears an expression of "sweet serenity" (*SF* 339). As Walsh points out, Porter uses caricature here and elsewhere as a means of conveying unexpressed hatred between the sexes (206-07).

The purpose of *The Praise of Folly*, in contrast, is not to tear down, but to mend. In a letter written in May 1515 to his friend Martin Dorp, Erasmus defended the *Folly* by insisting that a satirist should not only criticize faults, but also supply the moral reference point that can be used to correct them.

> In whatever books I've published, I always aimed exclusively at the same single objective, to do some good by my efforts. . . . In the *Enchiridion*, I laid out very simply the pattern of a Christian life; in my little book on *The Education of a Christian Prince*, I declared directly the things that a prince ought to be taught. . . . And now Folly says, though jokingly, precisely the same thing as the *Enchiridion*. I wanted to mock, not to attack; to benefit, not to wound, to comment on men's manners, not to denounce them. (229, 231)

The *Enchiridion* (1504), which has the English title *Handbook of the Christian Soldier*, is Erasmus' most representative and perhaps greatest work. Intended as a spiritual guide for educated laymen, it presents his argument that the *philosophia Christi*, the philosophy of Christ, is the best guide to life. The goal of improving the mind and the quality of life by studying ancient texts was the essence of Renaissance humanism. In the words of Robert M. Adams:

> Its basic concern is several potentials of the human mind—to learn and communicate approximate truths, to govern some part of itself and the world outside it, to reach agreement on the rudiments of civilized existence. (326)

Erasmus expanded this concept to include the study of the New Testament and the writings of early Christians. He wrote extensively about the use of Scriptures and classical texts in the education of young boys.

Northern humanists such as Erasmus and Brant were influenced primarily by classical and Biblical texts. Porter and her fellow modernists knew the classics, but they were also influenced by the study of (at least the awareness of) Darwin, Nietzsche, Freud, and Frazer, and by the death of liberal humanism associated with their work. In *Ship of Fools*, as shown in the work of Joan Givner, Janis Stout, and Thomas Austenfeld, she shows a simultaneous fascination with Renaissance humanism and twentieth-century violence. Although she was drawn to Erasmus' belief in grace, she could not make it her own. Her attraction to humanism stems from what Walsh refers to as the illusion of Eden. This longing for a simpler world pervades the Miranda stories, but even there, as Darlene Unrue suggests, it is undercut by awareness of twentieth-century history. This tug between humanism and modernism, between idealism and realism, results in a tension that is one of the strengths of such gems of fiction as "Flowering Judas," "Old Mortality," and "Pale Horse, Pale Rider." The diminution of this tension is one of the weaknesses of *Ship of Fools.*

The divergence in the concept of folly in Erasmus and Porter can be illustrated by looking at their views of childhood. Erasmus believed that the nature of a child could be re-formed through education. His passion for the classics was related to his conviction that ancient virtue could be a model for modern virtue. He published the first Greek edition of the New Testament and the first critical editions of several classical Greek texts, often printed on facing pages with Latin translations so that they could be read by his contemporaries. He also produced critical editions of the early church fathers—not only the Latin figures, but also the previously untranslated Greek fathers. These scholarly editions have been superseded, but appearing at the intersection of the medieval and modern worlds, they did much to re-shape the mind of Europe.

Erasmus wrote five influential treatises on educational theory, used by teachers throughout Europe in his own day and still read in colleges of education. The Cleanth Brooks and Robert Penn Warren of his day, he wrote textbooks in the humanities that were widely used for over a generation. He transformed university education by challenging the scholasticism that had dominated European universities for centuries. His treatise, *Early Liberal Education for Children* (1509), is a classic, and his books for adolescents, such as *Good Manners for Boys* (1530), are full of practical wisdom. His pedagogical passion is also reflected in his handbooks, including his guide for rulers, *The Education of a Christian Prince*, and his manual for the ordinary Christian, the *Enchiridion.* This commitment to education is the essential backdrop for *The Praise of Folly* (1511).

The Folly is a mock-encomium spoken by the goddess Folly. Despite the fact that she is universally adored, Folly feels that she has been insufficiently praised, so to right this wrong, she gives an elaborate speech praising herself. In the first part, where the satiric butt is primarily everyman, universal human nature, the tone is tolerant, evoking amusement, but not contempt or scorn. In the latter part, where the butt includes grammarians and theologians (intellectuals like himself), the tone deepens without sacrificing its humorous edge. In the letter to Dorp, Erasmus maintains that humor is essential in his pedagogy:

> Horace reminds us . . . : "Telling the truth in a joke–what's wrong with it?" . . . Lucretius tells us that doctors rub a bit of honey on the rim of a cup from which a patient is to drink a bitter dose. (231)

He adds that his decision to don the mask of Folly was at bottom pedagogical: "I felt I had found a way to insinuate myself into diseased minds, and minister to them under the guise of pleasure" (231). Erasmus grants the Augustinian doctrine that children incline towards selfishness, but denies that this inclination is determinative. He argues forcefully that the nature of children can be re-shaped by having them read the classics and the New Testament under the supervision of a loving teacher.

Porter's view of human nature is directly stated in essays from the 1940s and 1950s and further illustrated in her portrayal of children in *Ship of Fools*. In one of her most revealing essays, "St. Augustine and the Bullfight" (1955), she recalls her first bullfight. She disliked violence and especially the idea of killing animals for sport. Much to her surprise, she found that she was thrilled at the danger and the violence of the kill. Her conclusion, confirmed by reading St. Augustine's *Confessions*, is that human beings are only superficially shaped by their environment. In certain circumstances, the facade of civility collapses and they experience an exhilaration that unmasks their true nature. In "Marriage Is Belonging" (1951), Porter claims, as Augustine does, that one can learn a great deal about human nature by observing children. Children "are human nature in essence, without conscience, without pity, without love, without a trace of consideration for others, just one seething cauldron of primitive appetites" (*CE* 190). This view of children can be seen in two of the most striking characters in *Ship of Fools*, the six-year-old twins, Ric and Rac. These little ones do not reflect an Erasmian concept, but an extreme Augustinian one.

Ric and Rac, the twin children of the Spanish dancers Manolo and Lola, are portrayed as incarnations of evil. They have been subjected to vicious beatings by their parents, leaving them howling in pain (*SF* 360), but given Porter's doctrine of innate depravity, the evil pre-existed the abuse and would outlast it. Even before they are old enough to understand the difference between right and wrong, they are so depraved that neither love nor education can touch them. Their wickedness is discussed by the other passengers and by many Porter critics. As remarked by the most perceptive person on board the *Vera*, Dr. Schumann, these six-year-olds are "little monsters," having "evil . . . in the egg of their souls" (*SF* 198). When La Condesa smiles at them, they stare at her "with utter malignance" (*SF* 198). They steal her pearl necklace, not because they have any use for it, but out of sheer malice, and they throw it overboard. They deliberately pour ink on the carpet in the writing room; they toss Frau Rittersdorf's pillow overboard, and try to do the same with the ship's cat. When Dr. Schumann steps in to save the cat, he finds himself looking with "dismay at their blind, unwinking malignance, their cold slyness" (*SF* 112). Father Garza refers to them as "devil-possessed," and Dr. Schumann responds with a question, "are they real devils who can take any shape, or [do they] make themselves invisible for their deeds of darkness?" (*SF* 318). Undeterred by their failure to kill the cat, Ric and Rac throw the Huttens' bulldog Bébé overboard.

But it is not just what they *do* that is reprehensible; it is what they *are*. When La Condesa expresses hope that the "little criminals" might grow out of it, Dr. Schumann observes that "Nothing of the sort will happen with these" children (*SF* 198). To her protest that "they are only children," the good doctor remarks that Ric and Rac are possessed by the devil. Father

Garza suggests that perhaps it is best not to exaggerate their wickedness, but instead to give them a good whipping, and Dr. Schumann responds, "I wish it might be so simple" (*SF* 319). Porter is relentless in portraying the little ones as malignant through and through. The other passengers secretly wish that Ric and Rac would fall overboard, and Porter's narrator piles on by describing them as "outside the human race" (*SF* 330). They are unredeemable because in Porter's caricature of childhood, they are static and one-dimensional, incapable of the development we see in the child Miranda in the Texas stories.

Another striking contrast with earlier concepts of childhood is the fact that these little demons are highly sexualized. The "fierce little faces" of the male Ric and the female Rac are "exactly alike except for the mysterious stigmata of sex" (*SF* 112). Porter repeatedly emphasizes their unity as twins. They are "of one mind and spirit," and they "lived twined together in a state of intense undeclared war with the adult world—or rather, with the whole world, for they did not like other children, or animals, either" (*SF* 71). They are often portrayed as entwined, entangled, as a single two-headed monster with four legs and four arms, an image that recalls Iago's dirty joke: "your daughter and the Moor are now making the beast with two backs" (*Othello* I.1.126). In the lifeboat, Ric and Rac are presented as "all tangled up giggling in the darkness. . . . [They] fought furiously, knees in ribs, claws in hair; the pain they inflicted on each other had a strong undertow of pleasure" (*SF* 195-96). After a beating by their parents, they crawl into bed and "lay there half naked, entangled like some afflicted misbegotten little monster in a cave, exhausted, mindless" (*SF* 360). As Walsh points out, Porter portrays these masochistic children as miniature adults. They ape the adults around them, demonstrating "the hostile, bestial, and incestuous character of . . . sexuality as Porter sees it" (210).

The bright line separating the sixteenth-century Erasmus and the twentieth-century Porter can be partially illuminated by contrasting their respective intellectual milieus. For him, it was northern humanism and the Protestant reformation. For her, it was the collapse of liberal humanism, the birth of modernism, and two world wars. In the late nineteenth century, under the influence of Darwin, social scientists began using evolutionary models in accounting for human behavior. In regard to children, no one was more important than Freud. Until he published his *Three Essays on the Theory of Sexuality* in 1905, children were regarded as innocent, as in Wordsworth's "Immortality Ode," and asexual, as in Coleridge's "Frost at Midnight." Because he was a physician, Freud focused on abnormal children, with emphasis on sexuality and violent emotions. While many of his theories, including the psycho-sexual development of children and the Oedipus complex, have been rejected, his insistence on the role played by sex and violence in childhood development permeated other fields, producing a shift in consciousness. Anthropologists, for example, suggested parallels between the development of individuals and of culture, thus associating childhood with primitive society and children with savagery. From one point of view, Porter's characterization of the evil twins is an extreme reflection of Augustine's theory of original sin; from another, it is like a composite snapshot of the dark views of childhood in the new social sciences.

The modernist divide separating Porter from Erasmus is also striking in regard to the relation between the sexes. Erasmus smiles with us and with Folly as she claims that a certain amount of imbecility is essential in all matters related to sex.

> What man would put his neck into the yoke of matrimony if . . . he first counted . . . the inconveniences of the estate; or what woman would let a man approach if she had fully calculated the pains and perils of childbirth, to be followed by the trouble of rearing a child? . . . would a woman who has gone through this procedure once ever want to do it again, unless my servant "Forgetfulness" were at hand to help her? (13)

Folly goes on to explain that only she can induce people to "make babies."

> Let me ask you if the head or the face or the breast or the hands or the ear, . . . which are . . . the more seemly parts of the body, actually beget either gods or man? No. . . . it's that other part, so stupid or even ridiculous that it can't be named without raising a snicker, that propagates the human race. (12-13)

Folly reminds the reader that as queen of foolishness, she helps to preserve marriage by encouraging the endless stream of flattery and games that enable the wife to please the husband and vice versa (21–22).

In Porter, the relation between the sexes is also seen in terms of play, but in her work, the game is deadly. In "The Necessary Enemy" (1948), she maintains that "the ugliest dilemma of marriage" is that it includes not only love, but hatred (*CE* 182). "The hatred in marriage," she claims, is "as real as love is real" and "has the advantage . . . because it works on a blind instinctual level, it is lawless." Her thesis is that hatred is part of the mysterious realm of sex; in marriage, hatred "is the necessary enemy and ally" of love (*CE* 186). In another essay, "Marriage Is Belonging" (1951), Porter associates marriage with cannibalism, "an ecstatic, reciprocal cannibalism" (*CE* 188) in which the male and female try to absorb and devour each other. In *Ship of Fools*, the relationship between Jenny and David is ambivalent on both sides, including both love and hate, and in addition, a cannibalistic inclination. "Boy eats girl and vice versa" (*CE* 188).

The motif of sexual relationships that include mutual hatred and the desire to absorb or kill one's partner is perfectly caught in Jenny's memory of a scene she glimpsed from a bus while passing through an Indian village in Mexico.

> As the bus rolled by, Jenny saw a man, and a woman, some distance from the group, locked in a death battle. They swayed and staggered together in a strange embrace, as if they supported each other; but in the man's raised hand was a long knife, and the woman's breast and stomach were pierced. The blood ran down her body and over her thighs, her skirts were sticking to her legs with her own blood. She was beating him on the head

> with a jagged stone, and his features were veiled in rivulets of blood. They were silent, and their faces had taken on a saintlike patience in suffering, abstract, purified of rage and hatred in their one holy dedicated purpose to kill each other. Their flesh swayed together and clung, their left arms were wound about each other's bodies as if in love. Their weapons were raised again, but their heads lowered little by little, until the woman's head rested upon his breast and his head was on her shoulder, and holding thus, they both struck again. (*SF* 144)

This unforgettable *danse macabre* is incorporated into Jenny's nightmares, but with a metamorphosis of the faces of the murderous lovers into the faces of herself and David, with "David's knife . . . raised against her pierced bleeding breast" (*SF* 145). She awakens in horror grasping her breast, almost feeling the blood. This memory of love and death, of reciprocal hatred and murder, with its phallic knife, its bloody stone, its piercing of the stomach and breast, is obviously indebted to Freud. The death ballet also points to the primitivism of the modernists which for Porter was mediated through her early experience in Mexico, a topic explored by Brinkmeyer and Titus. The scene has religious resonance as well, for the couple is participating in a rite requiring saintlike patience, a holy rite of purification which has the ultimate aim of reciprocal murder. The ritualistic nature of this performance and its linkage of sexuality and blood sacrifice connect it to the intense interest that Porter and the early modernists had in primitive religion. The text that inspired her generation's interest was Frazer's *Golden Bough*, a major reference point in Eliot (*The Waste Land*), Yeats, and Lawrence, writers whom she knew and admired. Frazer's fifteen-volume encyclopedia of religion and magic is replete with stories of fertility rites in which sexual performances ending in death are part of a commemoration of death and rebirth in nature. Frazer assembled his great catalog primarily from explorers and missionaries who had lived in primitive societies, including Spanish missionaries who lived among the Aztecs of ancient Mexico.

For Erasmus, folly, not hatred, is the necessary enemy and ally. In *The Praise of Folly*, it is foolishness that keeps us laughing and thus keeps us going. But for Porter in *Ship of Fools* (though not in her best stories), it is hatred. Both writers are indebted to St. Augustine, but whereas her view of human nature is severely Augustinian, his is only mildly so. One explanation for her darker view is that she was a witness to history in a century that was rife with corruption and violence. In inviting us, as she does, to reflect on the *Praise of Folly* and *Ship of Fools* together, she reminds us that not only children and lovers, but nations were entangled in hatred and reciprocal murder.

Works Cited

Adams, Robert M. "Draining and Filling: A Few Benchmarks in the History of Humanism," in Erasmus, *The Praise of Folly and Other Writings*. Norton Critical Edition. New York: Norton, 1989. 326-38.

Austenfeld, Thomas Carl. *American Women Writers and the Nazis: Ethics and Politics in Boyle, Porter, Stafford, and Hellman*. Charlottesville: University Press of Virginia, 2001.

Brinkmeyer, Robert H. Jr. *Katherine Anne Porter's Artistic Development: Primitivism, Traditionalism, and Totalitarianism*. Baton Rouge: Louisiana State University Press, 1993.

Erasmus, Desiderius. *The Praise of Folly and Other Writings*, trans. and ed. Robert M. Adams. Norton Critical Edition. New York: Norton, 1989.

Givner, Joan. *Katherine Anne Porter: A Life*. 1982. Rev. ed. Athens: U of Georgia P, 1991.

Porter, Katherine Anne. *Letters*, ed. Isabel Bayley. New York: Atlantic Monthly, 1990.

———. Letter to Andrew Lytle, "Bastille Day 1947." Katherine Anne Porter Papers, Special Collections and University Archives, University of Maryland Libraries.

———. *Ship of Fools*. Boston: Little, Brown, 1962.

———. "Marriage Is Belonging," in *The Collected Essays and Occasional Writings*. Boston: Houghton Mifflin, 1970. 187-92.

———. "The Necessary Enemy," in *Collected Essays*. 182–86.

———. "St. Augustine and the Bullfight," in *Collected Essays*. 91–101.

Stout, Janis P. *Katherine Anne Porter: A Sense of the Times*. Charlottesville: University Press of Virginia, 1995.

Swift, Jonathan. *The Writings of Jonathan Swift*, ed. Robert A. Greenberg and William B. Piper. Norton Critical Edition. New York: Norton, 1973.

Titus, Mary. *The Ambivalent Art of Katherine Anne Porter*. Athens: University of Georgia Press, 2005.

Unrue, Darlene Harbour. *Katherine Anne Porter: The Life of an Artist.* Jackson: University Press of Mississippi, 2005.

———, ed. *Critical Essays on Katherine Anne Porter.* New York: G. K. Hall, 1997.

Walsh, Thomas F. *Katherine Anne Porter and Mexico: The Illusion of Eden.* Austin: University of Texas Press, 1992.

"After All, What Is This Life Itself?"

Humanist Contexts of Death and Immortality in Katherine Anne Porter's *Ship of Fools*

Dimiter Daphinoff

There is a painting in the Yale University Art Gallery that gives visual expression to some of the central concerns of early modern culture which the twentieth-century American writer, Katherine Anne Porter, takes up in her novel *Ship of Fools.* As with so many of Hieronymus Bosch's works, the dating of *The Allegory of Intemperance* is uncertain, but it is generally assumed that it must have been completed some time between 1495 and 1500 as part of a triptych illustrating the Seven Deadly Sins.[1] The famous companion panel, the *Ship of Fools*, is now in the Louvre in Paris. Given the immediate European popularity of Sebastian Brant's *Narrenschiff*, published in 1494, Bosch is likely to have designed his triptych as a visual interpretation of Brant's poem.

Image 1. Hieronymus Bosch: *The Allegory of Intemperance*, c. 1495-1500

Image taken from the website of the Yale University Art Gallery, New Haven, CT. December 1, 2012.

This essay, whose starting point is a striking verbal echo of Erasmus' *Praise of Folly* in Katherine Anne Porter's *Ship of Fools*, proposes to investigate the interrelated themes of death, immortality, and folly in Porter's novel in the context of their treatment by Porter's great predecessors Brant, Erasmus, and More. It aims to show that the uncompromising indictment of the fools on board Porter's ship lacks the moral certainties that render the satires of Brant and Erasmus, in particular, effective through the alternatives they imply.

While *The Allegory of Intemperance* does not feature a ship, it presents another kind of vessel, a wine barrel on top of which sits a well-fed man with a fool's hat, a pipe, and a branch. He seems thoroughly self-satisfied and oblivious of the world around him.[2] His tub is pushed by slender naked servants who are on the point of either deserting their master or doing some mischief, as the swimmer in front of the barrel suggests—he is stealing some of his master's wine. The shore in the foreground is strewn with items of clothing. In their arrangement they appear ominous, in particular the black heap on the left that suggests, at least to the modern reader, Byron's Don Juan hiding under Donna Julia's sheets when the jealous husband takes the lovers by surprise (*Don Juan* I.137-187). The clothes point to the tent on the right-hand side of the picture in which a man and a woman are about to celebrate their union with a cup of wine. Bosch seems to suggest that while the foolish fat man on the barrel stands for the sin of gluttony, the pair in the tent represents the sin of lust (*luxuria*). What strikes the observer is the heedlessness of the glutton, who is about to fall into the sea (either owing to his sheer weight or to the envy of his underfed companions), but also the show of affection that the couple in the tent perform. Indeed, the woman turns her body slightly away from her partner and is more interested in the drink than in the prospect of an intimate embrace.

Gluttony and lust figure prominently in the catalogue of misbehavior in Sebastian Brant's *Narrenschiff* (*The Ship of Fools*).[3] The follies Brant describes are all traditional forms of transgression and sin. Many passages in Brant's poem correspond to Bosch's vision, for example the chapters on gluttony and drinking (ch. 16), on the "Power of Fools" (ch. 46) or those dealing with the dangers of lust (ch. 13, 50). An extract from chapter 108, entitled "The Schluraffen Ship," will suffice to illustrate the similarities between painting and poem:

Each port, shore we investigate
And travel far with dreadful fate,
As yet however we've not scanned
The port where we would like to land,
Our traveling will never end
For no one knows to where he'd wend.
[...]
Oh stay at home, ye men of sense
And let our fate a lesson be:
Don't go to sea with levity,
[...]
Hence fools are drowning more and more.
Let each one haste to wisdom's shore [...].
(*The Ship of Fools*, 350, 354)

Indeed, the ship bound for Narragonien ("Narragon"), the Land of Fools, is about to sink, as both Brant and his engraver make clear in chapter 103, "Of the Antichrist." The woodcut shows the ship of fools that has capsized, presided over by Antichrist, who visibly enjoys the scene, while—close to the beholder—St. Peter draws a boat to the shore.[4] And while the fools, although they are about to drown, still try to save some valuables from the sinking ship, the passengers in St. Peter's boat patiently and piously wait to be delivered. They are the unerring children of the Church, represented by St. Peter, at a time when some fools elsewhere are sailing to uncertain shores, misguided by Antichrist. Only two decades before Luther provoked the great schism, Brant viewed those who fail to place their faith in the true, i.e., in the Catholic Church, as sinners irretrievably lost.

Yet Brant's warning is nowhere more gripping than in chapter 85 ("Not Providing for Death"). As in most sections of his poem, Brant's didactic message is not all too subtle. His *memento mori* draws on the traditional dichotomy of body and soul that goes back to Plato, but seems more closely related to the medieval allegories depicting man unprepared for his ultimate destination. Brant's satire chastises in particular man's foolish hope that he might be spared:

> But folly cheats us shrewd and sly,
> That we neglect the truth each day:
> That Death won't let us tarry ay,
> Our pretty horse he'll take away,
> Our greening wreaths and garlands fair.
> [...]
> Impartially Death takes away
> The things o'er which our life holds sway.
> "You die, but you, my friend, will bide,"
> Yet no one stays a long, long tide,
> Who e'en a thousand years did stay
> Death ultimately took away. (*The Ship of Fools,* 279, 280)

To say that Brant is obsessed with death may sound exaggerated, but only if one forgets that his fools are on a voyage of perdition and that they are not shown reaching their destination, the land of *Narragon.*

Herein lies a significant difference between Brant's late medieval poem and Katherine Anne Porter's twentieth-century novel *Ship of Fools*: Porter's ship reaches her destination, Bremerhaven, though whether this is a blessing is a moot point. United despite their class divisions in their patriotism and anti-Semitism, the Germans on board the *Vera* yearn for a "Fatherland" which would soon prove worse than Sebastian Brant's Narragon.

Image 2. *The Ship of Fools*, p. 331

Image 3. *The Ship of Fools*, p. 278

In a letter from Berlin to Malcolm Cowley, dated 25 September 1931, shortly after arriving in Germany on board "a North German Lloyd tramp steamer" (Liberman 136), Katherine Anne Porter describes Germany as a country marked by the lost World War I and the harsh conditions of the Treaty of Versailles: "Here I feel the atmosphere of great poverty, strain, and thrift [...], great numbers of men in early middle age with scarred, mended heads, glass eyes, artificial legs and arms" (136). And she goes on to compare the people she meets in the streets to figures painted by Albrecht Dürer, "great masses of sculpture full of senseless energy without direction, hanging dangerously off every cornice and façade—streets like burnished iron and great platters of cheap harsh food" (137). What Porter may not have known at the time, but what has been proven since, is that some of the woodcuts in Brant's *Narrenschiff* are the work of Albrecht Dürer himself (137). That the *Ship of Fools*, like Brant's *Narrenschiff*, which Porter read in Basel in 1932, invites allegorical reading is a commonplace. Death is omnipresent in Porter, but she fails to provide the Christian alternative that Sebastian Brant obtrusively displays. On the other hand, Porter's fools also lack the consolations that the goddess Folly has in store for her followers, the happy-go-lucky fools of Erasmus' *The Praise of Folly*. The religious enthusiast Wilibald Graf seems an exception. Convinced that his God had promised him that he would see his native Germany again, Herr Graf wonders:

> What was death? Why had he been afraid? There remained the greatest reward of all: immortality for the suffering bewildered soul. Immortality. It is not a matter of belief, what is there to believe? How can anyone form even an idle wish around anything so infinitely formless? It is a matter of faith—no, a *hope*, a fixed changeless longing for a continued existence in another place, under another appearance, in a different element; continued existence at least until all questions are answered, and all unfinished things are done. (Porter 183)

Yet even Wilibald Graf has doubts: could this wish for immortality be merely a manifestation of self-love? In his yearning for relief in eternity,

Herr Graf is not alone on the ship. Although not all passengers are able (or willing) to articulate their sense of loss, they too suffer from disillusionment and frustration—the clumsy Swiss teenager Elsa as much as the bohemians Jenny and David, the middle-aged American Mrs. Treadwell as much as the childless Frau Hutten or Dr. Schumann. Maybe, thinks the dying old man in his wheelchair, "maybe heaven itself is only this: that Wilibald Graf may never once remember he was Wilibald Graf, miserable lost pilgrim in this terrible world. Is that what is meant, perhaps, by the blessed words 'forgiveness of sins'?" (183-84). Like him, most bourgeois passengers are obsessed with the idea of death, and Porter does not refrain from orchestrating their individual follies in a climactic entertainment in honor of the captain that unites the traditions of carnival and the medieval Dance of Death (*danse macabre*).

At its most drastic, death occurs when, in an allusion to the parable of the Good Samaritan (Luke 10:25-37), one of the most destitute of the travellers jumps overboard to save the life of a dog, and drowns in the event. His gesture of pity and respect for life in all its forms provokes mixed feelings: the owner of the dog, Professor Hutten, mimes incredulity ("Who could be such a fool?" [320]), the priest condemns the act as "a blamable disregard for his life, which is not his to throw away so lightly—Imagine, my dear Doctor? to save the life of a dog?" (318), while the stewardess, who is ordered to bring a bowl of broth to the dog, is scandalized: "One should be a dog in this filthy world! A rich man's dog drinking broth made from the bones of the poor. [...] And the man is dead! Dead to save the life of a dog!" (321-22). The altruism of this latter-day Good Samaritan, who saves but is not himself saved, brings together two of the novel's central concerns, death and folly, and it is typically contrasted with the wickedness of the ferocious twins Ric and Rac who, by throwing the dog into the sea, had caused the disaster in the first place.

A lighter version of the theme of death and immortality is given in the portrayal of the unnamed bride and groom, who form a contrast to the fools on the ship. Yet they, too, are fools in their self-absorption and naive expectation of enduring love. The bride shrinks from contact with the dying invalid Wilibald Graf, and

> repent[s] at once of her uncharitable feelings, [...] caused by her horror of age and ugliness and sickness and her fear of them, and her greater fear of death, which was the one alternative, the only possible escape from them. Feeling rather sensible and calm, and joyously well and immortal, she said in a dreaming voice, "I hope we die young." Her husband [...] gave her a little shake. "Die young? We'll never die. We're going to live together until the end of the world!" They laughed together for happiness, without a trace of irony, and kissed hastily and guiltily, for fear they might be seen. (439-40)

The bride and the groom would have pleased the goddess Moria in Erasmus' *Praise of Folly. Sub speciae aeternitatis*, Porter's young lovers are blind and oblivious, but at the moment of their embrace they are blissful and blessed. It is precisely because Folly has endowed them with pleasurable self-absorption and erotic desire that they can endure the general misery on board and leave the ship unscathed and unchanged, unlike the other young pair, Jenny and David, whose tense relationship recalls the couple in Hieronymus Bosch's sinister painting *The Allegory of Intemperance.*

The contrast between the two pairs of lovers in Porter's novel leads quite naturally to a discussion of some central concerns in Erasmus' *Encomium Moriae* (1511). Divided into three parts of unequal length, tone and content, *The Praise of Folly* is perhaps best known for its female speaker's unabashed self-praise as a dispenser of happiness. Starting out with the rhetorical question, "what can be sweeter or more precious than life itself?" (Erasmus 18), Folly soon repeats it emphatically in variation: "After all, what is this life itself—can you even call it life if you take away pleasure?" (19)

Attentive readers of Katherine Anne Porter's *Ship of Fools* will detect an echo of Folly's tongue-in-cheek question in Frau Schmitt's rueful confession early on in the novel: "I am tempted though I know it is a sin sometimes to ask myself—what is life but that, after all?" By "that," she has just explained, she means "only grief and disappointment" (Porter 29). Erasmus' Folly would have a remedy for the likes of Frau Schmitt, since she concurs with the latter that life, looked at squarely, is indeed "sad, cheerless, dull, insipid, and wearisome unless you season it with pleasure, that is, with the spice of folly" (Erasmus 19). Frau Schmitt, who has just lost her husband, is returning home with his coffin on board to face old age, and old age, Folly knows, is prone to infirmity and depression. Instead of brooding, the old should put their trust in her, in Folly, and thus "enjoy perpetual youth and live happily ever after" (22). If they refrain from any contact with wisdom, old people "would never feel the slightest discomfort of old age," an argument for which Moria adduces "the authority [...] of the proverb which asserts that Folly is the only means of preserving youth, otherwise so evanescent, and keeping harsh old age at a distance" (23). This is a much sounder advice, the reader is told, than to ask pagan deities or mythological figures for eternal life, for Moria asserts: "Mine are those herbs [...], mine are the magic formulas, mine is the fountain which not only recalls lost youth but also (what is even better) preserves it forever unimpaired" (24). The recipes she proposes—drinking, partying, gaming etc.—aim at dispelling the *tedium vitae* from which Frau Schmitt suffers and which gradually seizes Porter's first-class passengers. Folly, then, praises herself for holding the key to eternal youth and, by implication, to the preservation of self in a state approaching immortality

It is typical of Erasmus' text, which operates throughout with multi-layered paradox, irony, and ambiguity, that the proverbial authority on which Folly bases her promise of eternal youth derives from the Bible, as Harry Vredeveld has shown (88-91). The allusion is to Proverbs 17:22 (*KJB*, 1611): "A merry heart doeth good like a medicine: but a broken spirit drieth the bones." Medieval medical textbooks, too, defined ageing as a progressive "cooling and drying of the body" (Vredeveld 82), which ultimately leads to death, a process accelerated by such factors as grief, fear, violent emotions, and excessive mental activity—the latter a hallmark of the much derided "wisemen" in Erasmus' encomium.

The use of a biblical text to corroborate a foolish promise looks ahead to the difficult third part of Erasmus' work in which the authority of the Scriptures is adduced again, this time, however, to prove that all Christians are fools—namely in the image of Christ himself who, according to Moria, "became somehow foolish in order to relieve the folly of mortals when he [Christ] took on human nature and appeared in the form of a man" (Erasmus 130). Much depends on how one reads this last section of *The Praise of Folly.* Is it, as has been suggested, one more of Folly's abstruse jokes? (Ghose 180). The book's tripartite division, however, seems to imply a dialectic reconciliation and resolution of its parts.[5] The benevolent attitude and humorous tone of the first section is followed by a harsh critique of the social, political, and ecclesiastical élite who neglect their civic responsibilities. Victoria Kahn holds that "[t]here is no consensus of interpretation for the *Praise of Folly*" (365), yet a consensus may emerge nonetheless, one that centers on the seeming irreconcilability of the foolish acceptance of a merry life in Part One and the equally forceful negation of this world by the Christian fools in Part Three. Moria's final stance would seem to be that since the representatives of learning and power fail in their duties, a rejection of wisdom, knowledge and social involvement for the sake of self-centered pleasure is perfectly justified, but so is, on the other hand, the acceptance of Christian folly as the only path to immortality which, of course, is not of this world (see Rebhorn 473).

Erasmus' *Praise of Folly* was written in Sir Thomas More's home in London and is dedicated to him. It can be safely assumed that the two friends discussed the work in progress and enjoyed together the intellectual challenge of Moria's paradoxical encomium, a veritable *jeu d'esprit* of the kind More—a fool himself, as Erasmus' pun suggests—was to attempt only a few years later in his *Utopia* (1516).

What has More to say about death and immortality in his visionary work? If the *Utopia* is seen as, among other things, a response to Erasmus' *Moriae Encomium*, one can observe a few significant differences. In the first place, the *Utopia* proposes an alternative to the world as More's (and Moria's) contemporaries knew it: not its acceptance sweetened by folly, but a radically new world erected and inhabited by the very wisemen whom Erasmus' subversive goddess ridiculed. Thomas More replaces Erasmus' Folly by Reason, and Reason establishes—and upholds—order, equality, and justice in Utopia, which are seen as the prerequisites of happiness. Moreover, in More's vision it is Reason, not Folly, that instructs the Utopians to seek pleasure. Pleasure in Utopia can take a variety of forms, from the simple gratification of the senses (e.g. scratching) through the pleasures of procreation, to those of the mind. However, the highest form of pleasure, and hence of happiness, is the contemplation of God:

> The Utopians define virtue as living according to nature since to this end we were created by God. That individual, they say, is following the guidance of nature who, in desiring one thing and avoiding another, obeys the dictates of reason.
>
> Now reason first of all inflames men to a love and veneration of the divine majesty, to whom we owe both our existence and our capacity for happiness. Secondly, it admonishes and urges us to lead a life as free from care and as full of joy as possible and, because of our natural fellowship, to help all other men, too, to attain that end. (More 92-3)

Edward Surtz sums up the line of More's argumentation as follows:

> [...] *reason* advises and incites us to lead a life as free from care and full of joy as possible, and to show ourselves helpful, in view of the fellowship arising from nature, in obtaining the same for all other human beings. Therefore *virtue* advises and incites us to lead a life as free from care and full of joy as possible [...]. (110)

However, the rational Utopians are convinced that there would be "absolutely no place [...] left for any pleasure," if the body were not healthy and sound. Health, therefore, is indispensable for any of the myriad of pleasurable sensations that are conductive to happiness. Or, in Hythlodaeus's own words: "Health [...] gives delight to itself" and is "the foundation and basis of all pleasures" (More 99). Physical and mental health ensure a long and carefree life, though not eternal youth. But "a calm and harmonious state of the body" (99) is a precondition for longevity and the happiness of the soul. In the rational world of Utopia, death is not feared, because a long life lived in joy and fulfillment, both physical and intellectual, morphs smoothly and imperceptibly into the next. Nor is immortality an issue. Reason knows that the soul is immortal, and the Utopians take pleasure in leading a virtuous life to keep the soul ready for the world beyond.

Seen this way, both Erasmus and More concur in giving pride of place to pleasure and happiness, though they reach their conclusion from radically different points of departure. While in Erasmus it is Folly herself who preaches a life of joy and pleasure, in More it is Reason that guides the Utopians to the same goal. Is More teaching his friend Erasmus a lesson in humanism? Or is he on the contrary paying him a tribute? Or is his insistence on reasonable as opposed to foolish pleasure one more of More's puzzling ambiguities? A possible answer could be that Erasmus and More's positions are not as antithetical as would seem at a first glance. Folly's prescriptions for a life free of sadness and fear are not her last word. If one takes the final section of *The Praise of Folly* seriously, not merely as an extension of an already extended joke, then the Christian folly which Moria evokes, and the reasoned "love and veneration of the divine majesty" (More 93), which for the Utopians represents the highest form of pleasure, would lead both types of mortals to the same end: to the pleasurable preparation of the soul for its immortality in the presence of God.

Looking back from here at Katherine Anne Porter's *Ship of Fools* one realizes how bleak the modern writer's view of humankind is. Sebastian Brant's satire of man's sins and follies was, though harsh and angry, still grounded in the firm knowledge of alternative modes of life. The humanists Erasmus and More, while adding a playful intellectual dimension to their critique of human presumption and contemporary forms of social organization, worked, like Brant, within an intact framework of Christian faith. They are effective as satirists just because they assume a common ground of shared values from which to chastise deviation. Porter, on the other hand, does not propose any alternatives to folly and destruction. Her *Ship of Fools* engages in an informed dialogue with its predecessors without, however, offering the consolations the latter have in store for their Christian readers. If, therefore, Porter's novel fails as a traditional satire, it triumphs as a literary document of great intellectual integrity. It suggests that in the wake of two world wars and the collapse of religious hope, constructive satire is no longer the appropriate genre to express one's dismay and desolation at man's meaningless voyage through life.

NOTES

1. See Charles Seymour, *The Rabinowitz Collection of European Paintings.* New Haven: Yale University Art Gallery, 1961. See also Anne M. Morganstern, "The Rest of Bosch's *Ship of Fools.*" *The Art Bulletin* 66.2 (1984): 295-302.
2. See also Kay C. Rossiter, "Bosch and Brant: Images of Folly." *Yale University Art Gallery Bulletin* 34.2 (1973): 18-23.
3. Quotations from Brant's *Narrenschiff* will appear in Edwin H. Zeydel's modern translation which follows the original German text closely, unlike Alexander Barclay's version (1509), which is a free adaptation in "Chaucerian stanzas" (Zeydel 28) designed for an English public. It is likely that Katherine Anne Porter knew the nineteenth-century reprint of Barclay's work. See [Sebastian Brant], *The Ship of Fools.* Trans. Alexander Barclay. 2 vols. Edinburgh: William Paterson, 1874.
4. See also Peter Skrine, "The Destination of the Ship of Fools: Religious Allegory in Brant's 'Narrenschiff'." *The Modern Language Review* 64, no. 3 (1969): 589.
5. See also Wayne A. Rebhorn, "The Metamorphoses of Moria: Structure and Meaning in *The Praise of Folly.*" *PMLA* 89.3 (1974): 463-76.

Works Cited

The Bible. Authorized King James Version, ed. Robert Carroll and Stephen Prickett. Oxford: Oxford University Press, 1997; repr. 2008.

Brant, Sebastian. *The Ship of Fools*, trans. and ed. Edwin H. Zeydel. New York: Columbia University Press, 1944.

Byron, George Gordon. *Poetical Works*, ed. Frederick Page. Oxford: Oxford University Press, 1970.

Erasmus, Desiderius. *The Praise of Folly*, trans. and ed. Clarence H. Miller. New Haven and London: Yale University Press, 1979.

Ghose, Indira. *Shakespeare and Laughter: A Cultural History.* Manchester: Manchester University Press, 2008.

Kahn, Victoria. "*Stultitia* and *Diatribe*: Erasmus' Praise of Prudence." *The German Quarterly* 55, no.3 (1982): 349-69.

Liberman, M. M. "Some Observations on the Genesis of *Ship of Fools*: A Letter from Katherine Anne Porter." *PMLA* 84, no. 1 (1969): 136-37.

More, St. Thomas. *Utopia*, ed. Edward Surtz. New Haven and London: Yale University Press, 1964; 1978.

Porter, Katherine Anne. *Ship of Fools.* Boston and Toronto: Little, Brown, 1962.

Surtz, Edward L. "The Defense of Pleasure in More's *Utopia.*" *Studies in Philology* 46, no. 2 (1949): 99-112.

Vredeveld, Harry. "'That Familiar Proverb': Folly as the Elixir of Youth in Erasmus' *Moriae Encomium.*" *Renaissance Quarterly* 42, no. 1 (1989): 78-91.

Paratexts and the Rhetorical Factor in Literature

Sebastian Brant and Katherine Anne Porter

Joachim Knape

As a rhetorician, I did not take Thomas Austenfeld's invitation to compare Sebastian Brant's *Narrenschiff* (1494) and Katherine Anne Porter's *Ship of Fools* (1962) for granted. When working within a strictly defined theoretical framework of rhetoric, it is not obvious that rhetorical analysis is appropriate for the fields of art and literature. If it is, then such an analysis must deal with a series of specific theoretical problems and challenges. In what follows, I will raise a few fundamental questions:

- Is literature a communicative fact?
- What relationship does rhetoric have with the phenomenon of licensed communication?

- To what extent can we speak about a rhetorical case (*causa rhetorica*) in literary texts?

And finally, a methodological problem:

- How can we compare two literary works whose authors (Sebastian Brant and Katherine Anne Porter) came from not only very different times, but were also working with two extremely different aesthetics?

My essay is an attempt to find initial answers to these questions. In this introduction I can only briefly touch on the problems listed above; I have written more extensively elsewhere.[1] First, the general question about communication. Within the construct of modern aesthetics, it is not self-evident that literature is both an art and a communicative fact. Since the beginning of the so-called Art Period in the eighteenth century and the emergence of the *l'art pour l'art* ideology, an idea of the *autonomy* of artistic work has developed. This has culminated in the contemporary idea of *performance*: that the meaning and purpose of an artistic work only emerges in the moment of its *performance*. Artistic messages are thus a phenomenon of a situatively linked *emergence*.[2] With reference to literature, this means that poets write only for themselves and then leave us their texts as mere stimuli for our own individual games. In this way, perhaps literature that has been fully detached from its author, like every other form of art, leads to an original experience of being.

If this is the case, there is in fact no communicative interaction between author and reader, but rather only a connection between the artistic object and its observer, or between the text and its reader. Some literary theorists have gone so far as to claim that the text "speaks" to us as a "narrator"; that the text only really comes into being when read "or, to be brief, that the narrator is the reading."[3] This kind of metaphorical talk about communicative contexts is not everyone's cup of tea, even if we can guess what is meant by it. What is certainly true is that wonderful things can happen in the individual reading of a text that no author can predict or that his text can predetermine. But this depends on the cognitive projections of each individual reader. Naturally, we also have to consider the seismographic theory of literature (as I'd like to call it) which assumes that artists merely absorb certain "vibrations" in their environment and encode them according to a sort of will-less *écriture automatique.*

If this were indeed the only possible way to view literature, then it would most certainly not be a proper object for rhetorical study. In this case, the rhetorician would have to leave everything that we call *literature* today to the field of literary criticism. When a rhetorician engages literary text genres, he must take a different approach. Rhetorical analysis begins with at least two assumptions: one, that literature always exists in a communicative context (that someone wants to communicate with someone else and chooses literary forms to do so) and two, that there is a calculated communicative power and certain communicative achievements in the text.[4]

To support these assumptions, we can first cite the fact that every use of language is a social act that automatically implies communication due its conventionality and which automatically generates corresponding inferences in the mind of the reader. That is simply how language works as a system. Further, experience shows that in practice, most readers (at least those not trained in post-modernism) assume that *the author* (and not the text itself) wants to tell them something with the text.[5] This explains the fascination with author figures. Second, there are enough historical paratexts (especially epitexts) written by authors themselves that suggest that they do, in fact, want to communicate *their* message; that *they themselves* want to influence us with the help of their texts.[6] The following investigation into the peritexts as paratexts of the two *Ships of Fools* is connected to these rhetorical assumptions.

Rhetoric still assumes that texts don't write themselves, but rather are the result of strategic calculations and intentional work. This goes for literature as well. Still, the aesthetic calculus of literature has specialized *frames* of action, expectation, and meaning.[7] Both the sender and the audience always assign communicative expressions (the text in this case) a certain communicative *status.*[8] Here, we can speak of either a *standard status*, for normal communicative acts, or a specialized *licensed status.* The difference between the two types of status can be characterized thus: "Human speech that shapes and creates its objects through linguistic performance, such as narratives (novels, short stories), lyrics, jokes, or hymns, relinquishes its claim to validity or the ability to make such a claim in order to bring fundamentally different communicative intentions into the equation."[9] The appropriate textual and genre characteristics are acquired in the learning process of life and give members of a language community corresponding signals for orientation (found, for instance, in paratexts, to be discussed below). "There is no doubt that a practice of aesthetic speech exists. Just pointing out the difference between assertive speech and aesthetic speech makes it clear that 'aesthetic speech' is a conventional expression in our language." What the philosophers Gerhardus et al. here call "aesthetic speech" denotes "artistic acts of production, artistic acts that utilize characters in a special way, and artistic acts that are done with the intention of creating objects with uncertain utility."[10]

Problems two and three above, dealing with the rhetorical case (*causa rhetorica*) and the relationship between rhetoric and literature, arise against this backdrop.[11] Rhetoric is always situated within the actual world, in the *life-world* as the founder of philosophical phenomenology, Edmund Husserl, called it.[12] In the moment of *immersion*, a short-term mental fusion and identification with the literary possible world, we briefly mentally step out of the actual world.[13] Rhetorical analysis must ask how a transfer from the possible world of literature to the facticity of the life-world could be possible, and whether (and how) our world views can be influenced by it (in a type of persuasion). As a rhetorician, I suspect that when an author really wants to influence someone, he or she will place explicit determinants in their paratexts or in the central text itself. If this is the case, then we can speak of the *rhetorical factor in literature*, which presupposes a *licensed* communicative frame. We will see that paratexts, in particular, form clearly marked bridges that can reach from the fiction to the life-world and are as such highly relevant for rhetorical study.

For the early modern humanist Sebastian Brant, the anchoring of literature in the life-world was self-evident. His *Ship of Fools*, a didactic instruction in verse, is thus based on a completely different aesthetic foundation (an aesthetic of diction) from Katherine Anne Porter's novel of the same name (with its aesthetic of fiction). I will discuss the problems that arise due to this difference in aesthetic production calculi in my comments on the fifth paratextual statement, further below.

Rhetorical inquiry takes place on a completely different plane from reflections on aesthetics. Given the premises of the modern concept of the novel, the question of the rhetoricity in Porter's *Ship of Fools* is quite different from that in Brant's. Can comparisons still be made? Readers of my following attempt may determine for themselves whether the entire analysis that I have attempted with the help of a few textual and medial comparative aspects makes sense *sub specie artis rhetoricae.*

*

In the year 1497, print editions of Jakob Locher's Latin version of Sebastian Brant's *Narrenschiff* (Ship of Fools) appeared in Basel and three other German cities (see Figure 1). This Latin version was the basis of the international success of Brant's work. Around ten years later, in 1509, the first English translation was published by Alexander Barclay (see Figure 2). All of these instances, however, represent later levels of reception. The original edition of Brant's *Ship of Fools* had already been printed in Basel in 1494, in German, by the publisher Johann Bergmann.[14] In this first edition, the central text of the *Narrenschiff* is framed by a total of five paratexts:

- Two title pages with woodcuts and their inscriptions (the second woodcut was also used by Katherine Anne Porter in 1962, see Figures 3 and 4).

- Brant's preface (see Figure 5).
- Brant's afterword: "End des Narrenschiffs" (The end of the Ship of Fools) (see Figure 6).
- A colophon with the date "1494", the publisher's motto "Nüt on vrsach" (nihil sine causa/nothing without a reason), and the publisher's name "Jo.(hann) B.(ergmann) von Olpe" (see Figure 6).

In the year 1962, Katherine Anne Porter's *Ship of Fools* appeared in Boston and Toronto. This edition includes twelve paratexts:

- Flap text on the dust cover.
- The spine of the book, with title and a decorative trim taken from the *Narrenschiff*, which doesn't appear in Brant's book until chapter 5 (see Figures 7 and 8).
- The author's handwritten signature on the front cover.
- A brief title page on the flyleaf inside the book.
- A separate page showing Porter's other publications (see Figure 9).
- The actual title page, including woodcut (see Figure 4).
- The imprint page, including the genre designation "this novel."
- A dedication to Porter's wealthy friend, Barbara Wescott (see Figure 10).
- A preface by the author (see Figure 11).
- A table of contents.
- An index of *Characters*, such as in a play script or screenplay, or possibly as if in a passenger manifest. The characters are grouped by nationality "German," "Swiss," "Spanish," etc. (see Figure 12). Like some other elements of the paratexts, these national identities were not given in the German translation published in 1963.
- At the end of the central text of the novel, the two dates: "*Yaddo, August, 1941*" and "*Pigeon Cove, August, 1961*" on page 497 (see Figure 13).

The peritexts (or more general: paratexts) at the front of the book are clearly marked as separate: each page is given a Roman numeral instead of the Arabic numerals used in the main text.

Why am I speaking at such length about paratexts? Because these elements are a part of the rhetorical side of the communicative act and represent a part of the rhetorical factor in a literary event, while the novel itself primarily—not entirely—represents the aesthetic-poetic side of communication.

In his 1987 work on the accessory parts of the book, French literary theorist Gérard Genette defined paratexts as

> what enables a text to become a book and to be offered as such to its readers and, more generally, to the public. More than a boundary or a sealed border, the paratext is rather a *threshold*[15] or —a word Borges used apropos of a preface—a "vestibule" that offers the world at large the possibility of either stepping inside or turning back. It is an "undefined zone" between the inside and the outside, a zone without any hard and fast boundary on either the inward side (turned toward the [central-]text) or the outward side (turned toward the world's discourse about the [central-]text), an edge, or, as Philippe Lejeune put it, "a fringe on of the printed text which in reality controls one's whole reading of the [central-]text".

Genette assigned a clear rhetorical function to these elements. For him, the symbiosis between the printed central text and its paratext

> constitutes a zone between [central-]text and off-text, a zone not only of transition but also of *transaction*: a privileged space of a pragmatics and a strategy, of an influence on the public, an influence that—whether well or poorly understood and achieved —is at the service of a better reception for the [central-]text and a more pertinent reading of it (more pertinent, of course, in the eyes of the author and his allies). (Genette, *Paratexts* 1f.)

Our topic deals with an inside and an outside, with the virtual world of the novel and the actual world of the author and his readers, with the intrinsic and extrinsic perspectives: the aesthetic-poetic viewpoint on the one hand and the pragmatic-rhetorical viewpoint on the other.

Let us take a look at the most important paratextual element for Porter's main text, her preface, in which she positions her work for us (see Figure 11). In this paratextual preamble, designed to steer our reception of the main text, Porter makes a total of seven statements that I will discuss in a different order in which they appear, in order to better demonstrate the systematic connections between them.

*

Her first statement is, "The title of this book is a translation of the German of 'Das Narrenschiff' [...] first published in Latin as 'Stultifera navis' in 1494." This statement is false. The woodcut that Porter selected for the title page of her book is, in fact, from the original 1494 edition, but this edition was published in German in Basel.[16] The decorative border used on the spine of Porter's 1962 edition is also taken from the 1494 German edition (see Figure 7).

*

Now her second statement: "I read it in Basel in the summer of 1932 when I had still vividly in mind the impressions of my first voyage to Europe." In other words, Porter connected Brant's series of fools with the experiences she had had with Europeans. We may be able to assume that she read Barclay's English translation of the work.[17] On the other hand, she may have read the inexpensive New High German translation by Junghans, which had been published continually since 1877 (one edition of which appeared in 1930).[18] She may have even known of the 1913 facsimile copy of the Basel first edition, which also contained all of the image and graphic elements of the original.[19]

By explicitly referencing Brant's work, and by borrowing his title, Porter sought to create a clear intertextual relationship between her work and Brant's *Narrenschiff*. This relationship is the intertextual nexus between *Narrenschiff* as the famous, early printing of the first large work of modern German literature[20] and at the same time, the most important poetic German contribution to European moralism in the Renaissance.

*

Porter's third statement in the preface is that the idea of a ship full of fools "is by no means new—it was very old and durable and dearly familiar when Brant used it; and it suits my purpose exactly." In other words, Porter sought to incorporate a very old model as the root idea of her work, one that also just happened to have been used by Brant.

Let's take a look at Figure 7. The 112 German *Spruchgedichte* (lyrics) of the *Narrenschiff* are a part of the medieval tradition of *Sangspruchdichtung* (i.e. didactic, gnomic, religious, or political songs) which traces its roots to wisdom poetry. The owl-woodcut border sidebar of the *Narrenschiff* (see Figures 7 and 8),[21] illustrates the core principle of the work: the contrast between *sapiens* and *insipiens*, wisdom and foolishness. We see the tree of life, and we see at the bottom and in the middle two fools with fools' caps, symbolizing foolishness, trying to climb the tree. They represent the 109 dumb, foolish, and unreasonable personality types that Brant called "fools/*stulti*" (after his role model, the Roman poet Horace). They clamber up the tree of life in order to ultimately achieve insight, knowledge, or even wisdom. This goal is represented by the owl at the top of the tree, the symbolic animal of the goddess of knowledge and wisdom, Pallas Athena. In the *Narrenschiff*, the final chapters 107 to 112 in particular thematize the postulate of wisdom symbolized by the owl.

For Brant, life was a search for and pursuit of self-awareness; elsewhere he once wrote, "Know thyself!" after the famous engraving on the temple of Apollo in Delphi.[22] In an adjunct to the 1497 Latin version of his work, Brant wrote, "Up, Up! Look in the mirror in which you seek to know the way of life, and the terrible end, of men."[23]

On the spine of the first edition of Porter's *Ship of Fools* (see Figure 7), all that remain are the two climbing fools. The top part of the decorative illustration is cut off. Where Brant had placed the owl at the top of the tree of life, the spine of the 1962 book has the name,

Katherine

Anne

Porter

Is *her name* supposed to stand for the *new owl of wisdom*? And what would a discussion of wisdom and awareness in her book look like? The de facto arrangement of the book's spine leads to such thoughts, stimulates our reasoning, and thus releases something specific in the communicative space. We don't know whether this is an intended message or not, because we don't know who conceptualized the careful, elaborate, and thoroughly planned book design of Porter's first edition. We also cannot say whether the designer associated some sort of sophisticated idea with cutting the owl out of the spine. The clearly deliberate replacement of Porter's name would certainly count as strong self-stylization by the author. We do not have any other information on this point, but it is highly likely that the author was (in some way) involved in the multiform medial framing and decoration of her novel; that is, in the design of the book as a book.[24] Even today, publishers discuss the design of books with their authors. Is it possible that Katherine Anne Porter had no interest in the design of exactly this book, her magnum opus? It is certainly the case that the graphic designer knew the woodcut ornatus of the original *Narrenschiff* from 1494 well. Perhaps Porter herself pointed out certain aspects of Brant's book, given that it was such a source of inspiration that she named her work after it and wanted to see its title woodcut printed on the title page of her novel.

*

This leads us to a series of poetological and aesthetic questions that are addressed by Porter's fourth statement in her preface. According to her assessment, Brant's *Narrenschiff* is a "moral allegory."[25] According to Quintilian's classical textbook on rhetoric, an allegory is an utterance that "either presents one thing in words and another in meaning, or else something absolutely opposed to the meaning of the words," and is "generally produced by a series of metaphors" such as a work by Horace, "in which Horace represents the state under the semblance of a ship (*navis pro re publica*)."[26] This definition also raises Brant's most important source of inspiration, namely Horace, who wrote in his ode to the "Ship of State,"

> You haven't a single sail that's still intact now,
> no gods, that people call to when they're in trouble (1.14.9f.)

and

> You must beware of being
> merely a plaything of the winds (1.14.15f.; transl. by A. S. Kline 2003).

As we can see, even Horace's ship allegory contains the melancholic and critical, not necessarily pessimistic but certainly not cheerful fundamental tone that we later see in both Brant's and Porter's works. This is just how ships of fools work; they are not places of happiness, but rather places of squalidness and mental weakness. Michel Foucault misinterpreted this literary fiction, and in his 1961 book *Folie et Déraison* even falsely believed that in the Middle Ages, mentally handicapped people were sent to live on ships of fools that floated up and down rivers.[27]

*

Let us move on to Porter's fifth paratextual statement. It can be found in the half-sentence, "when I began thinking about my novel." Here, Porter is speaking about her decision to write a novel, and about the conceptual phase of the work. Such considerations remain firmly within the field of poetics, because Porter's statement is also a declaration of the genre of her work. It should be a modern novel, one that has clear structural differences from the series of the 112 *Spruchgedichte* on individual types of foolishness found in Brant's image of a ship full of fools. This is a significant difference, and it speaks to the aesthetic core of the difference between the new and old ship of fools.

Brant dealt with the 109 different types of fools in individual chapters, each with (1) a motto, (2) an image, and (3) a didactic poem (*Spruchgedicht*). The poems dealing with each of the negative behavioral deviations are argumentative in nature. The panopticon of foolishness in the *Narrenschiff* is a mirror, ultimately one that reflects vice, deficiency, weakness, stupidity, and sin[28] in a way that should be personally recognizable to all readers, so that each can find their way to a new understanding. In many areas of life, Brant saw foolish people who had problems dealing with norms and finding their right way through life.[29] In Brant's time, which lacked psychology as a discipline, all of these themes were coded moralistically. Porter's work also deals with these same themes, but her version handles them differently.

Brant's work only occasionally contains rhetorically functionalized narrative or descriptive elements. The fictional is provided by the framework of the ship allegory and the sketches of individual types of fools in the text. In Porter's novel, this dynamic is turned on its head. Porter's fictional virtual world is built through narrative, and only occasionally does she integrate argumentative and descriptive elements. In short, Brant's priority is arguing, while Porter's is telling.

In her modern novel, Porter tells the story of at least thirty people or groups of people (families, couples, twins, etc.). We encounter some of these people as real characters, as opposed to the woodcut-like sketches, the more abstract types of sinners found in Brant. Still, Porter's series of figures, which are all presented as equals in the work, demonstrate clear structural similarities with Brant's 109 fools. But while every one of Brant's figures gets its profile exclusively from an abstract discussion of negative morality, Porter's figures get their profiles primarily psychologically through their actions and through the mental processes that the author gives us a glimpse of. Components of an ethical discourse occur only secondarily (for instance, when protagonists reflect on the morality or amorality of the small children Ric and Rac). Thus, Porter presents us with a psychologically interpreted moral universe. Porter tells the common story of a common voyage of figures across the Atlantic. In doing so, her narrative utilizes a principle of film montage known as shot and cut, with alternating sequential syntagma; she thus incorporates a non-linear narrative flow. All of these partial episodes are presented—and this is important, and in the same way that each figure is presented with their idiosyncrasies—on equal footing. This fragmentation of character portraits throughout the work forces the readers to use their imagination to construct a holistic synthesis of each character.

On Deck A there is no main, or even secondary plot. This is a part of an important contrast to Brant's ethically individualist conception of fools; this is the reason why he handles each fool separately. In addition to profiling her individual characters, Porter modeled a social and socio-ethical context of interaction through her depiction of the overall ship. This is missing from Brant's work. Porter's readers can imagine a two-tier *Vera*-world, in which the exploited and non-privileged are penned up "in steerage" in the third class ("the oppressed and intimidated," 365), where revolutionary potential rears its head. Above deck, in the first and second classes that we get a glimpse of, we see a world of delusion, of ideology, and vapidly romanticized belief. Seen psychologically, readers are confronted with unhappiness, worry, and fear, with misunderstanding and neuroses. It is significant that the "bride and groom" on board (who represent the existence of human happiness in the world) play no role in the narrative; their existence is only briefly mentioned. We experience how the Jew Löwenthal and Freytag, who has been branded as a Jew, also spin within the whirlpool of resentment due to their inner bondage;

they are unable to free themselves. Not even the two American artists are able to free their minds. It is a world in which moral considerations, dominant in Brant's work, are psychologized as nothing more than subjective prejudices or learned group egos. It is a world of mutual racism, social discrimination, of boundaries and structural violence. And simultaneously, this entire upper class is largely and only provisionally held together through their mutual class-disdain of those in steerage.

Thus, in Porter's work we experience a world of ancient European thought that cannot rid itself of authoritarian structures. It is an image of prestabilized order and ever recurring sameness, as the not coincidentally pious Catholic Dr. Schumann articulates it in the story (197). This train of thought and action is most clearly demonstrated by the captain of the ship, who represents an authoritarian-fascist social model as a substitute for the lost monarchy. He understands the fundamental model of an authoritarian system of privilege and hierarchically ordered social relationships as a part of God's order (174, 248, 424-430). Against the background of this world image (which, at the narrated time 1931, was beginning to decline), a pessimistic outlook on the world develops, as expressed in quotes such as, "There is no such thing as freedom" (Herr Graf, 442), or, "Well, what do you expect of this world?" (Frau Lutz, 393). The Spanish students and the shady dancers of the Spanish Zarzuela troupe break into this model of social order as antagonists. Someone has paid for their passage on the upper deck. In contrast to the Germans and Swiss, they represent the opposing model of deviation and chaos. This is most clearly seen from the perspective of the devilish kobolds, Ric and Rac. In reading the novel, what we imagine is the virtual world,[30] the virtual cosmos of the ship *Vera*, whose name, not coincidentally, contains a programmatic statement of realism: "vera" in Latin = the truth, the real. The sum of the characters and the sum of the events constitute the basis for the virtual *Vera*-world in the novel.

*

In her sixth paratextual declaration, Porter provides an interpretation of this world in stating, "I took for my own this simple almost universal image of the ship of this world on its voyage to eternity." Sebastian Brant also established an important level of coherence in his work through the ever-recurring thematic image of the ship (see Figures 14 and 15). For Porter, the ship becomes a strictly bordered, concrete space for interaction that the characters cannot escape. In the quotation from the preface at the top of this paragraph, Porter uses two important terms: "world" and "image." She creates a fictional world in the virtual imaginative space of the novel, a *possible world* in the sense of Saul A. Kripke's *Possible World Theory.*[31] The world of the *Vera* is *potentially factual*; it is an indirect reflection, an "image" as Porter puts it. But what is it a reflection of? Doubtless, it is a segment of the real world in 1931/1932 as found in the memory and interpretation of the author. This image is neither photographic, nor is it an image that reflects real facts. It is a constructed simile, a *Verisimile*, a truth analogon: something *similar to the truth* whose concrete referents (the text-external referent people in the real world) are unknown to us. As readers, however, we *could* connect the characters to historical figures if we were to believe that Porter's work was not a "novel" but rather a "historical travelogue." The genre declaration of "novel" seems to give us some clarity on this issue. As the term "novel" usually indicates, the work follows a specific Western-European aesthetic tradition, namely the tradition of the aesthetics of fiction, as Genette called it in his *Fiction and Diction.*

*

What seems to be clarity provided by the declaration of the work's genre is called into question by Porter's seventh and last paratextual statement. The last sentence of the preface states, "I am a passenger on that ship." What is this supposed to mean? It is clear that no real historical person can stand on the fictional ship of a novel. It is also clear, however, that this is not a reference to an actual historical voyage ("my voyage," she says in the second sentence of the preface) taken by the real-world author Katherine Anne Porter in 1931/32. A more appropriate interpretation might be that it is a recourse to Brant's paratext, in which he also claimed to be sitting in his own ship of fools. Even he belonged to the order of fools, as Brant states in the "Apology of the Poet,"[32] and thus would have to find his own place on the ship of fools.[33]

With such comments, both Brant and Porter consciously disturb the ontological levels between the virtual and the real world, and between fictionality and factuality. They suggest that we use our imaginations, our capacity for emotional sympathy, or our abstract thought to establish a connection between the levels of fictionality and factuality. Brant and Porter are telling us that even in the moment of immersion or illusion, we can fantasize ourselves into this poetic world. In this moment of imaginative participation, poetry creates in us every conceivable form of experience. That is the poetic communicative performance of fictional-aesthetic literature.

In contrast to the expectations of postmodern literary theory, we can also assume that both Brant and Porter acted rhetorically; that is, they wanted to express some sort of message to their readers. I refer here to Porter's sixth statement, in which she states that her *Ship of Fools* is "the ship of this world on its voyage to eternity." This is a commitment to an allegory, something quite surprising for a modern author. Thus, it is a commitment to a rhetorical figure, with whose help we can decode the poetically encrypted references relating to, for instance, philosophical viewpoints. Paratexts are a part of the rhetorical strategy of an author to make his poetic construct relevant to the real world. In this respect, the clear commitment to an allegory in Porter's work is important. In an allegory, the aesthetic-poetic and rhetorical-real world levels of communication work together. The allegory invites us to interpret a second statement from that which is first said in the text, to see a second something behind the concrete fiction, and, if we choose, to transfer this something into the facticity of the *life-world*. Katherine Anne Porter gives us a hint: the concrete ship *Vera* sails in the virtual world from *Vera*cruz, Mexico, to Bremerhaven, Germany. This is the first level of understanding. At the same time, however, the ship represents the world, as Porter says in her paratext, a world that is on its course to eternity. This broaches a second level of understanding. We can understand this process of understanding as a progression from the concrete to the abstract. In doing so, we transform the semantics (denotations and connotations) of an aestheticized text so that we can integrate them into our lives. In other words, we take something out of our internal experiences of a fictional world and apply it to the real world. That is the rhetorical performance of literature.

*

What, then, can we say is the rhetorical message in Porter's case? To this final question there are two general answers and one concrete one. Every reader can, if he so chooses, make an individual and idiosyncratic inference or abduction. Everyone can derive a message that is meaningful only to him- or herself. A professional interpreter can seek to utilize hermeneutic literary critical methods to derive an historically justified message. Or, we can leave the authors to speak for themselves, by interpreting the paratexts and epitexts (i.e. other historical sources related to the central text) they provide us.[34] If there are no epitexts provided, then options 1 and 2 above are our only recourse.

In all of these cases, we must always take into account the historically dominant understanding of the roles of authors in society. The law professor Sebastian Brant understood himself as a teacher around the year 1500 and integrated explicit theorems and supporting arguments into his *Narrenschiff* that leave little room for variable interpretations. His work stands on the border between standard communication in the life-world and the exclusive, licensed or specialized communication of art.[35] Katherine Anne Porter takes the role of the modern writer, for whom the status of a "novel" is quite clear. This type of author often understands himself or herself as nothing more than an analyst, a seismograph and recorder of the course of the world. Therefore, and in contrast to Brant, Porter does not give us any explicit directive. But if we are to take her conception of the *Vera*-world seriously, then we can only consider certain specific—rather unpleasant—*insights* into the world as her rhetorical message. And these insights were also, I think, important to Porter.[36]

Figure 1. Title page of Locher's *Stultifera Navis* (Basel 1497).

I

Stultifera Nauis.

Narragonice pfectionis nunq̄ ſatis laudata Nauis: per Sebaſtianū Brant: vernaculo vul=garicq̄ ſermone & rhythmo/ p cūctoꝝ mortaliū fatuitatis ſemitas effugere cupiētiū directione/ſpeculo/cōmodoq̄ & ſalute: proq̄ inertis ignaueq̄ ſtultitie ppetua infamia/exe=cratione/& confutatione/nup fabricata: Atq̄ iampridem per Iacobum Locher/cognomēto Philomuſum: Suēuū: in latinū traducta eloquiū: & per Sebaſtianū Brant: denuo ſeduloq̄ reuiſa/& noua q̄dā exactaq̄ emendatōe elimata: atq̄ ſupadditis qbuſdā nouis/admirādiſq̄ fatuoꝝ generi=bus ſuppleta: fœlici exorditur principio.

·1497·

Nihil ſine cauſa.

Io. de. Olpe.

Figure 2. Title page of Barclay's *The Ship of Fools*, ed. Jamieson (1874).

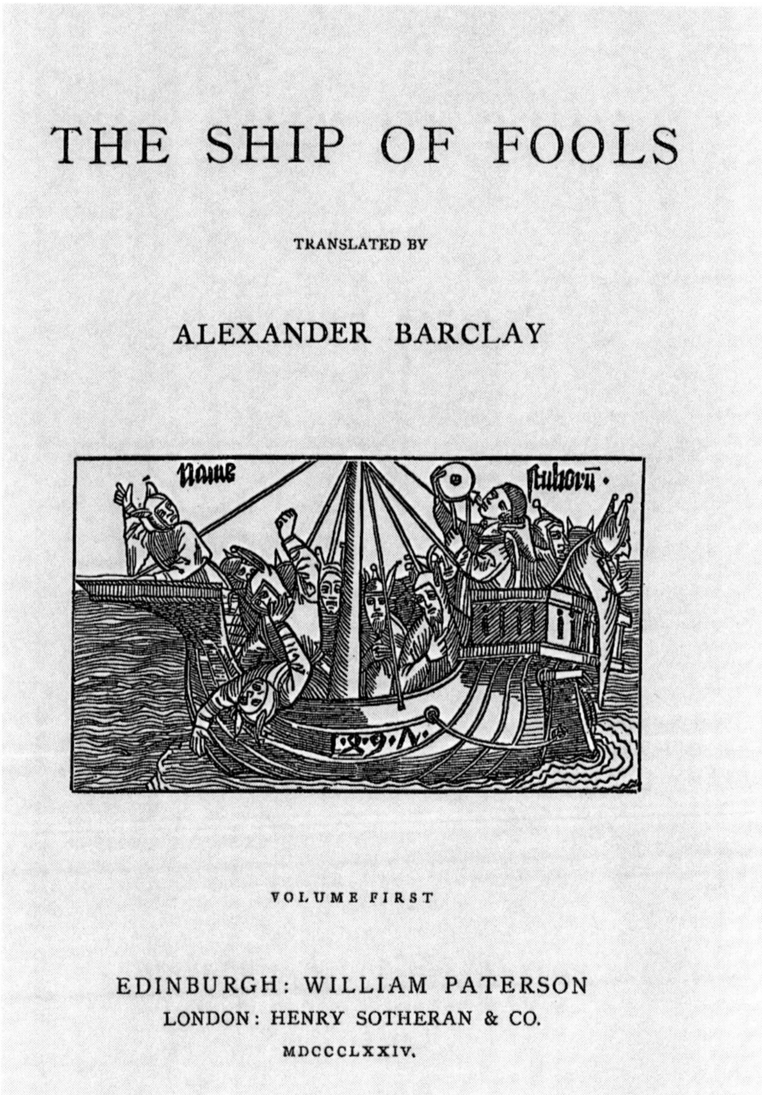

THE SHIP OF FOOLS

TRANSLATED BY

ALEXANDER BARCLAY

VOLUME FIRST

EDINBURGH: WILLIAM PATERSON
LONDON: HENRY SOTHERAN & CO.
MDCCCLXXIV.

Figure 3. Second title page of Brant's *Narrenschiff* (Basel 1494).

Figure 4. Title page of Porter's *Ship of Fools* (1962), iii.

Katherine Anne Porter

SHIP OF FOOLS

An Atlantic Monthly Press Book

Little, Brown and Company • Boston • Toronto

Figure 5. Brant's *Narrenschiff* preface (Basel 1494).

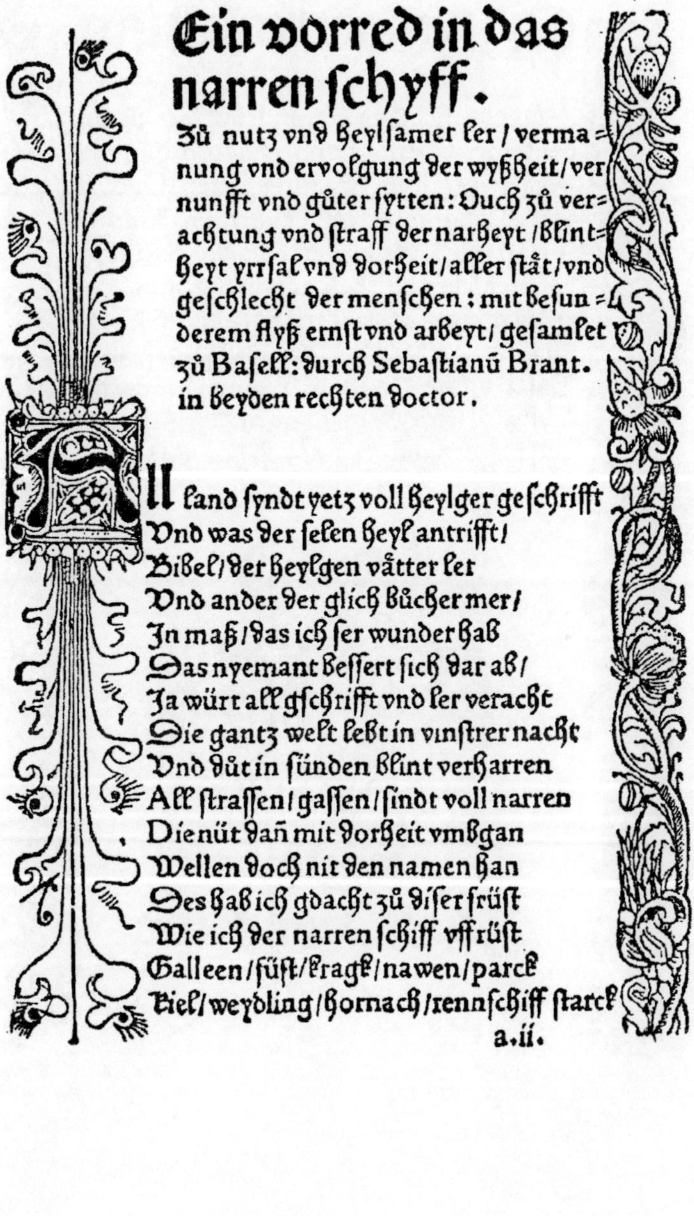

Ein vorred in das
narren ſchyff.

Zů nutz vnd heylſamer ler/ verma=
nung vnd ervolgung der wyßheit/ ver
nunfft vnd gůter ſytten: Ouch zů ver=
achtung vnd ſtraff der narheyt/ blint=
heyt yrrſal vnd dorheit/ aller ſtåt/ vnd
geſchlecht der menſchen: mit beſun=
derem flyß ernſt vnd arbeyt/ geſamlet
zů Baſell: durch Sebaſtianū Brant.
in beyden rechten doctor.

All land ſyndt yetz voll heylger geſchrifft
Vnd was der ſelen heyl antrifft/
Bibel/ der heylgen våtter ler
Vnd ander der glich bůcher mer/
In maß/ das ich ſer wunder hab
Das nyemant beſſert ſich dar ab/
Ja würt all gſchrifft vnd ler veracht
Die gantz welt lebt in vinſtrer nacht
Vnd důt in ſünden blint verharren
All ſtraſſen/ gaſſen/ ſindt voll narren
Die nüt dañ mit dorheit vmbgan
Wellen doch nit den namen han
Des hab ich gdacht zů diſer früſt
Wie ich der narren ſchiff vff rüſt
Galleen/ füſt/ kragk/ nawen/ parck
Kiel/ weydling/ hornach/ rennſchiff ſtarck

a.ii.

Figure 6. Last page of Brant's *Narrenschiff* (Basel 1494).

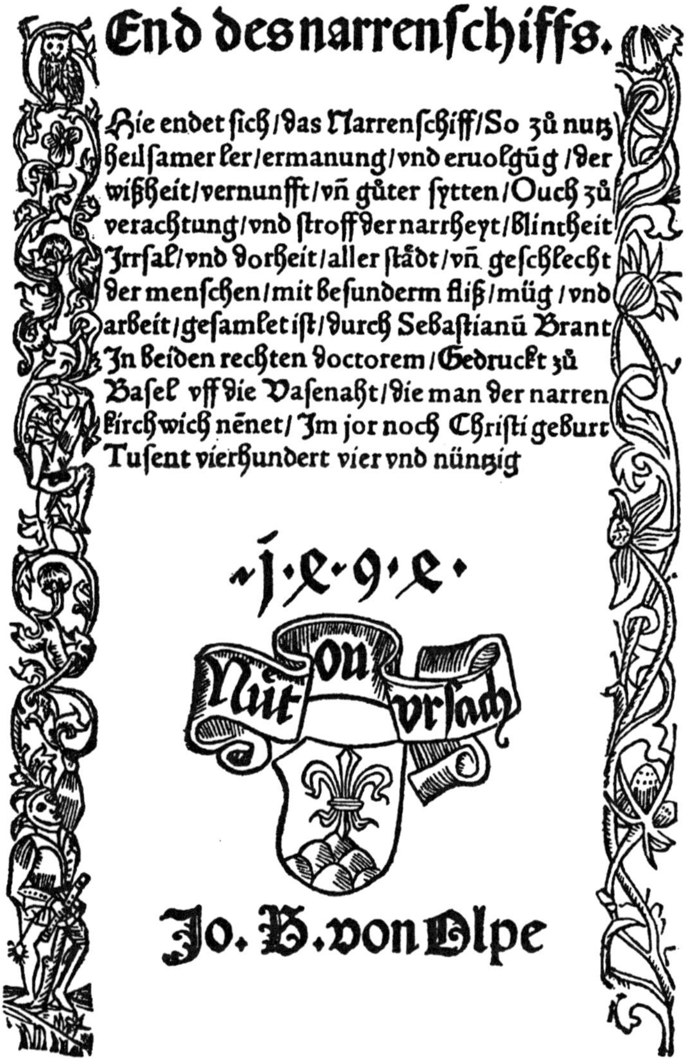

End desnarrenschiffs.

Hie endet sich / das Narrenschiff / So zů nutz
heilsamer ler / ermanung / vnd eruolgũg / der
wißheit / vernunfft / vñ gůter sytten / Ouch zů
verachtung / vnd stroff der narrheyt / blintheit
Irrsal / vnd dorheit / aller ståt / vñ geschlecht
der menschen / mit besunderm fliß / müg / vnd
arbeit / gesamlet ist / durch Sebastianũ Brant
In beiden rechten doctorem / Gedruckt zů
Basel vff die Vasenaht / die man der narren
kirchwich nẽnet / Im jor noch Christi geburt
Tusent vierhundert vier vnd nüntzig

Nüt on vrsach

Jo. B. von Olpe

Figure 7. Spine of Porter's *Ship of Fools* (1962) and sidebar of Brant's *Narrenschiff* chapter 5 (Basel 1494).

Figure 8. First page of Brant's *Narrenschiff* chapter 5 (Basel 1494).

Figure 9. Porter's publications listed in her *Ship of Fools* (1962), ii.

BOOKS BY KATHERINE ANNE PORTER

FLOWERING JUDAS

KATHERINE ANNE PORTER'S FRENCH SONG BOOK

PALE HORSE, PALE RIDER

THE LEANING TOWER

THE DAYS BEFORE

SHIP OF FOOLS

Figure 10. Dedication to Barbara Wescott in her *Ship of Fools* (1962), v.

FOR BARBARA WESCOTT

1932: Paris, Rambouillet, Davosplatz, Salzburg, Munich, New York, Mulhocaway, Rosemont :1962

Figure 11. Preface of Porter's *Ship of Fools* (1962), vii.

The title of this book is a translation from the German of *Das Narrenschiff,* a moral allegory by Sebastian Brant (1458?-1521) first published in Latin as *Stultifera Navis* in 1494. I read it in Basel in the summer of 1932 when I had still vividly in mind the impressions of my first voyage to Europe. When I began thinking about my novel, I took for my own this simple almost universal image of the ship of this world on its voyage to eternity. It is by no means new — it was very old and durable and dearly familiar when Brant used it; and it suits my purpose exactly. I am a passenger on that ship.

K. A. P.

Figure 12. Porter's *Characters* in her *Ship of Fools* (1962), xi.

Characters

On board the North German Lloyd S.A. *Vera,* between Veracruz, Mexico, and Bremerhaven, Germany, August 22–September 17, 1931.

German

Ship's Captain Thiele.
Dr. Schumann, ship's doctor.
The purser, and a half dozen young ship's officers.
Frau Rittersdorf, who keeps a notebook.
Frau Otto Schmitt, recently widowed in Mexico.
Herr Siegfried Rieber, publisher of a ladies' garment trade magazine.
Fräulein Lizzi Spöckenkieker, in the ladies' garment business; from Hanover.
Herr Professor Hutten, Frau Professor Hutten } Former head of a German school in Mexico, and his wife; traveling with them is their white bulldog Bébé.
Herr Karl Baumgartner, Frau Baumgartner, Hans Baumgartner } Lawyer from Mexico City – hopeless drunkard; his wife Greta, and their eight-year-old son.
Herr Karl Glocken, a hunchback, who has sold out his little tobacco and newspaper stand in Mexico, and is returning to Germany.
Herr Wilibald Graf, a dying religious enthusiast who believes he has the power of healing.
Johann, his nephew and attendant.
Herr Wilhelm Freytag, "connected with" an oil company in Mexico, returning to Germany to fetch his wife and her mother.
Herr Julius Löwenthal, Jewish manufacturer and salesman of Catholic Church furnishings, returning to his home in Düsseldorf for a visit with his cousin Sarah.

Swiss

Herr Heinrich Lutz, Frau Lutz, Elsa Lutz } A hotelkeeper from Mexico, returning to Switzerland after fifteen years, with his wife and their daughter, eighteen years old.

xi

Figure 13. Last page of Porter's *Ship of Fools* (1962), 497.

The sight of her weakness and defeat gave him pleasure like no other.

"Do you know," he said, falsely, "maybe we shall never leave each other. Where could we go?"

"We'll think of somewhere," she said, "let's wait."

"Here we go talking again," said David. "Let's think of something pleasant."

"You think of something, David darling," said Jenny, "something wonderful."

David leaned with great discretion and a very straight face and whispered, "Tonight in Bremen we'll sleep in the same bed for a change." Jenny made a slight purring sound at him, and he watched her face grow radiant.

The band played "*Tannenbaum*" at last, and kept it up until the gangplank was down, and the passengers began to descend rapidly and silently. As the musicians were wiping the mouthpieces of their instruments, wrapping up their drums and putting away their fiddles, their mouths were wide with smiles, their heads towards the dock, towards the exact narrow spot where the *Vera* had warped in and cast her anchor. Among them, a gangling young boy, who looked as if he had never had enough to eat in his life, nor a kind word from anybody, and did not know what he was going to do next, stared with blinded eyes, his mouth quivering while he shook the spit out of his trumpet, repeating to himself just above a whisper, "*Grüss Gott, Grüss Gott,*" as if the town were a human being, a good and dear trusted friend who had come a long way to welcome him.

Yaddo, August, 1941
Pigeon Cove, August, 1961

{497}

Notes

1. Knape, *Modern Rhetoric* 139-149.
2. Cf. Knape, *Kunstgespräch* 17.
3. Weimar: *Wo und was ist der Erzähler?* 504. Translation is my own.
4. For more on power and text achievements see: Knape, *Textleistung*.
5. This fact was self-evident for literary critics of earlier times, e.g. for Booth, *The Rhetoric of Fiction*.
6. The theory of rhetoric always assumes that the writers of texts have motives for their actions, communicative intentions, and a reason for their communication. The question is, of course, what kind of motives, intentions, and reasons they have. The philological problem of whether we can later interpretatively deduce these elements from their texts is not a topic that rhetorical theory is concerned with (rather, it is a complication in philological methodology).
7. Goffman, *Frame Analysis*.
8. Knape, *Modern Rhetoric* 15.
9. Gerhardus et al., *Schlüssiges Argumentieren* 105. My translation.
10. Gerhardus et al., *Schlüssiges Argumentieren* 106.
11. Knape, *Zur Problematik literarischer Rhetorik*.
12. Husserl, *The Crisis of European Sciences* §§ 33-34.
13. For more on *immersion* see: Ryan, *Narrative as Virtual Reality* 14.
14. Brant, *Narrenschiff*, ed. Knape 2005.
15. The French title of the book is *Seuils*, which means "thresholds."
16. This error may be due to the fact that the second title page of the 1494 first edition (see Figure 3) contains Latin engravings and psalm verses. This may have led to the impression that the rest of the book was also written in the Latin language.
17. Barclay, *Ship of Fools*, ed. Jamieson 1874 (see Figure 2).
18. Brant, *Narrenschiff*, transl. Junghans 1877.
19. Brant, *Narrenschiff*, facs. ed. Schultz 1913.
20. Knape, *Poetik und Rhetorik* 105-168.
21. One of the recurring decorative elements found as borders on each page.
22. Knape, *Poetik und Rhetorik* 158.
23. In: Locher *Stultifera Navis*, ed. Hartl 2001, 34f.
24. For more on the difference between "text" (novel) and "medium" (book), see: Knape, *Modern Rhetoric* 261f.

25. Porter may have even found a version of this completely acceptable interpretation in: Pompen *The English Versions* 295-299.
26. Quintilian, *Institutio oratoria*, transl. Butler, 8.6.44.
27. Foucault, *Madness and Civilization* chapter I; see also Kasten and Kemper.
28. Brant, *Narrenschiff*, ed. Knape 2005, Preamble (verses 29-44).
29. Among the "problem areas" that Brant observed were education, friendship, challenging the wrath of God, the correct evaluation of a given situation, the handling of overpowering physical temptation, the balance between the worldly sphere and the divine sphere, the relationship between wisdom and wealth, an affection for the world and the improvement of man, marriage and the relationship between a husband and his wife, fear in the social realm, the stubbornness of men, attitudes towards the religious, work ethic, the relationship between subordinates and their superiors, the deadly sins, politics and law, gratification and the gifts of God and the world, human self-care and human self-awareness, the relationship between men and women, belief in untruths, self-awareness and an awareness of others, rudeness, false priesthood, a happy social life, behavior in social roles, wealth, the betterment of man, attitudes towards God's judgment, attitudes towards the worldly and religious ideas of salvation, greed, and everyday hustle and bustle. See also Knape, *Poetik und Rhetorik* 152 and Gaier, *Studien* 110-188.
30. Ryan, *Narrative as Virtual Reality.*
31. According to Kripke's theory, the world would have to be contrafactual.
32. Brant, *Narrenschiff*, ed. Knape 2005, chapter 111.
33. In: Locher *Stultifera Navis*, ed. Hartl 2001, 34f.
34. For "epitext" see: Genette, *Paratexts* 344-403.
35. Knape, *Rhetorik der Künste* 900.
36. An earlier, shorter version of this essay appeared in Joachim Knape, *Modern Rhetoric in Culture, Arts, and Media* (De Gruyter 2013). I would like to thank De Gruyter publishers for permission to reprint it here.

Works Cited

Barclay, Alexander. *The Ship of Fools*, ed. T. H. Jamieson. 2 Vols. Edinburgh: Paterson, 1874.

Booth, Wayne C. *The Rhetoric of Fiction.* Chicago 1961.

Brant, Sebastian. *Das Narrenschiff*, trans. Hermann A. Junghans. Leipzig: Reclam, 1877.

———. *Das Narrenschiff.* Facsimile of the first edition by Franz Schultz. Strassburg: Trübner, 1913. Reprint ed. by Dieter Wuttke. Baden-Baden: Koerner, 1994 (Saecvla Spiritalia 6).

———. *Das Narrenschiff*, ed. Joachim Knape. Stuttgart: Reclam, 2005.

Foucault, Michel. *Madness and Civilization: A History of Insanity in the Age of Reason*, trans. from the French by Richard Howard. Repr. London: Routledge, 1999 (French Original: *Histoire de la Folie à l'Age Classique: Folie et Déraison.* Paris: Plon, 1961).

Gaier, Ulrich. *Studien zu Sebastian Brants Narrenschiff.* Tübingen: Niemeyer, 1966.

Genette, Gérard. *Paratexts: Thresholds of Interpretation*, trans. Jane E. Lewin. Cambridge: Cambridge University Press, 1997 (Literature, Culture, Theory 20) (French Original: *Seuils.* Paris: Seuil, 1987 [Poétique]).

———. *Fiction and Diction*, trans. Catherine Porter. Ithaca: Cornell University Press, 1993 (French Original: *Fiction et Diction.* Paris: Éd. du Seuil, 1991 = Collection poétique).

Gerhardus, Dietfried/Kledzik, Silke M./Reitzig, Gerhard H. *Schlüssiges Argumentieren.* Göttingen: Vandenhoeck & Ruprecht, 1975.

Goffman, Erving. *Frame Analysis. An Essay on the Organization of Experience.* New York: Harper & Row, 1974.

Husserl, Edmund. *The Crisis of European Sciences and Transcendental Phenomenology.* Translated with an Introduction by David Carr. Evanston: Northwestern University Press, 1970 (German Original: *Die Krisis der europäischen Wissenschaften und die transzendentale Phänomenologie: eine Einleitung in die phänomenologische Philosophie*, ed. Walter Biemel. Dordrecht: Nijhoff, 1954 = Husserliana. Gesammelte Werke 6).

Kasten, Ingrid. "'Narrheit' und 'Wahnsinn'. Michel Foucaults Rezeption von Sebastian Brants 'Narrenschiff.'" In Johannes Janota et al., eds., *Festschrift für Walter Haug und Burghart Wachinger.* Vol. 1. Tübingen: Niemeyer, 1992. 233-254.

Kemper, Raimund. *"Il était un petit navire ..." Zur Archäologie der "Narrenschiff"-Phantasien Michel Foucaults.* Frankfurt/M etc.: Peter Lang, 1996 (Bremer Beiträge zur Literatur- und Ideengeschichte 15).

Knape, Joachim. *Poetik und Rhetorik in Deutschland 1300–1700.* Wiesbaden: Harrassowitz, 2006 (Gratia 44).

———. "Rhetorik der Künste / Rhetoric and the Arts." In Ulla Fix, Andreas Gardt, Joachim Knape, eds., *Rhetorik und Stilistik / Rhetoric and Stylistics. Ein internationales Handbuch historischer und systematischer Forschung / An International Handbook of Historical and Systematic Research.* 1. Halbbd. / Vol. 1. Berlin, New York: De Gruyter, 2008. 894-927 (HSK. Handbücher zur Sprach- und Kommunikationswissenschaft / Handbooks of Linguistics and Communication Science 31.1).

———. "Zur Problematik literarischer Rhetorik am Beispiel Thomas Bernhards." In Joachim Knape, and Olaf Kramer, eds., *Rhetorik und Sprachkunst bei Thomas Bernhard.* Würzburg: Königshausen & Neumann, 2011. 5–24.

———. "Das Kunstgespräch." In Joachim Knape, ed., *Kunstgespräche. Zur diskursiven Konstitution von Kunst.* Baden-Baden: Koerner, 2012. 11-62, here 24 (Saecvla Spiritalia 47).

———. *Modern Rhetoric in Culture, Arts, and Media. 13 Essays.* Berlin, Boston: De Gruyter. 2013a.

———. "Textleistung. Eine moderne rhetorische Kategorie, erprobt am Beispiel mittelalterlicher Chronistik." In Klaus Ridder and Steffen Patzold, eds., *Die Aktualität der Vormoderne. Epochenentwürfe zwischen Alterität und Kontinuität.* Berlin: Akademie, 2013. 135–159 (Europa im Mittelalter. Abhandlungen und Beiträge zur historischen Komparatistik 23).

Kripke, Saul A. *Naming and Necessity.* Cambridge: Harvard University Press, 1980.

Locher, Jakob. "Stultifera Navis." In *Die 'Stultifera Navis'. Jakob Lochers Übertragung von Sebastian Brants 'Narrenschiff'.* Vol. 1.2. Ed. and trans. Nina Hartl. Münster: Waxmann, 2001 (Studien und Texte zum Mittelalter und zur frühen Neuzeit 1).

Pompen, Fr. Aurelius. *The English Versions of the "Ship of Fools." A Contribution to the History of the Early French Renaissance in England.* London: Longmans & Co., 1925.

Porter, Katherine Anne. *Ship of Fools.* Boston and Toronto: Little, Brown, 1962.

Quintilian, Marcus Fabius. *Institutio Oratoria.* 4 volumes. With an Engl. translation by H. E. Butler. Reprinted. Cambridge and London: Loeb, 1963/1966/1966/1961 (The Loeb Classical Library 124-127).

Ryan, Marie-Laure. *Narrative as Virtual Reality: Immersion and Interactivity in Literature and Electronic Media.* Baltimore: Johns Hopkins University Press, 2001.

Weimar, Klaus. "Wo und was ist der Erzähler?" *Modern Language Notes* 109 (1994): 495-506.

"Before the Voyage Ended"

An Examination of the Serial Publication of *Ship of Fools*, 1944–1959

Beth Alvarez

Prior to its April 1962 publication, more than half of the text of *Ship of Fools* had previously appeared in a total of twelve installments in seven periodicals. This exploration of the relationship between the previously published portions of the novel and the 1962 work is informed by primary source materials at the University of Maryland Libraries. Surviving among Porter's papers are manuscript copies of six of the excerpts (*Partisan Review*, Fall 1945; *Harper's*, October, November, December 1950, November 1953; *Mademoiselle*, July 1958). Her papers also hold Porter's personal copies of eleven of the twelve serials in which the excerpts were originally published (*Sewanee Review*, October 1944; *Accent*, Summer 1946; *Sewanee Review*, January-March 1947; *Harper's*, October, November, December

1950, November 1953; *Atlantic*, March, April 1956; *Mademoiselle*, July 1958; *Texas Quarterly*, Autumn 1959). There is also correspondence with editorial staff of the seven periodicals in her papers and additional relevant correspondence in the papers of Seymour Lawrence and Cyrilly Abels. My research began with the manuscripts and correspondence, followed by reading the twelve excerpts in the order in which they were published. After reading the text of the entire novel, I compared it with the texts of the excerpts and noted differences between them. What follows are the results of these efforts and some preliminary conclusions. Appended to the paper are charts detailing the relationship between the excerpts and the novel.

Although it has long been known that the genesis for *Ship of Fools* was the log or notes Porter made during her first voyage to Europe in the late summer of 1931, Porter initially conceived of the work, originally titled "Promised Land," as one of five short novels to be published in a single volume. (The other works were to be "Noon Wine," "Old Mortality," "The Man in the Tree," and "Pale Horse, Pale Rider" [KAP to Genevieve Taggard, January 5, 1937]). Porter reported working on the short novel in correspondence with Albert Erskine (KAP to Albert Erskine December 7, 1937, and March 22, 1938), Monroe Wheeler (KAP to Monroe Wheeler, December 15, 1937), and Josephine Herbst (KAP to Josephine Herbst, January 2, 1938). By spring 1939 when the three short novels collected in *Pale Horse, Pale Rider* were published, Porter confided to Josephine Herbst that "Promised Land" had grown into a novel (KAP to Josephine Herbst, March 21, 1939). Indeed, Porter signed a contract with Harcourt, Brace for "Promised Land" dated April 27, 1939, agreeing to deliver the manuscript on January 1, 1940. That contract was modified on December 19, 1940, extending the deadline for receipt of the manuscript to May 15, 1941 (Agreement between Katherine Anne Porter and Harcourt, Brace and Company Inc. relative to Promised Land). It is probably impossible to determine exactly how much of the full-length novel Porter completed before she composed her "Author's Apology" dated May 1941, but Donald Brace's May 5, 1941, letter to Porter acknowledged receiving the first fourteen pages of the novel. "I think you have managed the start of the story beautifully. I don't deny that I wish there were more, but at any rate we are fourteen pages better off than we were. . . ." In that "Author's Apology," Porter explained the genesis of the novel:

> This novel was begun as a journal during my first voyage to Europe in August-September, 1931, from Vera Cruz to Bremerhaven on the North German Lloyd S. S. Werra. A small part of this journal was sent as a letter to a friend. . . . From these notes a book began to take form almost at once, and I found myself writing in long scenes and situations which grew immediately out of present experience, so that all the main points of the story were written then and there, before the voyage ended. However, I distrust, for myself, snap judgments and instantaneous conclusions, preferring to view one experience in light of others, earlier and later, so after the first general outline and the main events were written, I put it aside and worked on it only at long intervals ever since. In my case, "working" quite often means long stretches of almost subconscious brooding and making vast heaps of notes whose order and sequence and meaning are known only to myself. ("Author's Apology," p. 1)

Also among Porter's papers is a remarkable nine-page synopsis of the novel. Porter's handwritten note on this document asserts, "Written in 1942 at request of one Richard Mealand connected with a moving picture agency" (No Safe Harbor Synopsis, p. 9; hereinafter cited as Synopsis). Mealand's May 21, 1941, letter to Porter corroborates Porter's note; in it, he asks to read "an available copy of the manuscript" (Richard Mealand to KAP, May 21, 1941). Sometime after November 17, 1943, Mealand, then story editor in the New York office of Paramount Pictures, received the synopsis and 219 pages of the novel's manuscript "plus 18 additional pages" (Richard Mealand to Donald Brace (cc), December 6, 1943). Donald Brace's November 17, 1943, letter to Porter reported that he is "letting" Mealand "read the script we have" and requested a carbon of the synopsis. Mealand's 1943 letter to Donald Brace states that he is returning the materials that Porter "sent me and asked me to turn over to you." This letter expresses admiration for the work but avers, "For the average director and producer it is much too subtle, much too concerned with purely individual observation and with attitudes on human failings" (Richard Mealand to Donald Brace (cc), December 6, 1943). The synopsis opens by stating the novel's theme, "the criminal collusion between people of average, conventional virtue and good will, with people whose aims are evil, and who live by manipulation of the apathy, indifference, or tacit assent of 'good' people" (Synopsis, p. 1). It outlines all of the major characters and events, concluding with a short description of the scene with the young German trumpeter that does, indeed, close the novel.

From the evidence of Mealand's December 1943 letter and the synopsis, which states "This outline takes up from page 229" (Synopsis, p. 1), one can conclude that Part I and some portion of Part II of the novel were completed by July 17, 1944. That is the date of Allen Tate's letter to Porter that mentions the first excerpt of the novel that was published in *Sewanee Review* in October 1944 (Allen Tate to KAP, July 17, 1944). In the completed work, the text of this excerpt coincides with the first fifteen pages of "Part II: High Sea." The excerpt is titled "Kein Haus, Keine Heimat," also the epitaph for "High Sea." It introduces Ric and Rac and their mischief; Herr Graf and his nephew; cabin mates David Scott, William Denny, and Herr Glocken; the Huttens and their bulldog; and Frau Rittersdorf. Comparing the text of the excerpt with that of the novel, one finds that, on every page of the novel, there are differences. Most of these are minor revisions: one word substituted for another; short descriptive phrases added; descriptions of characters, physical details, and events sharpened; sentences restructured; and inconsistencies eliminated or corrected.

A representative example of the minor stylistic revisions appears on page 75 of the novel. The text of the excerpt reads "Sometimes they talked German together, making small comments on the affairs of the ship, and the two young men never seemed to feel that Herr Glocken's general experience of life was particularly different from their own" ("Kein Haus, Keine Heimat," p. 470). The passage in the novel reads, "Sometimes they talked German together, gossiping about the affairs of the ship, and the young men never made Herr Glocken feel that their general experience of life was particularly different from his own" (*Ship of Fools*, p. 75; hereinafter cited as SOF).

The significant revisions—new portions of text, which point up or exaggerate negative aspects of characters—are less numerous. For example, passages added to David Scott's musings about Jenny Brown draw a much more negative picture of him: "There had never been a really great woman painter, nothing better than some superior disciple of a great man; it disturbed him to see a woman so out of place; and he did not believe in her talent for a moment. The best she could hope for was to be a good illustrator . . ." (SOF, p. 77). Frau Rittersdorf's anti-American sentiments are made pointedly stronger: "the gradual mongrelization of that dismaying country by the mingling of the steerage sweepings of Europe and the blacks had resulted only in mediocrity of feature and mind impossible to describe!" (SOF, p. 83).

"The High Sea," the second of the excerpts, appeared in fall 1945 in *Partisan Review*. In the completed novel, it appeared in the section titled identically and is placed approximately forty-five pages after the excerpt published in October 1944, about sixty pages into the 289 pages of this part of the novel. The ship is six days out of the port of Veracruz. The wife of the attaché of the Mexican Legation in Paris, her baby, and Indian nurse are introduced as are Wilhelm Freytag, the ship's doctor, Mrs. Treadwell, Jenny Brown, the steerage passengers including the fat Mexican political agitator, Herr Lutz and his daughter Elsa, the two Mexican priests, Frau Schmitt, and the adult members of the zarzuela company. This excerpt contains Freytag's conversation with Mrs. Treadwell in which he explains why he and his wife "are leaving Germany for good" ("The High Sea," p. 521; SOF, p. 141), a key incident that sets in motion what Porter described in the 1943 synopsis as one of the two main lines of the action: "the banishment of Freytag from the Captain's table because he has a Jewish wife" (Synopsis, p. 2).

Again there are revisions on nearly every page, but this section was much more heavily reworked than the earlier one. Revisions address minor differences, the doctor's surname is Sacher, the action is explicitly described as taking place on a Saturday and a Sunday, and words and phrases are revised throughout. However, there are significant additions. Most of these are Freytag's ruminations, primarily about his wife and his situation (SOF, p. 140). Other more extensive additions to the text of this portion of the novel show Mrs. Treadwell's insensitivity, develop Jenny Brown's character and her relationship with David Scott, and enhance the depiction of Frau Schmitt.

The third of the four excerpts to be published in the 1940s appeared under the title "The Strangers" in *Accent* in summer 1946. In the novel, this portion of the text appears on pages 154 to 184 and follows almost immediately after the text of the excerpt published in fall 1945. However, in the novel, the excerpts of 1945 and 1946 are separated by an additional page and a half developing the character of Herr Löwenthal, who appears only briefly and has no dialogue in "The Strangers" excerpt. It is likely that Porter or the editorial staff of *Accent* excised this text in order to make the excerpt a cohesive whole. Other characters introduced anew are the ship's captain, Frau Lutz, Herr Rieber, Lizzi Spöckenkieker, the Baumgartner family, Arne Hansen, the Cuban students, La Condesa (although named the Countess through the excerpt), and the steerage wood carver. Four members of the zarzuela company, Amparo, Pepe, Lola, and Concha, first appear here as individualized characters. For the novel, Porter made some minor revisions for plot consistency. It is made clear that Frau Schmitt was not in attendance at the Lutheran services. As both Herr Graf and his nephew are named Johann in the excerpt, Herr Graf becomes Wilibald in the novel. When first mentioned in the excerpt, the Cuban students are described as "Spanish" ("The Strangers," p. 217).

Much of this excerpt consists of conversations about religion and politics, and the novel contains quite a bit of new text that expands and sharpens them. The exchange between Frau Schmitt and Frau Baumgartner about saints is considerably enhanced (SOF, p. 159). Hansen's political beliefs and cynical attitudes about civilization are expanded (SOF, p. 162). Significant additions to the text develop Jenny's character—her conversation with Freytag reveals her sympathies and actions on behalf of the working class as well as her clear-eyed though negative views of romantic love (SOF, 164-165, 168, 169). Freytag's reactionary conservatism is also laid out ("he had seen police breaking up picket lines before cigarette factories in Mexico and had approved of it thoroughly" [SOF, p. 165]) and his "sick and sentimental and false" views of romantic love (SOF, 168). There are also passages that demonstrate the "degeneration of his character" (SOF, p. 170, 177) that Porter described in the 1943 synopsis (Synopsis, p. 3). New text for Father Carillo, one of the Mexican priests, clarifies his own prejudices while further developing the Mexican political agitator ("As for the fat man who had pushed the man still kneeling in prayer, he was of the lowest order of rabble rouser and meanest of leaders, a Mexican on his way to Spain for the sole purpose of making trouble there and linking Mexican labor uprisings with those of Spain" [SOF, p. 172]).

The last of the excerpts to be published in the 1940s, "Embarkation" appeared in *Sewanee Review* in the January-March 1947 issue. In the novel, it coincides with pages 3 to 23 of "Part I, Embarkation," and comprises nearly a third of that portion of the work. Characters introduced who had not previously appeared in published excerpts include the Mexican bride and groom and the young German ship's officers and common sailors. Of the primary characters, only Freytag and La Condesa do not appear in this opening episode. Although there are minor stylistic revisions on virtually every page, the excerpt is essentially identical to the opening of the published novel except for the following passage exchanged between two male citizens of Veracruz on the terrace of the Palacio Hotel:

> The older man said, "After all, I have not paid any rent for more than a year, I may never pay rent again. This bombing seems to me a useless sort of thing to do."

> The younger one said, "Nobody in the whole Tenant's Union pays rent, as for that, but still, it is better to keep the question before the public. Also I am told that the Swedish Consul was heard to criticize the Light Consumers' Strike. . . it does no harm to give these foreigners a little jolt, now and then. . . ." ("Embarkation," p. 6)

Porter substitutes a full page for this ten-line section, emphasizing a point made in the 1943 synopsis, that "individual human life has no value in the battle for power" (Synopsis, p. 1). She sharpens the cynicism of the Veracruz workers, whose "festival planned in celebration of the bombing" (SOF, p. 7) is held even though the only casualty was one of their own, "a young Indian servant boy" (SOF, p. 6). More significantly, however, Porter creates entirely different personas for the two Veracruzanos—one is transformed into a landlord who has not collected rent in a year and the other into a factory owner whose shoemakers have struck four times in seven months. Instead of suggesting that foreigners such as the Swedish consul are rightfully the object of violence, the men discuss using machine guns, troops, and hand grenades against the workers and conclude that the workers do not realize that they are simply fighting for a change of masters and can "never win" (SOF, p. 8).

October 1950 saw the publication of "The Prisoner," the first of four excerpts that appeared in *Harper's Magazine*. It, like the others published in *Harper's*, was illustrated. Only one other excerpt, published in *Mademoiselle* in July 1958, was illustrated. About ten of the pages appear in Part I of the novel (SOF, pp. 36-39, 46-47, 52, 61-62, 64-68) and five in Part II (SOF, pp. 98-103). The action of the excerpt takes place on board ship both before and after its stop at Havana. It is primarily concerned with developing the character of Elsa Lutz, the putative "prisoner" of the title, her parents, her relationship with them as well as the character of Hansen. The other significant characters depicted in the excerpt include Freytag, the Cuban students, Jenny Brown, and three of the members of the zarzuela troupe, Concha, Manolo, and Amparo. It is likely that Porter or the staff of *Harper's* deleted the only significant passage of the novel missing from this excerpt in order to keep the focus on Elsa

Lutz. The missing passage (SOF, pp. 62-64) is a nearly two-page interior monologue of Freytag, in which he contemplates the situation of the steerage passengers and confronts "his own fears taking monstrous shapes in his imagination" (SOF, p. 63). This passage serves to develop Freytag as a character and delineates a picture of his wife and both of their families; it also skewers his sense of entitlement, class sentiments, and materialism (SOF, pp. 62-63).

"Under Weigh," the second of the excerpts published in *Harper's,* appeared in November 1950. This excerpt coincides with about sixteen pages of Part I of the novel (SOF, pp. 23-24, 25-36, 39-44) and follows directly after the portion of the text published in January 1947. It continues to develop the plot and fills in details for additional characters: William Denny and his cabin mates, David Scott and Herr Glocken; Mrs. Treadwell; Frau Schmitt (whose surname is spelled Schmidt in the excerpt); the Baumgartner family; Frau Rittersdorf; the Huttens; the ship's doctor; and Jenny Brown. The text is substantially identical to that in the novel with three major exceptions. Two relatively long portions devoted to Elsa Lutz are missing as they appeared in the previous month's *Harper's*, having been separated and incorporated to make that excerpt more cohesive as a separate piece. Like the October *Harper's* excerpt, text that had been excised or is completely new appeared when the novel was published. It, too, further develops one of the major characters, William Denny, and, like the passage on Freytag, the depiction of Denny is negative. Both in the interior dialogue and the incident described, Porter clearly outlines Denny's ugly prejudices (SOF, p. 24).

The other notable differences between the excerpt and the published novel are revisions that make characters more negative. David is more suspicious and misogynist ("For even when Jenny seemed intelligent, or sincere, he still distrusted her female mind, crooked and cloudy by nature: she was . . . meaning to trap him into small confidences and confessions that later she could use as a weapon against him when needed" [SOF, p. 27]). Mrs. Treadwell is made more indifferent and self-absorbed ("She turned back to the dull little thing across from her, accepting this voyage and this society as a long boredom like any other, not to be denied, opposed or ignored, but to be fled from, lightly from point to point, moment by moment she would find a split second of relief from boredom in the very act of flight which gave her the fleeting illusion of invisibility" [SOF, p. 30]).

"The Exile," the third of the three excerpts published by *Harper's* in 1950, appeared in December of that year. It coincides with approximately fifteen pages (SOF, pp. 105-109, 111-122) of Part II of the published novel that follow the section of the novel that appeared in the October 1950 issue of *Harper's*. The title of the excerpt indicates the primary subject, the Spanish Countess who is being deported from Cuba to exile in the Canary Islands. As with the previously published excerpts, there are minor revisions on virtually every page. The noblewoman is named the "Countess" rather than La Condesa throughout, and the ship's doctor's surname has not yet been changed from Sacher to Schumann. For publication in the novel, the conversation of Jenny and David is slightly enhanced, and the Countess's imperiousness to subordinates and contempt for society is more strongly expressed. Two longer missing sections have been eliminated, perhaps to keep the focus on the Countess in the excerpt. Both are about two pages in length. The first is a scene at the captain's table at lunch, which concludes with actions and exchanges, sparked by Freytag's refusal to eat ham, insinuating that all the other tablemates share prejudices toward Jews. The second missing passage depicts the Huttens' episode of seasickness after leaving the captain's table; it does nothing to advance the plot but does more fully develop Frau Hutten's subversive resentment of "conscience, duty, attentiveness, obedience—all the granite foundations of her marriage" (SOF, p. 110).

Nearly three years elapsed before "The Seducers," the last of the excerpts to be published in *Harper's*, appeared in November 1953. At ten pages, it is the shortest of all the excerpts. Unlike the other excerpts previously published in *Harper's*, it appears pretty much intact, as the corresponding text was published on consecutive pages of Part II of the novel (SOF, pp. 194-204); it follows ten pages after the excerpt published in summer 1946. The ten missing pages (SOF, pp. 184-194) were not published until the novel's appearance in 1962. One of the "seducers" of the excerpt's title certainly is "La Condesa," whom the doctor characterizes as "a mischief-maker, a taker of drugs, a seducer" ("The Seducers," p. 38; SOF, p. 203) but also refers to Herr Rieber and Lizzi Spöckenkieker, Ric and Rac, and the doctor himself, who are the other major characters who appear in this portion of the text, the action of which takes place one evening on the deck of the *Vera*. In this excerpt, the noblewoman named the "Countess" in previous excerpts finally becomes "La Condesa," as she is named in the novel. Porter made many incidental revisions throughout this portion of the text for the novel, but the more significant ones include additional description and dialogue for the doctor, whose surname in this 1953 excerpt remained Sacher. It functions to develop the characters and relationship of "La Condesa" and the doctor. Porter or the staff of *Harper's* may have chosen to publish this portion of the novel because it prominently featured the Spanish noblewoman, the central character of the excerpt that had been published in December 1950.

The ninth and tenth excerpts of the novel to be published appeared under its eventual title, "Ship of Fools" in *Atlantic Monthly* in spring 1956. By the time these excerpts were published, Porter had made the momentous decision to change publishers for her full-length novel, but had not yet changed its title. Text at the head of both excerpts explains that they have been "drawn from Katherine Anne Porter's forthcoming novel, *No Safe Harbor*, which will appear under the Atlantic-Little, Brown imprint" ("Ship of Fools," *Atlantic Monthly,* March 1956, p. 33; "Ship of Fools," *Atlantic Monthly,* April 1956, p. 56). In the first excerpt, published in March 1956, and the one published a month later, the text is divided into sections demarcated by Arabic numerals. The five sections in the March segment very closely follow pages 44 to 61 of the published novel with some omissions. In the novel, the action on pages 44 to 51 takes place on the first day of the voyage, all of it in "Part I: Embarkation." The portion that continues in the middle of page 51 and continues through page 61 depicts the activities of some of the characters during the ship's stop in Havana, most notably, the boarding of 876 Spanish steerage passengers, sugar workers and their family members being deported by the Cuban government to their home country.

There are some notable omissions in the excerpt as published. Eight paragraphs of text on pages 46 and 47 and one paragraph on page 52 were previously published in October 1950. The passage developing the characters of Herr and Frau Baumgartner on pages 48 and 49 is not included. Other notable differences include introducing a five-line passage further developing the character of Herr Löwenthal (SOF, p. 49), excising the phrase "put on his phylacteries" ("Ship of Fools," *Atlantic Monthly,* March 1956, p. 34) in the Löwenthal passage to which a reader of the excerpt had objected as being inaccurate, adding a paragraph to make a transition from the first day on the ship and the stop in Havana (SOF, p. 51), clarifying some of Jenny and David's attitudes and beliefs about art, and adding a ten-line passage pointing up the conflict between the two artists in which David is markedly less sympathetic. ("He would give up talking to Jenny about Indians, or about her painting, either; she was sentimental about the one and obstinate about the other . . . ." [SOF, p. 56]). When this excerpt appeared in March 1956, essentially all of "Part I: Embarkation" had been published.

The second *Atlantic* excerpt, published in April 1956, resumes the story after the excerpt published in October 1944. All these passages belong to "Part II: High Sea," and the actions depicted take place on the first three days after the ship departs Havana. The parts numbered 1 through 3, which coincide with pages 86 to 94 of the novel, are primarily devoted to the development of Jenny Brown's character. The new text adds details of her family background and old-fashioned upbringing, inserts the character's negative assessment of David and their relationship, as well as her insight into her own flaws and shortcomings. Porter also pointed up the portrait of Freytag emphasizing his reflexive German patriotism and disdain for radicals.

In the novel, the parts of this excerpt numbered 4 and 5 appear about twenty-five pages after the first three parts. Virtually all of these twenty-five pages had appeared in *Harper's* in October and December 1950. The only substantial changes in part 4 of this excerpt are to the depiction of the Baumgartners (Frau Baumgartner observes that her husband "simply never knew when to stop—drinking, making faces, anything. Her heart sank as she perceived that now in a split second he would go too far, and he did" [SOF, p. 123]) and to that of David Scott. As she had for Jenny's character, Porter elaborates on the friction between the lovers and their censorious views of one another. A representative passage describes David Scott's recurrent "repulsion against Jenny's lack of discrimination, her terrible gregariousness, the way she was always ready to talk to anybody, anywhere, join up with any sort of party, go anywhere she was invited, take up with the most gruesome assortment of loons and clowns and thugs and drunks and perverts, and male model types like this Freytag" (SOF, p. 126).

The fifth section of the April 1956 *Atlantic* excerpt is unique. It alone reprints passages that had previously been published, in *Partisan Review* in fall 1945. This section makes use of about three and half pages of the fifteen-page 1945 excerpt and includes three fairly extensive new sections of text. Focused on Freytag, it ends with the dramatic revelation that his wife is Jewish. Of course, this would have come as no surprise to anyone who had read the excerpt published in fall 1945 in which Freytag confides this fact to Mrs. Treadwell. In the novel, Porter retained virtually all of the text introduced in April 1956 (SOF, pp. 134, 138). It consists of Freytag's interior monologues developing his growing realization of and dismay about the serious consequences of his marriage ("And what it would be like to know always. . . that they were in flight, harried over one frontier, and then another, without power to choose their place or to refuse what shelter might be offered?" [SOF, p. 134]. "The solid earth was slipping from underfoot, the house shaking overhead, the long flight was beginning, and he could not even imagine the end" [SOF, p. 134]. "Before he could stop it, suppress it, before he even realized he had thought the fearful thought, it formed in actual words shockingly in his waking mind: 'If that were Mary walking yonder, even at this distance, at first glance, anybody—even I!—anybody would know she is a Jew. . . '" [SOF, p. 138]). One minor but significant revision introduced in this section is to the name of the ship's doctor—it first appeared as Dr. Schumann here.

The thirty-two-page excerpt published in *Mademoiselle's* July 1958 issue was, until the publication of the *Texas Quarterly* excerpt that followed it, the longest among them. Although it may seem surprising that a long section of the novel was published in what was putatively a fashion magazine for young women, its managing editor was Porter's friend and eventual agent Cyrilly Abels. During her tenure at the mass market publication, Abels was responsible for publishing the work of other major American literary figures, such as James Baldwin and Flannery O'Connor. This is the only excerpt, other than the four published in *Harper's*, that was illustrated. The head note states, "This is a section of Miss Porter's novel, *No Safe Harbor*, which Little, Brown will publish later this year. The action takes place on board ship in the early 1930s. The theme is Good and Evil, the central problem of life as well as literature. Its brilliant writing, keen wit and perceptive insights show why Miss Porter is called the first lady of American letters" ("Ship of Fools," *Mademoiselle*, p. 26).

Also remarkable is that, unlike the text for all of the other published excerpts, the revisions are almost entirely confined to insertions of large portions of new text. When revising the text of the other ten excerpts of the novel, Porter made small revisions on nearly every page. The experience of reading and comparing the *Mademoiselle* excerpt with the text of the published novel is strikingly different from that of reading and comparing the previously published excerpts with the novel's text. It seems simply to be a finished portion of the novel, edited into a tight narrative suitable for publication in *Mademoiselle.* Although many of the novel's other major characters appear fleetingly in the excerpt, Frau and Herr Hutten, the episode of their bulldog's being thrown overboard, and the Basque carver Etchegaray's drowning are the focus of the episode. Taking place on one single evening, the portion of the novel to which it corresponds commences about two hundred pages into the 290 pages of "Part II, High Sea" and ends about forty pages before the beginning of "Part III: The Harbors." Although there is virtually no minor revision to the text of the sort observed in the previously published ten excerpts, Porter did, however, sharpen the negative portrait of Frau Rittersdorf, by adding text for her diary (SOF, p. 268), her thoughts (SOF, pp. 269, 271), and her dialogue with Tito of the zarzuela company (SOF, p. 272); these revisions all develop her character as more censorious, rigid, pettily imperious, small minded, and parochially German.

The last of the excerpts appeared in the autumn 1959 issue of *Texas Quarterly*. By far the longest of the excerpts, equivalent to fifty-nine pages of the novel, it includes all but about four pages of the section to which it corresponds (SOF, pp. 205-267). This portion directly precedes the text published in *Mademoiselle* more than a year previously. Like all of the excerpts published since March 1956, it is titled "Ship of Fools." However, the note at the end of the excerpt announces both the novel's forthcoming publication and the change of its title: "One of the most significant literary events of the decade will be the publication by the Atlantic Press of Katherine Anne Porter's long-awaited novel, *Ship of Fools*" ("Ship of Fools," *Texas Quarterly,* p. 151). This portion includes some of the most significant actions of the plot—Mrs. Treadwell betrays Freytag's confidence that his wife is Jewish to Lizzi Spöckenkieker, which ultimately leads to the scene at the captain's table and Freytag's banishment to the table with Löwenthal, the only Jew on board the ship. Like the excerpt published in *Mademoiselle*, there is virtually none of the minor revision observed in the first ten excerpts that were published.

Several of the differences between the excerpt and the published novel were made for publication in *Texas Quarterly*. The Spanish noblewoman is named the "Countess" throughout, rather than "La Condesa." Porter eliminated the three-page episode that concludes with the suggestion of sado-masochistic sex between Pepe and Amparo (SOF, pp. 222-225) as extraneous to the central Freytag episode (KAP to Frances C. Hudspeth, March 1, 1959). The most significant revisions to this portion of the novel's text occur on pages 235 to 237 of the published novel, in the episode in which La Condesa smashes the bottles of German sparkling wine that the Captain has sent her. The new text serves two purposes. It further develops La Condesa's biography—the search for her revolutionary activist sons resulted in the burning of her Cuban hacienda and ultimately her deportation into exile. Additional dialogue clarifies her relationship with the doctor.

Having come to the end of this exploration of the relationship between the serially published excerpts and the completed novel, a few conclusions can be drawn. Examination of the excerpts shows that Porter executed the plan articulated in the synopsis created at the request of Paramount Picture's Richard Mealand in 1943. The synopsis includes an explicit statement of the novel's theme, summarizes the opening scene in Veracruz, provides a lengthy description of the "two main parallel lines" of the action—"the banishment of Freytag" (Synopsis, p. 2) and the Spanish zarzuela company's actions "to exploit the occasion as they can" (Synopsis, p. 3), provides details of "the personal histories" (Synopsis, p. 4) of all of the major characters, and briefly sketches all the episodes of the plot. Everything outlined in the synopsis appeared in the completed novel.

It is clear, by autumn 1959, when the *Texas Quarterly* excerpt appeared, that Porter had definitely completed the first 323 pages, or 65 percent, of the novel. More than 85 percent of these 323 pages had been published in twelve separate excerpts over the course of fifteen years. Evidence in Richard Mealand's December 6, 1943, letter to Donald Brace and the "No Safe Harbor" synopsis strongly suggest that at least the first 184 pages of the published novel, and possibly the first 204 pages, were essentially complete by the time Mealand received 219 pages of "No Safe Harbor" "plus 18 additional pages." Porter states in the synopsis that the "outline takes up from page 229." As the synopsis is nine pages in length, the 219 pages of the manuscript explicitly described by Mealand plus nine additional pages are equal to the 228 pages of the novel that Mealand must have read in late 1943. The serial publication of the excerpts from the novel provides some support for this conclusion. All four of the excerpts published between October 1944 and January-March 1947 appear between pages 3 and 184 of the published novel. Additionally, the four *Harper*'s excerpts published between October 1950 and November 1953 (prior to Porter's change of publishers) appear between pages 23 and 204 of the 1962 publication.

One can also conclude that Porter's decision to change publishers in 1955 spurred her to devote concerted effort to revising and completing the novel between 1955 and 1959. The texts of the excerpts published in *Mademoiselle* and *Texas Quarterly*, in July 1958 and autumn 1959 respectively, unlike the ten published previously, are virtually identical to the corresponding text of the published novel. Although the two excerpts published in *Atlantic Monthly* in March and April 1956 appeared after Porter had contracted with Atlantic-Little, Brown to publish *Ship of Fools*, she had previously agreed, as early as 1954, to send Seymour Lawrence a portion of her novel for publication in *Atlantic Monthly* (Seymour Lawrence to KAP, June 30, 1954; KAP to Seymour Lawrence, April 2, 1955). The excerpts published in 1956 clearly were drawn from a draft completed before Porter became an Atlantic-Little, Brown author. In the published novel, the texts of the *Atlantic Monthly* excerpts appear between pages 44 and 128, within the first 204 pages that may have been drafted as early as 1943. Porter must have extensively revised that draft, composed more of the novel, and sent the revised and completed portions to the publisher before the 1958 and 1959 excerpts were published. Porter's December 1958 letter to Frank Wardlaw about possible publication in *Texas Quarterly* provides corroboration: she wrote that she was "a little uneasy" about the "large swatch of manuscript out of the middle of [her] working copy of SHIP OF FOOLS" that she had sent for consideration as it was "not replaceable except at the cost of having it all copied again from the publisher's copy" (KAP to Frank H. Wardlaw, December 26, 1958). The pieces published in 1958 and 1959 appear between pages 205 and 323 of *Ship of Fools* and clearly were completed no later than December 1958.

The evidence of the serial publication points to Porter's completion of the novel between late 1958 and September 1961, when she departed from the Yankee Clipper Inn in Rockport, Massachusetts, where she had two month-long residences (June and August-September 1961) in order to finish and revise the work. None of the text on pages 323 to 497, the last page, were published prior to the April 1962, publication of the work. In that roughly two-and-a-half-year period, Porter may have written 35 percent of the novel. It also seems likely that she revised the manuscript and added or restored passages to stitch together previously written episodes, as passages never published until 1962 are interspersed between pages 23 and 317 among texts that had been published between 1944 and 1959. Porter's correspondence with Donald Brace and Richard Mealand, the 1943 synopsis, and the serial excerpts of the novel suggest that, by May 1941 when she completed her "Author's Apology," Porter had a clear plan for her novel that she executed, more or less, in the order laid out in the synopsis during the twenty-year period during which the novel was written.

Finally, by comparing the excerpts with the completed novel, it appears that many of Porter's revisions to *Ship of Fools* emphasize a negative, pessimistic, and cynical view of mankind. Although the 1943 synopsis outlines such a view, the published novel is darker. Over the course of her twenty-year "voyage" to complete the novel, Porter suffered painful personal experiences and witnessed national and world events that inform the novel. The former include the untimely deaths of family members and friends, unhappy love affairs, repeated episodes of ill health, and financial troubles. Historical events also contributed to Porter's darkening views: wars, the development and employment of nuclear weapons, the Cold War, the civil rights struggle, and the Second Red Scare. These private and public occurrences allowed Porter ample opportunity to observe the human failings that are central to *Ship of Fools.* Ostensibly describing the novel in a February 20, 1958, letter to Cyrilly Abels, Porter conveyed her own uncharitable assessment of her fellow human beings:

> It is a long exposition of the disastrous things people do to each other out of ignorance, prejudice, presumptuousness, self-love and self-hate, with religion, or politics, or race, or social distinctions, or even just nationality or a difference in customs. . . —and—this is the other side of the question, out of inertia, moral apathy, timidity, indifference, and even a subconscious criminal collusion, people allow others to do every kind of wrong, and even, if the wrong doers are successful, finally rather approve of them, perhaps envy them a little. (KAP to Cyrilly Abels, February 20, 1958)

Table 1a. Serially Published Excerpts of *Ship of Fools* in Chronological Order

Title of Excerpt	Serial Title	Date of Publication	Page numbers in SOF	Total Pages	Working Title of Novel
"Kein Haus, Keine Heimat"	*Sewanee Review*	October 1944	71-86	15	No Safe Harbor
"The High Sea"	*Partisan Review*	Fall 1945	131-152	22	No Safe Harbor
"The Strangers"	*Accent*	Summer 1946	154-184	30	No Safe Harbor
"Embarkation"	*Sewanee Review*	January 1947	3-23	20	No Safe Harbor
"The Prisoner"	*Harper's* (illustrated)	October 1950	36-39, 46-47, 52, 61-62, 64-68, 98-103	18	No Safe Harbor
"Under Weigh"	*Harper's* (illustrated)	November 1950	23-24, 25-36, 39-44	18	No Safe Harbor
"The Exile"	*Harper's* (illustrated)	December 1950	105-109, 111-122	17	No Safe Harbor
"The Seducers"	*Harper's* (illustrated)	November 1953	194-204	10	No Safe Harbor
"Ship of Fools"	*Atlantic Monthly*	March 1956	44-46, 49-51, 51-52, 52-61	13.5	No Safe Harbor

Table 1b. Serially Published Excerpts in Chronological Order, continued

"Ship of Fools"	*Atlantic Monthly*	April 1956	86-94, 122-128, 132-136, 136-137, 138	19.5	No Safe Harbor
"Ship of Fools"	*Mademoiselle* (illustrated)	July 1958	267-272, 281-299, 302-303, 308, 312-15, 317-323	32	No Safe Harbor
"Ship of Fools"	*Texas Quarterly*	Autumn 1959	205-222, 225-267	59	Ship of Fools
				274	

Table 2a. Excerpts in Numerical Page Order

SOF Page Numbers	SOF Subtitle	Title of Excerpt	Serial Publication	Date of Publication
1-2	Part I, Embark-ation			
3-23		"Embarkation"	*Sewanee Review*	January 1947
23-24		"Under Weigh"	*Harper's*	November 1950
24-25				first published in 1962
25-36		"Under Weigh"	*Harper's*	November 1950
36-39		"The Prisoner"	*Harper's*	October 1950
39-44		"Under Weigh"	*Harper's*	November 1950
44-46		"Ship of Fools"	*Atlantic Monthly*	March 1956
46-47		"The Prisoner"	*Harper's*	October 1950
48-49				first published in 1962
49-52		"Ship of Fools"	*Atlantic Monthly*	March 1956
52		"The Prisoner"	*Harper's*	October 1950
52-61		"Ship of Fools"	*Atlantic Monthly*	March 1956
61-62		"The Prisoner"	*Harper's*	October 1950

Table 2b. Excerpts in Numerical Page Order, continued

62-64				first published in 1962
64-68		"The Prisoner"	*Harper's*	October 1950
69-70	Part II, High Sea			
71-86		"Kein Haus, Keine Heimat"	*Sewanee Review*	October 1944
86-94		"Ship of Fools"	*Atlantic Monthly*	April 1956
94-98				first published in 1962
98-103		"The Prisoner"	*Harper's*	October 1950
103-105				first published in 1962
105-109		"The Exile"	*Harper's*	December 1950
109-111				first published in 1962
111-122		"The Exile"	*Harper's*	December 1950
122-128		"Ship of Fools"	*Atlantic Monthly*	April 1956
128-131				first published in 1962
131-152		"The High Sea"	*Partisan Review*	Fall 1945
132-137, 138		"Ship of Fools"	*Atlantic Monthly*	April 1956
152-153				first published in 1962

Table 2c. Excerpts in Numerical Page Order, continued

154-184		"The Strangers"	*Accent*	Summer 1946
184-194				first published in 1962
194-204		"Seducers"	*Harper's*	November 1953
204-205				first published in 1962
205-222		"Ship of Fools"	*Texas Quarterly*	Autumn 1959
222-225				first published in 1962
225-267		"Ship of Fools"	*Texas Quarterly*	Autumn 1959
267-272		"Ship of Fools"	*Mademoiselle*	July 1958
272-281				first published in 1962
281-299		"Ship of Fools"	*Mademoiselle*	July 1958
299-302				first published in 1962
302-303		"Ship of Fools"	*Mademoiselle*	July 1958
303-308				first published in 1962
308 (23 lines)		"Ship of Fools"	*Mademoiselle*	July 1958
308-312				first published in 1962
312-314		"Ship of Fools"	*Mademoiselle*	July 1958
314 (8 lines)				first published in 1962

Table 2d. Excerpts in Numerical Page Order, continued

314-315 (31 lines)		"Ship of Fools"	*Mademoiselle*	July 1958
315 (8 lines)				first published in 1962
315 (6 lines)		"Ship of Fools"	*Mademoiselle*	July 1958
315-317				first published in 1962
317-323		"Ship of Fools"	*Mademoiselle*	July 1958
323-360				first published in 1962
361-362	Part III, The Harbors			
363-497				first published in 1962

WORKS CITED

Agreement between Katherine Anne Porter and Harcourt, Brace and Company Inc. relative to Promised Land, April 27, 1939, modified, December 19, 1940, cancelled, December 30, 1955, Contracts –(Harcourt, Brace, & Co.), 1930-1975, Series 4, Box 4, Katherine Anne Porter Papers, Special Collections, University of Maryland Libraries.

Brace, Donald. Donald Brace to Katherine Anne Porter, May 5, 1941, Harcourt, Brace and Company, Inc., 1940-1944, Series 1, Box 10, Katherine Anne Porter Papers, Special Collections, University of Maryland Libraries.

———. Donald Brace to Katherine Anne Porter, November 17, 1943, Harcourt, Brace and Company, Inc., 1940-1944, Series 1, Box 10, Katherine Anne Porter Papers, Special Collections, University of Maryland Libraries.

Lawrence, Seymour. Seymour Lawrence to Katherine Anne Porter, June 30, 1954, Atlantic Monthly Press, 1940, 1953-1955, Series 1, Box 4, Katherine Anne Porter Papers, Special Collections, University of Maryland Libraries.

Mealand, Richard. Richard Mealand to Katherine Anne Porter, May 21, 1941, Paramount Pictures, Inc., 1941-1946, Series 1, Box 14, Katherine Anne Porter Papers, Special Collections, University of Maryland Libraries.

———. Richard Mealand to Donald Brace (cc), December 6, 1943, Paramount Pictures, Inc., 1941-1946, Series 1, Box 14, Katherine Anne Porter Papers, Special Collections, University of Maryland Libraries.

Porter, Katherine Anne. "Author's Apology," *Ship of Fools*–(Author's Apology), May 1941, Series 2, Box 16, Katherine Anne Porter Papers, Special Collections, University of Maryland Libraries.

———. "Embarkation." *Sewanee Review* 55 (January-March 1947): 1-23.

———. "The Exile." *Harper's Magazine* 201 (December 1950): 70-78.

———. "The High Sea." *Partisan Review* 12 (Fall 1945): 514-29.

———. "'Kein Haus, Keine Heimat.'" *Sewanee Review* 52 (October 1944): 465-82.

———. No Safe Harbor Synopsis, *Ship of Fools*—(Synopsis), 1942, 1960, Series 2, Box 16, Katherine Anne Porter Papers, Special Collections, University of Maryland Libraries.

———. Katherine Anne Porter to Genevieve Taggard, January 5, 1937, Porter, Katherine Anne, 1924-1939, Series 1, Genevieve Taggard Papers, Manuscripts and Archives Division, New York Public Library.

———. Katherine Anne Porter to Albert Erskine, December 7, 1937, Erskine, Albert, 1935-1937, Series 1, Box 57, Katherine Anne Porter Papers, Special Collections, University of Maryland Libraries.

———. Katherine Anne Porter to Monroe Wheeler, December 15, 1937, Wheeler, Monroe, 1936-1939, Series 1, Box 40, Katherine Anne Porter Papers, Special Collections, University of Maryland Libraries.

———. Katherine Anne Porter to Josephine Herbst, January 2, 1938, Porter, Katherine Anne, 1927-1962, Series 1, Box 21, Josephine Herbst Papers, Beinecke Rare Book and Manuscript Library, Yale University.

———. Katherine Anne Porter to Albert Erskine, March 22, 1938, Erskine, Albert, March 1938, Series 1, Box 57, Katherine Anne Porter Papers, Special Collections, University of Maryland Libraries.

———. Katherine Anne Porter to Josephine Herbst, March 21, 1939, Porter, Katherine Anne, 1927-1962, Series 1, Box 21, Josephine Herbst Papers, Beinecke Rare Book and Manuscript Library, Yale University.

———. Katherine Anne Porter to Seymour Lawrence, April 2, 1955, Correspondence, 1955, Series I, Box 1, Seymour Lawrence Papers, Special Collections, University of Maryland Libraries.

———. Katherine Anne Porter to Cyrilly Abels, February 20, 1958, Correspondence, 1958, Series 1, Box 1, Cyrilly Abels Papers, Special Collections, University of Maryland Libraries.

———. Katherine Anne Porter to Frank H. Wardlaw, December 26, 1958, *Texas Quarterly*/University of Texas Press, 1958-1959 and undated, Series 1, Box 16, Katherine Anne Porter Papers, Special Collections, University of Maryland Libraries.

———. Katherine Anne Porter to Frances C. Hudspeth, March 1, 1959, University of Texas at Austin, 1939-1975, Series 1, Box 53, Katherine Anne Porter Papers, Special Collections, University of Maryland Libraries.

———. "The Prisoner." *Harper's Magazine* 201 (October 1950): 88-96.

———. "The Seducers." *Harper's Magazine* 207 (November 1953): 33-38.

———. "Ship of Fools." *Atlantic Monthly* 197 (March 1956): 33-38.

———. "Ship of Fools." *Atlantic Monthly* 197 (April 1956): 56-63.

———. "Ship of Fools." *Mademoiselle* 47 (July 1958): 25-43, 85, 89-90.

———. "Ship of Fools." *Texas Quarterly* 2 (Autumn 1959): 97-151.

———. *Ship of Fools*. Boston: Little, Brown, 1962.

———. "The Strangers." *Accent* 6 (Summer 1946): 211-29.

———. "Under Weigh." *Harper's Magazine* 201 (November 1950): 80-88.

Tate, Allen. Allen Tate to Katherine Anne Porter, July 17, 1944, Tate, Allen, 1930-1976 and undated, Series 1, Box 37, Katherine Anne Porter Papers, Special Collections, University of Maryland Libraries.

"Mad with Virtue and Piety"

Faulkner's Ike McCaslin and Porter's Dr. Schumann

Robert H. Brinkmeyer, Jr.

In this paper I want to bring into dialogue William Faulkner's *Go Down, Moses* and Katherine Anne Porter's *Ship of Fools.* At first glance the two novels appear to have nothing to do with each other: *Go Down, Moses,* which appeared in 1942, focuses on the lives of an extended family in rural Mississippi over the course of more than a hundred years; and *Ship of Fools,* which appeared in 1962, follows the complicated interactions of various shipmates on a 1930s voyage across the Atlantic. While I am not suggesting any specific matters of influence—Porter clearly knew the work of Faulkner, but I've yet to find any evidence that she had read *Go Down, Moses*—the two novels (both of which had their origins in the late 1930s, despite their vastly different publication dates) dovetail in terms of several key concerns and themes, particularly regarding issues of idealism, responsibility to history and one's community, and what might be called the negative collusion with evil. Especially striking are the parallels between two principal characters, Faulkner's Ike McCaslin and Porter's Dr. Schumann. In my discussion here, I want to focus primarily on these two figures, and particularly on the way that the noble, but finally misguided, idealism of Ike McCaslin sheds light on Dr. Schumann's similarly admirable but ultimately flawed commitment to a principled life. Typically understood as the moral center of *Ship of Fools*, Dr. Schumann emerges in this reading as more complicated and less trustworthy, not the moral compass of the novel but finally another of its foolish denizens.

In *Go Down, Moses,* Ike McCaslin has repudiated his inheritance of the family plantation (and his place as family leader) in an attempt to cleanse the family—and more generally, the South—of its sinful treatment of black people. Rather than following in the path of his father, Ike has chosen the way of his surrogate father, Sam Fathers, a Native American (who is also part black) who instructs him in the ways of the wilderness and the hunt. Sam teaches Ike not merely technical skills, but more crucially the sacred Native American rituals honoring the hunter's intimate ties to the land and to his prey. Whereas Ike's fellow hunters easily return to their daily lives in town and farm after their two-week hunting excursions, Ike upon coming of age attempts to structure his life year-round according to Sam's spiritual teachings. Following Sam's inspiration, Ike embraces a profound asceticism in which, through self-control and restraint, he strips himself of needless attachments and material goods to pursue his spiritual quest. With Sam beside him, Ike enters "his novitiate to the true wilderness," a training so consciousness-altering that "it seemed to [Ike] that at the age of ten he was witnessing his own birth" (187). Even though he withdraws from active participation in the affairs of his family and community, he nonetheless seeks to pass along his spiritual wisdom, by teaching the rituals of the hunt to the youth of his community and by presenting himself as a man who has successfully stepped outside of history and freed himself from its terrible burdens.

A life structured by such deep spirituality, however, comes at a profound cost to Ike's humanity, especially with regard to his ability—or actually, his inability—to empathize fully with those whose lives are driven by the passions that Ike has sought to extinguish within himself. The most striking example of Ike's cold-heartedness comes in "Delta Autumn," when Ike talks with Roth Edmonds's spurned black lover and the mother of his son. Roth, the grandson of Ike's cousin Cass Edmonds, has left Ike to hand over his final message to his lover—a packet of money. Rather than showing her any sympathy, Ike upbraids her for getting involved with Roth, even after he comes to realize that the woman is a distant family relative. In the end Ike spurns Roth's mistress as callously as Roth has. When she tells him she is going to move North, Ike all but pushes her on her way: "Then go," he says, adding, "Get out of here! I can do nothing for you! Cant nobody do nothing for you!" (344). His parting advice is for her to marry a black man and to "forget all this, forget it ever happened, that [Roth] ever existed"—as if extinguishing her feelings and her memories were that simple, as if forgetting were possible. To Ike's admonition, the woman responds with a striking retort: "Old man, have you lived so long and forgotten so much that you don't remember anything you ever knew or felt or even heard about love?" (346).

I mention this episode because the woman's stinging admonishment of Ike bears a striking resemblance to the sharp reproach that La Condesa delivers late in *Ship of Fools* to Dr. Schumann, another well-intentioned but misguided idealist. Not long before La Condesa must leave the ship to begin her exile on Tenerife, Dr. Schumann breezily advises her that she will have nothing to fear in her new life. Stunned by his callous disregard for the realities of the future she now faces, one of unending isolation and painful separation from loved ones, La Condesa responds, "You may say I have nothing to fear—how easy for you, who are going home! But I am going to be a prisoner here. Never think once I am left here at their mercy they won't put me in a dark dirty place by myself." Still not grasping the realities of exile, Dr. Schumann once again attempts to comfort La Condesa, sounding a good bit like a travel consultant:

"You are not going to be a prisoner except on this whole island. A most beautiful place, and you may live where you and how you choose in it." Aghast, La Condesa replies, "her voice rising but not in question": "As I choose? Alone? Friendless? Without a *centavito?* Without my children, not even knowing where they are? And how shall they find me? Oh, my friend, have you gone mad with virtue and piety, have you lost your human feelings, how can you have forgotten what suffering is?" (367).

In their rejoinders, both Roth's mistress and La Condesa zero in on the crucial failing shared by Ike and Dr. Schumann: whatever their good intentions, the two men have so detached themselves from their inner feelings and emotions that they cannot empathize adequately with the sufferings of others, particularly of those who revel in rather than restrain their passions. Ike's and Dr. Schumann's failures of deep empathy stem from their ascetic withdrawals from the dizzying complexity of passionate human relationships. Ike's severe asceticism, as I have already mentioned, derives primarily from Native American beliefs, as taught by Sam Fathers, particularly those honoring the sanctity of the natural world and rituals of hunting. At the same time, however, as we learn in Ike's discussions with his cousin Cass justifying his relinquishment of his family inheritance, Ike also draws from Christian theology and history, specifically from the example of the Desert Fathers, who renounced the affairs of society and retreated into desert sanctuaries, pursuing spiritual quests through ascetic discipline and practice. As Peter Brown has written of the early Christian ascetics, the journey into the desert was a passage "of liberating precision. It delimited the towering presence of 'the world,' from which the Christian must be set free, by emphasizing a clear ecological frontier. It identified the process of disengagement from the world with a move from one ecological zone to another, from the settled land of Egypt to the desert. It was a brutally clear boundary, already heavy with immemorial boundaries" (216).

Ike's desert is of course the Mississippi wilderness, an ecological (and spiritual) zone set off from settled land and informed by a spirit described at one point as "profound, sentient, gigantic, and brooding" (169). It is here that Ike goes to free himself from his identity as a McCaslin and all the responsibilities and burdens that that identity entails, quietly pursuing the realm of the spirit. That realm, described in one of Ike's visionary moments, is "a dimension free of both time and space" wherein he sees "the names, the faces of the old men he had known and loved and for a little while had outlived, moving again among the shades of tall unaxed trees and sightless brakes where the wild strong immortal game ran forever before the tireless belling immortal hounds, falling and rising phoenix-like to the soundless guns" (337-38). As ascetic hero, Ike resists the temptations of the body together with the corrupting influences of materialist society. He still lives *in* society—in a simple house, working as a carpenter (modeling himself, like most Christian ascetics, after Christ) —but is not really *of* that society. His home—his true home—as we learn in "Delta Autumn," is the woods, specifically wherever he stakes his tent during his hunting trips.

If not quite so obviously, Dr. Schumann also lives by a tightly configured asceticism, grounded in religious belief and rigid self-control that in many ways mirrors Ike's. Dr. Schumann's desert—his sanctuary to which he can retreat for spiritual succor and security—is the sea on which he spends most of his life. While Dr. Schumann has of course not literally set off on a solo cruise, he has done so figuratively: for by working as a ship's doctor, rather than as a doctor in Germany, Dr. Schumann signally cuts himself off from his family and from his homeland, thereby largely freeing himself from the demands and responsibilities that come with being a husband and a citizen. That isolation is underscored throughout the text, as Dr. Schumann is almost always by himself, observing others but not becoming involved with them. Significantly, when we first see him, Dr. Schumann is gazing down from a high deck upon the boarding passengers, viewing them with eyes that are "without speculation or curiosity, but with an abstract goodness and even sweetness" (17). Dr. Schumann's elevated position and disinterested gaze point to his fundamental detachment from everyday people and concerns, as well as to the abstract nature of his virtues, whose principles are rarely tested in everyday life. In other words, Dr. Schumann affirms his goodness in principles rather than actions.

Even when Dr. Schumann is in a group or with a patient he is for all intents and purposes alone, remaining detached and often silent. Unlike a family doctor who would normally develop an extended, professional relationship with his or her patients (getting to know them as individuals rather than merely as faceless sufferers in need of treatment), Dr. Schumann, as a ship's doctor, almost exclusively tends to passengers whom he barely knows and who will soon, at the end of the voyage, pass quietly out of his life; they in effect remain strangers, bodies in need of medical help. His position thus allows him to remain all but alone—until La Condesa comes along (whose relationship with Dr. Schumann I will discuss shortly). Likewise, in social gatherings, such as meals at the captain's table, Dr. Schumann remains essentially locked within himself. During meals he rarely speaks, and when he does, he usually does so only sparingly. When the conversation veers in ways that make him uncomfortable, he's likely to retreat deeper within himself, remaining silent or leaving the table rather than engaging with the group.

One of the most striking scenes illustrating Dr. Schumann's disengagement occurs when, at one of the dinners, his German tablemates are disparaging Jews. To draw him into the conversation, Frau Rittersdorf says to the doctor: "You have said nothing, good Doctor! What do you think about the Jews?" To his credit, and befuddling his tablemates, Dr. Schumann responds: "I have nothing to say against them. I believe we worship the same God." Lizzi Spöckenkieker pushes back, first by identifying Dr. Schumann's Catholicism and then by asking, "Do not Catholics worship the Virgin Mary first, and then God?" Here's the description of Dr. Schumann's response:

> "No," said Dr. Schumann, crossing his knife and fork in the form of an x, laying down his napkin carefully, and rising without

> emphasis. "Allow me to be excused, if you please," he said, and left them. (230)

This is Porter at her best, using a few spare words to describe Dr. Schumann's controlled, polite, and forceful rejection of his tablemates' anti-Semitism. A small but telling detail—Dr. Schumann's crossing his tableware into an *x*—signals not only his rejection of the tablemates' anti-Semitism but also the dangerous ends to which their prejudice leads. As suggested in Dr. Schumann's motion, the anti-Semitism of the Germans transforms the Christian cross into an x, a letter often suggestive of endings and of death (one thinks, for instance, of the x-ed out eyes of cartoon characters who have died); and with only one more small adjustment, as is easily imagined, the *x* becomes a Swastika.

But for all of Dr. Schumann's magnificent, exacting formality in refuting his tablemates' anti-Semitism, one is also struck by how quickly he retreats from the table. While the good doctor has forcefully expressed his opinion, he does so in a mere two brief declarations that all but shut down further discussion. And then he departs. Perhaps he thinks that there is no sense in arguing with these Germans about Jews, as their thoughts are already made up; or perhaps he thinks he has made his point the best way he can; or perhaps he thinks that really there is nothing else to be said, that one either believes Jews are a threat to Germany (and the world) or one doesn't. Whatever his thinking, Dr. Schumann's dramatic departure from the table proves anything but an effective challenge to the anti-Semitism of his tablemates. None of the Germans at the table questions anything about his or her own beliefs about the Jews. Their immediate response is to question whether Dr. Schumann, who suffers from a heart problem, should be looked after, since the episode clearly has sent his blood pressure soaring. Then they ponder whether Dr. Schumann, given his thinking and his name, might actually be a Jew himself.

Dr. Schumann's dignified attempt but utter failure in meaningfully affecting his tablemates' anti-Semitism parallels in some crucial ways Ike

McCaslin's failure in influencing the values of people within his family and community. In embracing his ascetic ethic, drawing from both Native American and Christian models, Ike seeks not only to reconfigure his own life but also to inspire others to join him in remaking their lives. Just as Sam Fathers taught him the ways of the hunt and the wilderness, practical as well as spiritual, Ike seeks throughout his life to teach these same ways to his community's youth. "In a way," Faulkner commented in an interview, speaking of Ike's efforts, "every little eight- or ten-year-old boy was his son, his child, the ones he taught how to hunt. He had passed on what he had" (54). And yet, as "Delta Autumn" makes clear, Ike's efforts at inspiring youth have finally come to naught. Now an old man pushing eighty, Ike is on a hunting trip with a generation of men whom he had trained as boys. But none of these hunters has become a follower of Ike and his teachings: rather than respecting Ike, they humor him, seeing his codes of conduct and his spiritual beliefs as silly and irrelevant. Hunting, which for Ike is practiced with humility, dignity, and honor, is for these modern men merely an opportunity for a raucous backwoods getaway of drinking, shooting, and bluster, a time for wallowing in excess rather than a time for practicing ascetic discipline and purification.

Ike's complete failure at inspiring a new generation of followers is driven home by Roth's cruel question concerning Ike's long life of spiritual commitment and withdrawal: "So you've lived almost eighty years. . . . I suppose the question to ask you is, where have you been all the time you were dead?" (329). For Roth (and more generally the community), Ike's asceticism is merely dreamy, pie-in-the-sky idealism that leads him to relinquish his responsibilities to family, community, and Southern history. To their eyes, Ike's ascetic struggles at becoming dead to the world (in order to be alive in the spirit, following the example of the Desert Fathers), is simply that—death, in the sense of being completely absent from the everyday world of human affairs. That Ike imagines that he can free himself from the burdens of local and regional history ("Sam Fathers set me free," he tells Cass, justifying his relinquishment of his inheritance and his place as family leader [286]) places him among many in Faulkner's fictional world—and more generally in Southern literature—who mistakenly believe such escape is possible. Indeed, perhaps the most suspect line in modern Southern literature is quite simply, "I'm free."

All this is not meant entirely to disparage Ike. His idealism in the face of his community's crass materialism is in some ways quite admirable. And certainly his failure to become a model for and leader of his community could be understood less as a judgment against Ike than against the community, in not recognizing Ike's nobility. But haunting Ike's efforts is the simple fact that while he is able to keep his own dream alive, everything that he hopes to save with his dream slides toward ruin: the wilderness, which is progressively diminished by loggers; his family, which declines with each generation, having no strong leader; his community, which increasingly abandons its traditional values for those of greed and the marketplace. A number of characters weigh in on Ike's relinquishment, suggesting that had Ike accepted his proper role as head of his family, not only his family but also his community would have been better able to endure the momentous changes that had rocked the region, particularly following the Civil War. Faulkner himself stated in an interview that Ike was the type of person who, when challenged by a daunting situation, says, "This is rotten, I don't like it, I can't do anything about it, but at least I won't participate in it myself, I will go off into a cave or climb a pillar to sit on" (246). In other words, Ike doesn't do anything about the problem other than retreat from it in ascetic fervor.

Similar issues and questions also plague Dr. Schumann, particularly with regard to his treatment of La Condesa. I have already noted Dr. Schumann's ascetic cast and his propensity to withdraw from difficult situations and into the security of his beliefs. Keeping control of his interior life is of course crucial for Dr. Schumann, and he grounds his defenses in his unbending Roman Catholicism and his exacting Germanic decorum. His strict formality in social situations is a visible manifestation of the strict formality of his interior life, though of course his emotions and instincts are always threatening to burst through those confines.

Not far into the novel, Dr. Schumann's lunge to save a cat from being tossed overboard by Ric and Rac reveals the ongoing struggle between emotion and reason that shapes his life. In saving the cat, Dr. Schumann acts instinctively, unthinkingly putting his own life in jeopardy because of his fragile heart condition. When he later reflects upon his actions, Dr. Schumann is baffled that he risked so much for so little, even wondering if, had he time to think about the situation, he would make such a leap to save the life of his wife. This disturbing consideration (he thinks he would do it but is really not sure) pushes him to think more generally about his efforts to maintain his strictly structured life, keeping it secure from onslaughts of emotion and, more generally, from pressing considerations that impinge upon his isolated self. As the narrator comments, Dr. Schumann longs "to move within his own familiar body, to stay safely within himself, a place he knew as home" (113).

As his thoughts here reveal, Dr. Schumann suffers from a version of the myopic focus on self and self-interest that besets all the passengers on the ship. Their common suffering, the narrator observes of the passengers, "did not by any means make them fellow sufferers. On the contrary, each chose to maintain his pride and separateness within himself" (11), thus creating a world, as Frau Schmitt notes, "where no one seems to understand or sympathize with another; it seemed all too often that no one really wished even to try to be a little charitable" (159). Some make this choice deliberately and openly, while others mask it, sometimes even from themselves. But in times of crisis, that ugly selfishness always emerges. In a revealing passage relevant to all the passengers, Mrs. Treadwell recognizes the possible threat to her stability when Herr Freytag speaks to her of his problems:

> Mrs. Treadwell moved away again, from the threat of human nearness, of feeling. If she stayed to listen, she knew she would weaken little by little, she would warm up in spite of herself, perhaps in the end identify with the other, take on his griefs and wrongs, and if it came to that, feel finally guilty as if she herself had caused them; yes, and he would believe it too, and blame her

> freely. It had happened too often, could she not learn at last? All of it was no good, neither for confidant nor listener. There was no cure, no comfort, tears change nothing and words can never get at the truth. No, don't tell me any more about yourself, I am not listening, you cannot force my attention. I don't want to know you, and I will not know you. Don't try to come nearer. (142)

Mrs. Treadwell's fears of weakening herself through connecting with other people mirror Dr. Schumann's fears of losing himself through intimacy, though in his case the most threatening intimacy is that generated by sexual desire (the passion, of course, against which ascetics most stridently struggled). As we learn, Dr. Schumann has a deeply passionate side to him that since childhood has troublingly tempted and tantalized him, threatening to shatter the strict formality taught to him by his elders. At age five, he tells La Condesa, he had seduced a cousin aged three and then later, at age six, he himself had been seduced by a playmate aged nine. "In our ignorance," he recalls, "we did preposterous things—not even parodies." "Both of my playmates," he adds, "were very nice, charming, virtuous girls who turned out well, married happily, and spanked their own children roughly for the least thing" (200). Dr. Schumann likewise grew into respectability (signaled so prominently by his *Mensur* scars), and yet, as he admits, he continues to be drawn to "the dancing and the music and the drink and the lovemaking and all that ecstatic confusion" (349) that can brighten his otherwise dull life.

"Ecstatic confusion" is precisely what draws Dr. Schumann to La Condesa. She lives the life (or at least, he imagines she does) that Dr. Schumann has always desired but has done his best to repress. "He loved La Condesa," he comes to realize, "because she was perverted, strayed, a taker of drugs, a woman who lived outside religion, outside law, outside morality, who was beautiful, willful, and he had no doubt, a born liar" (350). Dr. Schumann reaches this understanding only late in the novel, after he has done all he could to smother his feelings and punish his temptress. At one point, recognizing the danger he is in, he vows to bring the relationship under control—that is, to make it one strictly between patient and doctor—declaring to himself that "she must be treated like an hysterical woman with no control over her acts. She could have been the death of him with her silly melodrama. Nonsense, there was to be no more of it" (196). But his efforts at self-control quickly come to naught. Not long after this vow, and still rippling with desire for La Condesa, Dr. Schumann "permitted himself a vengeful meditation" on the evils of women; rather than an hysterical woman, Dr. Schumann now concludes, La Condesa is merely what all women are, "the crockery-smashing sex, the outraged scullerymaid, the exasperated housewife of the lower classes, the jealous mistress—the sex that brought confusion into everything, religion, law, marriage; all its duplicities, its love of secret bypaths, its instinct for darkness and all mischiefs done in darkness" (237). He then wonders who La Condesa is out to smash—just him or could there be other men too?

If Dr. Schumann's professionalism and his sexism cannot check his desire for La Condesa, neither can religious faith. Central to Dr. Schumann's efforts at ascetic withdrawal is his unbending Catholic faith, which provides him with a means to understand—and to resist—his transgressive desires. At one point, Dr. Schumann admits that he believes in Original Sin as securely as he does "the Real Presence" (200), and he makes it clear he sees himself in constant battle with diabolic enticements. As the voyage progresses and his feelings for La Condesa increase, he more and more invokes his Catholicism to portray himself as caught in the wiles of the grand temptress. Late in the novel, angry at himself for not reining in his desire, he is filled with "a savage impulse to strike" La Condesa, whom he now characterizes as "this diabolical possession, this incubus fastened upon him like a bat, this evil spirit come out of her hell to accuse him falsely, to seduce his mind, to charge him with fraudulent obligations to her, to burden his life to the end of his days, to bring him to despair" (316). His rage ironically pushes him toward the type of racist (though not specifically anti-Semitic) thinking that he had previously scorned in others and that would, as we know, soon become cemented in Nazi policy: "His agitation grew as he felt the oppression of the increasing millions of subhuman beings, the mindless grave-stuff not even fit to be good servants, yet whose mere mass and weight of negative evil threatened to rule the world" (317). This is in 1931; one wonders what Dr. Schumann will be thinking, should his heart hold out, in 1933. Put another way: not only has Dr. Schumann done nothing in his work to stem the tide of Nazi thinking in those about him, but he has also done nothing to stem the tide of that thinking within himself.

As does Ike, Dr. Schumann thus in the end fails to save—or even influence—the world in which he lives from the powerful forces of history. Ike's and Dr. Schumann's ascetic strategies for coping are of course in some ways commendable, above all in their devotion to their craft—the good hunter, the good doctor—and particularly when seen against the worlds in which the two men live, worlds in which most people overlook the moral and ethical in their pursuit of money and power. And yet those ascetic strategies, which pull them away from active involvement within their families and communities, ultimately fail because they lead Ike and Dr. Schumann to sequester themselves in the cold and distant world of the individual consciousness. In their isolation Ike and Dr. Schumann not only lose sight of (and sympathy for) others, but their communities also lose sight of them. With the dynamics of their withdrawal diametrically opposed to the dynamics of modernity, their communities merely dismiss them as unhinged outsiders, men to humor but not to follow. Their virtues go unrecognized. And so, mistakenly believing that they stand outside history, Ike and Dr. Schumann end up having history pass them by. "Kein Haus, Keine Heimat" (the epigraph to *Ship of Fools*' central section) describes their situation well: isolated and given to petulance, they live without home or homeland, their lives emptied of the meaning and fellowship nurtured by deep connections with time, place, and community.

WORKS CITED

Brown, Peter. *The Body and Society: Men, Women, and Sexual Renunciation in Early Christianity.* New York: Columbia University Press, 1988.

Faulkner, William. *Faulkner in the University: Class Conferences at the University of Virginia, 1957-1958*, ed. Frederick L. Gwynn and Joseph L. Blotner. Charlottesville: University Press of Virginia, 1959.

———. *Go Down, Moses.* 1942. New York: Vintage International, 1990.

Porter, Katherine Anne. *Ship of Fools.* Boston: Little, Brown, 1962.

Ship of Fools the Film

In Context

Christine Hait

The present volume celebrates the fiftieth anniversary of Katherine Anne Porter's *Ship of Fools* by bringing the novel into conversation with the various Ships of Fools that preceded it, including Sebastian Brant's and Alexander Barclay's. Another Ship of Fools merits inclusion in this fleet, the Ship of Fools that Porter's novel inspired: director Stanley Kramer's 1965 film version of the novel. Porter scholars typically put the novel and Kramer's film in an exclusive relationship, focusing on the translation of the novel to film and asking questions about the film that lead back to the novel. Understandably, they probe the film for assistance in the ongoing effort to accurately evaluate the novel. Especially when understood in a variety of contexts, the film does help with the evaluation of the novel. The film can be placed in the context of films from 1965 that look back at the rise of Hitler and its aftermath.

Nineteen-sixty-five was a hallmark year for American films about Hitler and the Holocaust, furthering what some call the "Americanization" (Doneson 61) of the Holocaust through American popular culture. Scholars interested in Hollywood's handling of the Holocaust have given significant attention to the film and, because of both it and *Judgment at Nuremberg*, to Kramer. The film version of *Ship of Fools* can therefore also be understood in the context of Kramer's career. One of many films that he produced or directed that take as their original source material a Broadway play or literary novel, it can be seen in the context of his varying successes and failures in film adaptation and his intense interest in literary form, story, and character. In addition, it is one of the films, including *Judgment at Nuremberg,* he made in collaboration with screenwriter Abby Mann, and as Robert Brinkmeyer observes, *Judgment at Nuremberg* and *Ship of Fools* are companion pieces that allowed Mann and Kramer to explore history from a distinctly liberal and progressive point of view. Understood in the context of the year 1965 and in the context of Kramer's other film adaptations and other cinematic explorations of the rise and fall of Nazism, *Ship of Fools* the film reminds us of the relevance and timeliness of the story Porter created, a relevance and timeliness that deserve acknowledgment in the continuing debate over the novel's worth. Porter's *Ship of Fools* merits continued study, and consideration of the film version may point to new directions for further study of the novel.

Because of its famously protracted period of creation, spanning decades, Porter's novel is difficult to pin down as a creative work emerging from a particular historical and cultural moment. Contemporary reviews and later scholarly analysis of the novel often emphasize its remarkably long and arduous road to publication.[1] Indeed, it has seemed at times that the story of its creation has interested readers more than the story *Ship of Fools* tells. With a few exceptions, the emphasis on the novel's journey to completion has substituted for discussion of the novel as a literary product published in an historical and cultural context. The novel's creation does not stand outside of time and history, as its reception might suggest, however. Instead, its form and content reflect the cultural conflicts and concerns of its time. Readings of Kramer's film point to worthwhile areas of study of the novel that help readers to view it as more than the tortured product of its author's heroic labor understood only in relationship to her artistic struggle and to her overall body of work. It is remarkable that a novel that outsold every other American novel in 1962 (Cowles) is not seen more clearly as a novel of its time.[2]

Janis Stout argues that in terms of its critical reception Porter's novel was doomed to failure. Because of the many years that had passed since Porter first imagined the project, the book was "dated" (212). She argues that the novel

> could not possibly have the impact in 1962 that it would have had in the late 1930s, when the tensions between Germany and the rest of the world that appear in the novel were actually building, or in the 1940s when the events leading up to the war were still relatively fresh in the minds of the public . . . . By 1962, however, the events and that atmosphere had already been examined and reexamined in countless books, articles, and films. Thus, one of the major themes of the novel was simply old hat. (212)

It is hard to square Stout's assessment of the novel with its status as the most widely read book of the year and to thus draw the sharp line she does between the interests of the novel's general readership and its critics. However, it is worth noting that Stout does at least note the novel's position within an ongoing discussion, even if it is to conclude that the subject matter had become "old hat." Few discussions of Porter's novel place it in the context of other American short fiction, novels, plays, and films exploring similar terrain.[3]

Press materials for the novel and many reviews tout its status as a long-awaited work by a highly acclaimed artist, but such statements may not fully explain its extraordinary popularity.[4] Certainly, the marketing of the novel was a grand success. However, one can also argue that 1962 was an opportune year for a novel with *Ship of Fools*' subject matter and point of view to appear. The success of *Exodus* as a novel (1958) and film (1960) and *The Diary of Anne Frank* as a book in English (1952), play (1956), and film (1959) may have suggested an American audience's developing interest in the subject matter of *Ship of Fools*. Particularly of note here, Mann's *Judgment at Nuremberg* teleplay (1959) and Kramer's movie version of it (1961) also paved the way for the success of Porter's *Ship of Fools*.[5]

One might argue, in fact, that the novel benefited from its long-delayed publication. Alan Mintz in *Popular Culture and the Shaping of Holocaust Memory in America* offers a compelling account of America's slow progression from post-World War II American "Victory" narratives to American Holocaust narratives. He asks,

> In the depths of the 1940s and 1950s, at a time when the term *Holocaust* as we now use it had not been invented, when survivors were silent and stigmatized, and when the destruction of European Jewry did not figure in public discourse, who could have predicted that the Holocaust would move so forcefully to the center of American culture? (3)

According to Mintz, it was not so much that Americans, American Jews in particular, were too traumatized by the Holocaust to speak of it in the years after the war. Instead, Mintz argues, immediately after the war,

> Jews were too deeply engaged in the energetic enterprise of entering American society and seizing the opportunities offered to them to be available to the subversive sadness provoked by the Holocaust. It was not until this project was complete and Jews felt more at ease in America as Americans and, moreover, the luster of America itself had dimmed, that American Jews were ready for this dark encounter. (7)

In addition, the capture and trial of Adolf Eichmann in 1960–1961, according to Mintz, "amounted to an epic retelling of the Holocaust narrative" (11) that reintroduced the Holocaust as part of America's "collective memory" and "a key event in the modern age" (11). The Eichmann trial ended on August 14, 1961, the same month and year in which Porter completed her novel.[6] Porter, like other Americans, had long wrestled with the tragic events that led to World War II and, like other Americans, witnessed in the years before *Ship of Fools*' publication increasing interest in and openness to narratives that might help give meaning and shape to public memory.

The novel is, then, in many ways, very much of its time, both in terms of the decades-long struggle with its subject matter that its author endured and its eventual publication in a year when interest in its subject matter was high. The rarity of contextualized readings of Porter's novel can be seen in contrast to the frequency of such readings of Kramer's film. Granted, the problem of an extended creation period doesn't apply to the film. After completing the novel in August of 1961, Porter published it in April of 1962, and sold the film rights to United Artists in the same month for $400,000.00 (Unrue, *Katherine* 249-252). The film opened three years later, in the fall of 1965, to an eager audience, one that had read the bestseller from which the film was derived and viewed other films that explored similar territory.

In 1965, film viewers could watch Julie Andrews both make the hills come alive with the sound of music and along with her Austrian singing family climb every mountain to escape the Nazis. They could watch Rod Steiger in the role of Sol Nazerman, a pawnbroker and concentration camp survivor, endure a lonely existence caged in a Harlem pawnshop in the film *The Pawnbroker.* And then of course they could—and many of them did—watch Vivien Leigh, Oskar Werner, Simone Signoret, and many others, voyage from Mexico to Europe in the early days of Hitler's rise to power in *Ship of Fools.* Hollywood in 1965 was clearly in a reflective mood, employing a variety of genres—musical, melodrama, and epic—to tease meaning or merely entertainment out of the world events of preceding decades.

Thus, when the Academy Awards ceremony came around, *Ship of Fools* competed against *The Sound of Music* for best film (*The Sound of Music* won) and Oskar Werner competed against Rod Steiger in *The Pawnbroker* for best actor (Lee Marvin, who played Denny in *Ship of Fools*, won for his performance in *Cat Ballou*). In all, *Ship of Fools* was nominated for eight Academy Awards and won two, for its black and white cinematography and art direction and set decoration.

Filmgoers in 1965 who went to theaters to see *The Sound of Music*, *The Pawnbroker*, and *Ship of Fools* encountered a dizzying variety. The black and white *Ship of Fools* and technicolor *Sound of Music* bookend the experiences of two decades, as the voyagers in a monochromatic *Ship of Fools* make their way toward a dreadful future and the Trapp Family Singers in a burst of color in *The Sound of Music* are released by the end of the movie into a bright future as survivors whose singing prowess provides the situation for their escape. (American audience members knew that the Trapp Family Singers had emigrated to the hills of Vermont.) *The Pawnbroker*, on the other hand, reveals the lives in the United States of European survivors not fortunate enough to have gained international fame in a family choir. Film viewers in 1965 continued their exploration of the lead-in to and the aftermath of world war with this powerful film directed by Sidney Lumet. It perhaps serves as the true book end to *Ship of Fools*, an example of social realism offering in black and white a picture of its solitary character contemplating the anniversary of his loved ones' deaths twenty-five years before in the concentration camps. Working in a vibrant multicultural Harlem, Sol is as removed as he possibly can be from the life viewers see in flashback, and the film is in itself a stark contrast between old and new worlds, with Sol embodying the impulse of the moment in 1965 to look back.

Critics then and now have debated the use of history in these three films from 1965. Judith Doneson charges both *The Pawnbroker* and *Ship of Fools* for blaming the victims of the Holocaust for a lack of foresight and a lack of understanding of their own suffering (112). Unlike critics who praised *The Pawnbroker* for drawing connections between the suffering of Holocaust victims and the racial prejudices African Americans faced in the 1960s, Doneson decries how the Holocaust is "demystified, available for all groups to use as needed in order to interpret specific events" (110). Annette Insdorf warns that as we move further in time from the realities of Nazism and closer to comforting myths, many people shrug off the complexity of history to embrace the simplifications offered by films (4). In her review, Pauline Kael declares *The Pawnbroker* a "terrible movie" but admits to finding it moving not because "it reveals how most or some or even a few concentration-camp survivors are or might be but because this is how we fantasize and fear that we could be—unable to feel again, deadened, past pain, past caring" (161). In contrast, Kael renames *The Sound of Music* the "Sound of Money" and rejects its "luxuriant falseness" (178), wondering humorously, "Wasn't there perhaps one little von Trapp who didn't want to sing his head off, or who screamed that he wouldn't act out little glockenspiel routines for Papa's party guests . . . ?" (177).[7] However, Kael reserves her most scathing assessment for Kramer's *Ship of Fools.*

Like Porter's critics who struggled to place her novel in the larger context of her work, critics of Kramer's film found in it an occasion to assess the career of its filmmaker. If Theodore Solotaroff[8] led the charge against Porter, then Pauline Kael can be said to have played the same role against Kramer. Her essay, "The Intentions of Stanley Kramer," published in 1965 in response to the opening of *Ship of Fools,* reviews Kramer's career, with Kael bitingly concluding that in "Kramer's work the artist's accuracy is missing. That is why he is so often congratulated for his *intentions*" (214). She finds Kramer and Mann a particularly deadly combination, prone as they are to self-congratulation and "holy hindsight" (209). She mocks their decision to recreate the character of Julius Löwenthal into a charming and sociable creature more German than Jew. "In their view the fools are those who do not see that Nazism is coming: such wisdom is easily acquired in 1965. Their charming Jew, the waltzing Löwenthal, is a humorous, compassionate man whose failing is that he considers himself a German: this will lead to his downfall" (211). According to Kael, Kramer and Mann "want to make movies that mean something" (210), but they also want to make money and feature big stars in spectacular productions. They are quick to point out the compromised positions of others and blind to their own (210).

Kael is often sharp and funny in her essay on Kramer. For example, she observes, "The cynics said Kramer and Mann counted on people going to see the movie to find out how the book they never finished came out" (209). However, admirers of Kramer's career and of his filmed version of Porter's novel certainly winced at her harsh dismissal of the film and its director. Readers of Kramer's 1997 autobiography, *A Mad, Mad, Mad, Mad World: A Life in Hollywood*, find a more endearing figure than Kael's essay suggests.

For one, Kramer certainly took a greater interest in literature and literary history than many Hollywood filmmakers. Kramer's opening to his autobiography's chapter on *Ship of Fools* reveals his awareness of Porter's predecessors who employed the Ship of Fools metaphor. In fact, the chapter begins with his declaration that what he has adapted is "the old satire" 471 years after the original version. He continues with a discussion of the popularity of Sebastian Brant's narrative in the early days of the printing press, and of Alexander Barclay's English version. Kramer shows knowledge of the foolish types in the early versions of the allegory, including, "a book collector who learns nothing from his books, a judge who supplements his income by accepting bribes, a priest who is even more corrupt than those he would save, and a slave of fashion without limits" (Kramer 202).

The detailed introduction that Kramer offers to Brant and Barclay suggests that these narratives stimulated his interest in adapting Porter's work. After reflecting on Brant's and Barclay's works as satires, Kramer asserts that Porter's *Ship of Fools* is not so much a satire as "a saddening observation of humankind's sorry condition and pending tragedy in 1933, when Adolf Hitler was coming into power without much resistance" (202).[9] Kramer emphasizes the pathetic rather than satiric nature of Porter's narrative and Porter as observer rather than satirist. In the chapter on *Ship of Fools* and throughout his autobiography, Kramer's belief in story and character is evident. Having adapted many literary works, when confronted with the challenge of adapting *Ship of Fools* for the screen, he was excited about the prospect of working with a novel he considered important and timely. He sought in the stories of others a means by which he could give expression to his own concerns as an American and as a filmmaker. A self-described gambler and risk-taker, he often risked his own money to bring to the screen a variety of stories, some, like *The Wild One*, taken directly out of the newspapers, but most, like *Home of the Brave*, *Cyrano de Bergerac*, *The Member of the Wedding*, and *The Caine Mutiny* adaptations of plays or novels. Perhaps led reluctantly to humility by the criticism of Kael and others, all the same, Kramer admits that most of his films were "too ambitious" and that he "fell short" of achieving his goals with them (16).

Robert Brinkmeyer, in his essay "*Ship of Fools*: From Novel to Film," agrees with Kramer's assessment of his shortcomings. Brinkmeyer notes that Porter and Kramer shared ambition, and that both novel and film may, ironically, be seen as examples of the human folly of overambition ("*Ship*" 65), although Brinkmeyer's evaluation of the film is more favorable than his evaluation of the novel. In general, Brinkmeyer expresses puzzlement that Kramer was drawn in the first place to Porter's work and finds sharp contrasts between them. What Brinkmeyer calls Porter's "political paranoia" and "misanthropy" ("*Ship*" 69) in *Ship of Fools* could not have appealed to the left-leaning Kramer, and Porter's depiction of Herr Löwenthal must have offended the Jewish director as well, Brinkmeyer speculates. Furthermore, his "tendency toward social realism" would have clashed with "the allegorical and ahistorical aspects of Porter's novel" (73). "What, then, attracted Kramer to the novel?" Brinkmeyer asks (71). His answer is that Kramer, swept up in the "hoopla" that greeted the novel's publication, "envisioned adapting what was being proclaimed as the great American novel into the great American film" (72).

Kramer admits to such aspirations, with pride (Lyman).[10] However, more than ambition unites Kramer and Porter. Kramer shares with Porter an anti-totalitarian point of view and a commitment to individualism. Kramer avows in an interview with Donald Spoto,

> Any American film that contains criticism of the American fabric of life . . .is accepted, both critically and by the mass audience overseas, as being something that could never have been produced in a totalitarian state. This in itself builds tremendous respect for American society among foreigners—a respect I've always wanted to encourage. (17)

For Kramer, his films' frequent explorations of American racism and other forms of discrimination and intolerance served as reminders to the world that American artists enjoyed freedoms unheard of in less democratic and open societies. His films fought totalitarianism by their very existence. Many critics, including Thomas Austenfeld and Robert Brinkmeyer, have studied Porter's increasing preoccupation over the course of her career with totalitarianism and her complicated response to it.[11] Although Brinkmeyer argues that Porter ironically slipped into totalitarian thinking in her later years even as she bemoaned totalitarianism (*Katherine*), Porter certainly considered herself anti-totalitarian in her world view.

In addition to their anti-totalitarianism, the individual's search for truth preoccupied both Porter and Kramer. Darlene Harbour Unrue has argued that the human struggle to know the truth is the essential theme of Porter's work (*Truth*). Kramer shared this preoccupation, telling Spoto, "I search for truth, but it's never there for me in its totality. All I ever seem to find is part of it" (17). Both Porter and Kramer recognized that they lived in difficult and confusing times, and that lies and obfuscation on the parts of both individuals and governments obscured the path to truth. In addition, both struggled to find their own truth and were wary of party lines and group think. Like Porter, Kramer was a complicated and at times contradictory figure. According to Spoto, Kramer described himself as "a mess of contradictions—conservative in some ways, liberal in others" (16). Porter, too, defies easy categorization.

Porter's career and Kramer's career followed similar trajectories. Early in her career, Porter garnered praise but little monetary gain from her remarkable short stories. She struggled to make a living and was known as a writer's writer unspoiled by popular success and protective of her artistic integrity. Early in his career, Kramer lost money on film projects that he pursued not because he imagined them as popular moneymakers but because of his commitment to the subject matter and to the stories the films told. *Home of the Brave*, *The Men*, *The Wild One*, and *Cyrano do Bergerac* are some of the early films Kramer made as an independent producer working outside of the better financed and more powerful system of major studios. Many of his early films were "little movies" made on a small budget with actors, like Marlon Brando, who had yet to be discovered.[12] In the decade before he made *Ship of Fools*, however, he won the New York Film Critics Circle award for best director for *The Defiant Ones*, and in films like *Inherit the Wind* was able to cast well-known actors. He was also becoming known to a middle-brow audience interested in movies with serious themes (Lyman). Porter and Kramer may have suffered for their art early in their careers, but both found wealth and popular success around the same time.

April of 1962 in particular was a high point in the careers of both Kramer and Porter. *Ship of Fools* was the Book of the Month selection, and on April 1 the novel received a lead review by Mark Schorer in the *New York Times Book Review*. Kramer was in the spotlight just a week later when *Judgment at Nuremberg*, nominated for eleven Academy Awards, won two Academy Awards, one for best actor for Maximilian Schell and one for best adapted screenplay for Mann, and Kramer himself received the prestigious Irving Thalberg Award (Lyman). In the same month, United Artists paid for the film rights to *Ship of Fools*. Kramer was truly at the height of his powers as a popular filmmaker. Although at times he was derided for his sentimentality and at times he made movies weighed down by their messages, Porter would have been considered fortunate to have him direct and produce her novel. With *Judgment at Nuremberg* receiving awards at the time of *Ship of Fools*' publication and the purchase of its film rights, Porter hoped Kramer and Mann would have as much success with *Ship of Fools.*

Although it is not clear that Porter saw *Judgment at Nuremberg*, it would have been surprising if she had not, especially once it was determined that Mann and Kramer would be adapting her novel. It seems reasonable to assume that her approval of their most recent collaboration—or at least her recognition that others approved of it—shaped her decision to permit them to adapt her novel and to cooperate with them during the process.[13] Porter clearly approved of the high-profile casting that distinguished *Judgment at Nuremberg* and expected the same for *Ship of Fools.* In a letter to Mann, she states that she likes the idea of casting Marlene Dietrich in the role of La Condesa (*Selected*, 295). She would, of course, have known that Dietrich starred in *Judgment at Nuremberg.* She expected the most prestigious actors of the day to be cast in her film: Another letter to Mann makes it clear that she could imagine Laurence Olivier in the role of Dr. Schumann (*Selected*, 299). Coming off of a film with a celebrated cast that included Spencer Tracy, Montgomery Clift, and Judy Garland, in addition to Dietrich, Kramer and Mann seemed to guarantee that the cast of *Ship of Fools* would be distinguished and newsworthy.

Porter could also be confident that Kramer and Mann would present capably at least one of the love stories at the heart of her novel. Viewers of *Judgment at Nuremberg* and *Ship of Fools* are sure to recognize the remarkable similarities between the films' star-crossed lovers: *Judgment at Nuremberg*'s Judge Dan Haywood and Mrs. Bertholt and *Ship of Fools*' Dr. Schumann and La Condesa. In fact, they came close to being performed by the same pair of actors. Not only did Porter picture Dietrich, who played Mrs. Bertholt, as La Condesa, but Kramer at one point considered Spencer Tracy, who played Judge Haywood, for the role of Dr. Schumann. Tracy was too sick, however, by the time that the film went into production to perform in the role (Kramer 205). If Tracy and Dietrich had been cast as Dr. Schumann and La Condesa, audiences would have seen quite clearly the strong connections between the pair of lovers in *Ship of Fools* and the pair of lovers in *Judgment at Nuremberg*. In fact, the relationship between Dr. Schumann and La Condesa may be so powerfully presented in Kramer's *Ship of Fools* because Kramer was returning to a kind of relationship that he had explored in *Judgment at Nuremberg*: a relationship of mature and dignified equals strongly attracted to each other but prevented by their positions from engaging in anything more than a brief affair. Dr. Schumann and La Condesa are doctor and patient, and Judge Dan Haywood and Mrs. Bertholt are a judge and a widow of a war criminal with a deep interest in the Nuremberg trials. Judge Haywood loses his lover because he stands up for what he believes is right, a decision that alienates him from Mrs. Bertholt, who refuses to take his phone calls after his sentencing to life in prison the four judges on trial. In his speech explaining his decision, he articulates a viewpoint that Kramer himself cherished, a viewpoint that valorizes the individual over nation or external authority. Haywood proclaims,

> A country isn't a rock. And it isn't an extension of one's self. It's what it stands for, when standing for something is the most difficult! Before the people of the world, let it now be noted in our decision here that this is what we stand for: justice, truth... and the value of a single human being! (*Judgment*).

Ultimately, Judge Haywood puts duty over love and morality over desire.

The very American and down-to-earth Judge Haywood and the very German and aristocratic Mrs. Bertholt are classic star-crossed lovers. The scenes in which they meet and come to respect and love each other despite their cultural and political differences are charged and poignant, as are the scenes between the star-crossed lovers in *Ship of Fools*. However, Dr. Schumann is a compromised figure, especially in comparison to the stalwart Judge Haywood, and he loses La Condesa, whom Porter describes in her list of characters as "a déclassée noblewoman" and a "political exile" (xii), because he is unable to stand up for his beliefs and face the scrutiny of the other passengers. At a key moment in the film, Dr. Schumann articulates the main theme of both the film and the novel. After listening to the Captain cast aspersions on her, he tells the Captain that La Condesa is the only one on the ship with integrity, and that they are the fools, not she: "We are the intelligent, civilized people who carry out orders we are given, no matter what they may be. Our biggest mission in life is to avoid being fools. And we wind up being the biggest fools of all." Nevertheless, he watches her depart the ship and lets her go. Like Judge Haywood, he puts duty over love, but in his case, duty requires conformity.

Judgment at Nuremberg and *Ship of Fools* explore male authority figures whose moral command is tested by subversive women committed to their own worldviews who bring love and duty into sharp contrast for the men attracted to them. Kramer himself identified with the characters of Judge Haywood and Dr. Schumann, the men in the films who communicate the moral dilemmas that the films explore. Kramer's widow states that Kramer identified with the leading man roles in all of his films ("Tribute"), and Brinkmeyer helps us to see that in *Ship of Fools* this role, reconfigured to suit Kramer's viewpoint, is the role of Dr. Schumann. His death near the end of the film is a significant change to the story. Dr. Schumann at the end of the novel reunites with his family. Brinkmeyer argues that Kramer "reconfigures Porter's condemnation of human folly . . . into a study of difficult choices involved in taking a stand for human values in a world that attempts to destroy those values." According to Brinkmeyer, "For Kramer, to conform when you know better is to die, spiritually if not literally" ("*Ship*" 76).

Conformity and compromise were subjects that Porter and Kramer, with their complicated careers and studious negotiation of art and commerce during the height of their popularity, knew something about. It is through failed romantic relationships that Porter and Kramer best communicate in their novel and film the many ways, large and small, that humans fail each other and compromise themselves. The film helps readers of the novel to see fully the role the characters of Dr. Schumann and La Condesa play in communicating the narrative's overall theme.

Even Spoto, who refers to the film as "a floating *Grand Hotel*" (266), notes that the relationship between Dr. Schumann and La Condesa could have easily been the stuff of soap opera but is instead "beautifully handled" (268). Brinkmeyer observes that "their relationship dominates the movie in a way that it does not in the novel" ("*Ship*," 76).

Conformity and compromise certainly were at work as Porter managed her conflicting responses to the film adaptation of her work. Not all of the changes that Kramer and Mann eventually made to the novel pleased her, and her hopes for future Hollywood work as a result of her association with Kramer and Mann were not met.[14] As Unrue notes, "Although publicly [Porter] said that she was pleased with the adaptation of her novel, she actually was displeased with some of the changes" and she thought "the film bore the marks of Hollywood sentimentality" (*Katherine*, 262). She did not mind the change of year to 1933, and for the most part admired the casting, cinematography, and set direction. [15] However, according to Unrue, she was displeased with the change of Karl Glocken to a dwarf who acts like a Greek chorus and Julius Löwenthal to a merry and wise Jew and with the killing off of Dr. Schumann at the film's end. Nevertheless, according to Unrue, "Kramer's direction . . . was brilliant, and he revealed a keen understanding of the original work" (*Katherine*, 263). He said that all of the characters were "'aspects of Katherine Anne Porter herself and of what she feels and responds to'" (qtd. in Unrue 263). In addition, it was "his shrewd directing of his excellent cast, his timing of the numerous scenes, and his playing off pairs of characters against each other that accounted for much of the success of the film" (*Katherine*, 263). Of all of the pairs of characters and of all the casting choices, it was Oskar Werner as Dr. Schumann and Simone Signoret as La Condesa who emerge as strongest in the film and embody the film's themes and values, including ideas about love and disease, ideas important to the novel, too.

Mary Titus points to the failure of love as the novel's major theme. She asks whether the novel is atonal, monologic, and static in its characterizations, as some critics suggest, or multistranded and dynamic in its characterizations, at least in one or two key instances (200). She notes the viewpoints of Porter scholars who see the novel as a commentary on love and its failures.[16] She states, "Their focus on love opens up a fruitful avenue for approaching Porter's final opus" (200). Relationships are the driving vehicle of the work, Titus argues (200). However, "love is a battle" in the novel (205), expressing "misogyny and misanthropy" (206). Titus concludes that *Ship of Fools* is "unremitting in its bitter view of human folly" (213).

Another "fruitful avenue" for approaching Porter's novel is followed by Titus and other critics. Love in the novel is not only a battle, Titus observes, but a sickness (209). She notes a statement in Porter's notes from the early 1920s: "'Love affects me as a great sickness of the heart, a crushing nostalgia that withers me up, that leaves me fruitless and without hope'" (209). Unrue's 2005 biography makes clear the extent to which the experience of Porter's maternal grandmother as an institutionalized mentally ill patient and her own sanitarium experiences as a tuberculosis patient haunt Porter's fiction. Recent explorations of the novel's use of the disease metaphor offer the kind of contextualized readings of the novel called for here. For example, Lisa Roney reads the novel in light of the views of health and disease popular in Porter's time. She asks readers of the novel to consider public policies of the period that reflected social concerns about the spread of disease, concerns that coincided with Nazi ideas about racial purification. The film's focus on the doctor-patient relationship of Dr. Schumann and La Condesa underscores the reading of the novel through the lens of not only love and loss but also illness and disease. Brinkmeyer's reading of the film also sheds light on this element of the narrative, noting the way that the film "cleans up" a scene of sickness and illness in the novel. He points out that in the novel "sailors hose down steerage to clean up the filth from the writhing, seasick passengers" who are clearly miserable, but in the film the sailors hose down steerage because Dr. Schumann wants the passengers there to enjoy a cleansing shower, and the scene is a happy one that contributes to the portrayal of Dr. Schumann as a compassionate and moral man attentive to the public health needs of his ship ("*Ship*," 75). Kramer's "cleaning up" of this scene indicates his awareness of the provocative nature of Porter's original scene of mass human misery and the impossibility of including it in his glossy star-studded Hollywood film, even in 1965 when Americans were slowly confronting the horrific images that accompanied their growing understanding of the Holocaust.

In *The Eve of Destruction: How 1965 Transformed America*, James T. Patterson argues that 1965 was a pivotal year in the United States, the "year that the 1960s became the Sixties" (xiii). The early years of the 1960s were for the most part a time of consensus and optimism. He is struck by "how buoyant and confident most white Americans were in late 1964 in contrast to their attitudes at the end of 1965" (xvi). Military escalation in Vietnam, the Watts riots, divisions in the civil rights movement, and "mounting cultural change and polarization" made 1965 the "hinge year" that opened the door to the Sixties. "The full force of the Sixties" was not felt until 1965, Patterson argues (xvi). Patterson points out that the world of film was changing, too, and he cites *The Pawnbroker* as a key film in this changing period, but not for the reasons that the film has been highlighted here. *The Pawnbroker* was the first mainstream American film to show a glimpse of a woman's bare breasts, making clear that Hollywood Production Codes were losing power in a more open and frank era (110). By 1967, Patterson points out, movies like *The Graduate* and *Bonnie and Clyde* would change filmmaking forever (245).

Kramer himself acknowledged as early as 1968 the way that filmmaking had changed: "The nouvelle vague, the neo-realists and the angry young men . . . opened the gates to interrupted dialogue, mismatching jump cuts, super-imposures, split screens and the camera as primary weapon in the director's bag. Technique covers a multitude of sins" (qtd. in Lyman). Kramer's *Ship of Fools* then can be seen as a film in the traditional Hollywood fashion, made in a transitional period. Kramer was not technically innovative, and as a result, his reputation suffered. But this is not to say that he did not make an important contribution to a changing cinema, having helped pave the way for films after 1965 that addressed directly America's pressing societal issues. As David Desser argues, even in more mainstream Hollywood fare in the mid-1960s, like *Ship of Fools*, "one could easily detect the restlessness and disillusionment that would threaten to break apart the fabric of American society later in the decade" (130). Like the film, *Ship of Fools* the novel expresses a "restlessness and disillusionment" that if not felt widely at the time of its publication, if Patterson is correct about the early 1960s, anticipates the public mood to come.

The history of American film is continuing to be written, and scholars are gradually gaining the distance needed to see the key developments in an art and industry only a little more than a hundred years old. That same kind of distance is useful as we read American literature of the twentieth century and see key developments, like modernism, more clearly. Porter, whose career spanned many decades of the century, is a writer whose best work has qualities that readers might call "timeless," yet she has also earned her reputation as a Southern writer of note and a significant modernist figure whose defining artistic work took place in the periods that we name the Southern Renaissance and the modernist period, both at their height in the 1920s and 1930s. Often overlooked is her contribution, through *Ship of Fools*, to the popular culture of the 1960s. As much as her novel engenders debate about its value, it also invites us to recognize Porter as a voice of her times, including her later decades. As understanding of the historical and cultural context in which she lived and wrote grows, especially understanding of the years in which she finished and published *Ship of Fools* and saw it adapted for the screen, her only novel will merit further consideration and further debate.

Notes

1. Examples include Stanley Kauffmann's review of the novel in *The New Republic* and Mark Schorer's review of the novel in *The New York Times Book Review.* Kauffmann refers to the novel as Porter's "crowning work" (23) and Schorer begins his review by claiming, "This novel has been famous for years" (1). Scholars who have highlighted Porter's ordeal completing the novel include Stout in her chapter on *Ship of Fools.*
2. Cowles, looking back at the *New York Times Book Review*'s list of best-selling novels for July 22, 1962, notes that Porter had stiff competition. Other writers on that July 22 list included J. D. Salinger, James Baldwin, Philip Roth, Vladimir Nabokov, and William Faulkner, whose death that month put his work in the spotlight.
3. One exception is Thomas Austenfeld who in *American Women Writers and the Nazis* brings *Ship of Fools* into conversation with a number of other American literary works exploring the Nazi rise to power, including Kay Boyle's *Death of a Man* and *Generation without Farewell,* Lillian Hellman's *Watch on the Rhine,* and Jean Stafford's stories.
4. Schorer declares that the novel would have been worth waiting for "for another thirty years" (1) and that it should be compared to the "greatest novels of the past hundred years" (5).
5. See Mintz for a detailed account of the many popular novels, films, plays, and television shows that preceded and followed *Ship of Fools* and that contributed to America's knowledge of the Holocaust.
6. See Solotaroff who discusses *Ship of Fools* in relationship to the Eichmann trial.
7. See also Desser, who notes that in *The Sound of Music* the "genocidal racism that helped the Nazis rise to power is repressed" (131).
8. Solotaroff calls the novel morbid and misanthropic and its author an "unreconstructed short-story writer."
9. Actually, Porter's novel is set in 1931. For the film, Kramer moved the year to 1933.
10. Kramer also criticized younger American filmmakers for their misplaced ambitions, for their desire to be more European, more like Jean-Luc Godard than John Ford, and for their lack of interest in "creating the Great American novel or the great American film, or indeed . . . exploring what it meant to be American" (Lyman).

11. See Austenfeld, 136-139.
12. See Verswijver, 78-80.
13. See Unrue, *Katherine*, 262–263; Givner, *A Life*, 467–471.
14. See Porter's correspondence with Mann in *Selected Letters of Katherine Anne Porter: Chronicles of a Modern Woman*, which makes clear her interest in Hollywood work and her hope that her association with Mann would result in a career in Hollywood (294-296). The failure of her hopes to be realized may be behind the particularly ugly portrait of Mann that she paints in a 1974 talk to the students at College of Notre Dame (Givner, *Conversations*, 173).
15. See Porter's correspondence with Mann in *Selected Letters of Katherine Anne Porter: Chronicles of a Modern Woman*, which includes Porter's ideas about casting (295).
16. In addition to the critics that Titus mentions, Schorer states that "the fated and clumsy human quest for love and affection" is the idea that gives the novel its thematic unity (5).

Works Cited

Austenfeld, Thomas. *American Women Writers and the Nazis: Ethics and Politics in Boyle, Porter, Stafford, and Hellman.* Charlottesville: University Press of Virginia, 2001.

Brinkmeyer, Robert. "*Ship of Fools*: From Novel to Film." *Twentieth-Century American Fiction on Screen*, ed. R. Barton Palmer. Cambridge: Cambridge University Press, 2007. 65-77.

---. *Katherine Anne Porter's Artistic Development: Primitivism, Traditionalism, and Totalitarianism.* Baton Rouge: Louisiana State UP, 1993.

Cowles, Gregory. "Inside the List." NYTimes.com. *New York Times*, 13 July 2012. Web 22 Nov. 2012.

Desser, David. "1965—Movies and the Color Line." *American Cinema of the 1960s: Themes and Variations*, ed. Barry Keith Grant. Piscataway, NJ: Rutgers University Press, 2008. 130–149.

Doneson, Judith E. *The Holocaust in American Film.* 2nd ed. Syracuse: Syracuse University Press, 2002.

Givner, Joan, ed. *Katherine Anne Porter: Conversations.* Jackson: University Press of Mississippi, 1987.

---. *Katherine Anne Porter: A Life.* New York: Simon and Schuster, 1982.

Insdorf, Annette. *Indelible Shadows: Film and the Holocaust.* 3rd ed. Cambridge: Cambridge University Press, 2003.

Judgment at Nuremberg. Dir. Stanley Kramer. MGM. 2004. DVD.

Kael, Pauline. *Kiss Kiss Bang Bang: Film Writings, 1965-1967.* New York: Marion Boyars, 1973.

Kauffmann, Stanley. "Katherine Anne Porter's Crowning Work." *The New Republic* 2 April 1962: 23-25.

Kramer, Stanley, and Thomas M. Coffey. *A Mad, Mad, Mad, Mad World: A Life in Hollywood.* New York: Harcourt Brace, 1997.

Lyman, Rick. "Stanley Kramer, Filmmaker with Social Bent, Dies at 87." *NYTimes.com.* New York Times, 21 Feb. 2001. Web. 22 Nov. 2012.

Mintz, Alan. *Popular Culture and the Shaping of Holocaust Memory in America.* Seattle: University of Washington Press, 2001.

The Pawnbroker. Dir. Sidney Lumet. Republic Pictures. 2003. DVD.

Patterson, James T. *The Eve of Destruction: How 1965 Transformed America.* New York: Basic Books, 2012.

Porter, Katherine Anne. *Ship of Fools.* Boston: Little, Brown, 1962.

---. *Selected Letters of Katherine Anne Porter: Chronicles of a Modern Woman,* ed. Darlene Harbour Unrue. Jackson: University Press of Mississippi, 2012.

Roney, Lisa. "Katherine Anne Porter's *Ship of Fools*: An Interrogation of Eugenics." *Papers on Language and Literature* 45, no.1 (Winter 2009): 82-107.

Schorer, Mark. "We're All on the Passenger List." *New York Times Book Review* 1 April 1962: 1, 5. Print.

Ship of Fools. Dir. Stanley Kramer. Sony Pictures Home Entertainment. 2007. DVD.

Solotaroff, Theodore. "*Ship of Fools* and the Critics." *Commentary* 34 (October 1962): 277-286.

The Sound of Music. Dir. Robert Wise. 20th Century Fox. 2004. DVD.

Spoto, Donald. *Stanley Kramer: Film Maker.* New York: Putnam's, 1978.

Stout, Janis. *Katherine Anne Porter: A Sense of the Times.* Charlottesville: University of Virginia Press, 1995.

Titus, Mary. *The Ambivalent Art of Katherine Anne Porter.* Athens: University of Georgia Press, 2005.

"A Tribute to Stanley Kramer." *Judgment at Nuremberg.* Dir. Stanley Kramer. MGM. 2004. DVD.

Unrue, Darlene Harbour. *Katherine Anne Porter: The Life of an Artist.* Jackson: University Press of Mississippi, 2005.

---. *Truth and Vision in Katherine Anne Porter's Fiction.* Athens: University of Georgia Press, 1985.

Verswijver, Leo. "*Movies Were Always Magical*"*: Interviews with Nineteen Actors, Directors, and Producers from the Hollywood of the 1930s through the 1950s.* Jefferson, NC: McFarland, 2003.

Transnationalizing Porter's Germans in Stanley Kramer's *Ship of Fools* (1965)

West and East German Responses

Anne-Marie Scholz

In the mid-twentieth century and just prior to the onset of mass commercial air travel, the transatlantic voyage provided novelists and filmmakers with a potent metaphor to gauge the relationship between tourism, travel, and the meaning and significance of "transnational" forms of interaction and transformation. An intriguing example of such an effort is the Jewish-American filmmaker Stanley Kramer's 1965 adaptation of Katherine Anne Porter's 1962 novel *Ship of Fools.* In her novel, Porter transformed the medieval German satire *Das Narrenschiff* into a modern narrative about transatlantic travel. Her version tells the story of a group of German, Spanish, and American as well as Swiss, Cuban, and Mexican passengers en route on the passenger ship *Vera* from Veracruz, Mexico, to Bremerhaven, Germany. It is set in the historically significant period of the early 1930s, when the Nazis were first coming into power. This essay will evaluate the ways that the metaphor of transnational travel was used to examine the meanings of "Germanness" in this period. It will also consider how these American depictions were received by German reviewers and critics in both West and East Germany.[1]

Both Kramer's film and Porter's novel were very interested in exploring questions of German national identity. They did so by using transnational interactions on board a ship traveling to Germany to shed light on the most sinister dimensions of nationalism and prejudice. The events in this story take place within this suspended space offered by a four-week ocean voyage. Although Porter set the story in 1931, Kramer changed the year to 1933 to emphasize the theme of the rise of fascism in Germany.

The film adaptation of *Ship of Fools*, intended to be "character" rather than "plot" oriented, as Stanley Kramer pointed out, featured an international cast. The Americans on board include Vivien Leigh as Mrs. Treadwell, a jaded southern divorcee; Lee Marvin as Denny, a failed baseball player with rough manners; and a young artist couple, unmarried and always in domestic conflict, Jenny and David, played by Elizabeth Ashley and George Segal. Among the Spanish characters are an exiled countess played by the French actress Simone Signoret and a flamenco dance troupe leader and pimp played by José Greco.

Most important to the story, however, are the German characters on board this ship. These include the ship's captain (Charles Korvan) and the ship's doctor, Schumann, played by the Austrian actor Oskar Werner. At the captain's table we find more Germans: a loud-mouthed National Socialist editor named Rieber (José Ferrer), his fellow Nazi flirt on the voyage, Lizzie Spöckenkieker (Christiane Schmidtmer), a German professor and his wife together with their bulldog, Bébé, and a soft-spoken German man travelling alone named Freytag (Alf Kjellin), whom we later learn is married to a Jewish woman. Those not placed at the captain's table, as they are not "acceptable" Germans, are the patriotic Jewish salesman Julius Löwenthal (Heinz Rühmann) and the dwarf Karl Glocken.

Kramer's angle on the potential for transformation among the culturally and ethnically diverse passengers aboard the *Vera* was far more optimistic than was Porter's, and he deliberately downplayed Porter's more virulent depictions of German nationalism. Instead, he gave more voice to the perspective of the "Other" by making the dwarf character, Karl Glocken, function as a chorus. Played by the American actor Michael Dunn, this character could mediate between different national interests, thereby transforming a German national issue into a transnational issue relevant across nations and cultures. Thus, the film opens with Glocken commenting on the foolishness of all aboard the *Vera* (Kramer w/ Coffey 204):

> My name is Karl Glocken, and this is a ship of fools. I'm a fool, and you'll meet more fools as we go along, this tub is packed with them: emancipated ladies, ball players, lovers, dog lovers, ladies of joy, tolerant Jews, dwarfs. All kinds. And who knows, if you look closely enough, you might even find yourself on board. (*Ship*)

When the vessel, after making stops in Cuba and Tenerife, arrives at its destination in Bremerhaven in 1933, Glocken again directly addresses the viewers, ironically encouraging them to consider identifying with all they have just borne witness to on the *Vera*. The ship's doctor has died of a heart attack; the Jewish salesman is warmly greeted by his family; the other passengers go their separate ways to the tune of a brass band. A swastika on the arm of a soldier picking up one of the passengers appears ominously as the film ends.

Transforming the relationship between Nazism and Germanness into a transnational theme—that is, one that would generate interest beyond German-speaking boundaries—was a central goal of Kramer's *Ship of Fools* as a big budget Hollywood production. Kramer had shown his interest in the continued influence and impact of National Socialism on postwar German society in his 1961 film *Judgment at Nuremberg*, which dramatized a fictional trial of four German judges condemned for their complicity with Nazism despite pressure from the U.S. Cold War authorities for leniency. Kramer's interest in the rise of fascism in Germany reflects his position as a Jewish-American filmmaker interested in history and politics. *Judgment at Nuremberg*, however, had not been a very popular film, in Germany or elsewhere, upon its release just a few months after the construction of the Berlin Wall (Etheridge 73-106; Muñoz Conde and Muñoz Aunión 82-89).[2] In *Ship of Fools*, Kramer adapted Katherine Anne Porter's novel to explore the origins of National Socialism. In this, his second film on "the German question" (rpm, "Die Deutsche Frage"), he decided upon a different approach, one that essentially transformed negative German characters in Porter's novel to more positive characters. Kramer's goal as a popular filmmaker, as one West German critic put it, was to "create films that appeal across cultural boundaries and manage to bring people together" (Färber 631-32). He thus sought to create a drama that could offer a meditation on the relationship between Nazism and Germanness that would also appeal to a world audience.

TRANSNATIONALIZING "THE GERMAN QUESTION": KRAMER'S VERSIONS OF PORTER'S GERMANS

Three characters portrayed on Kramer's ship are especially relevant to his effort to transnationalize issues pertaining to German history: the Jewish-German businessman Löwenthal, the National-Socialist publisher Rieber, and the dwarf Glocken. Kramer's version of transnationalism began with his casting. Heinz Rühmann, a well-known German actor, was chosen to play the Jewish businessman in Kramer's film.[3] In his autobiography, Kramer mentioned having seen Rühmann's performance in West German reception (1965) the 1960 film production of *Der Brave Soldat Schwejk*, originally a Czech satirical pacifistic play about a military deserter ("Heinz Rühmann und das Narrenschiff," "Der Brave").[4] Kramer also recalled that he had chosen Rühmann because he was interested in playing this role. Rühmann had indicated to Kramer that he "felt guilty for being a German" and wanted to make up for it. Anticipating resistance from German actors because of what he perceived as the overall negative reception of his previous film dealing with Germany, *Judgment at Nuremberg*, Kramer apparently appreciated Rühmann's enthusiasm for the role, and took Rühmann's rationale seriously (Kramer w/Coffey 209-11).

Yet while Kramer actively politicized the German question in his discussion of Rühmann's role in the film in his 1997 autobiography, he did not address questions about Rühmann's own ambiguous relationship to the Third Reich. In fact, Rühmann actually resembled one of the German characters in the film—a man with a Jewish wife. Rühmann had been married to a Jewish woman when the National Socialists came to power, whom he then divorced. He was known to keep his distance from politics during the Third Reich, but had actively pursued his acting career under the Nazis and was thus spared military service (Strauven 2007). As the critic L. Wronkow, who praised Rühmann's performance, noted ironically in 1965 in the *Aufbau*, a German-Jewish newspaper published in New York, here was an actor playing a German Jew who, during the Third Reich, "managed to fulfill all the National Socialist's racialist criteria" (Wronkow).

Kramer also significantly transformed Löwenthal's character by making him far more appealing than he was in Porter's narrative. In Porter's novel, the character Wilhelm Freytag, a German man also banished to a separate table during meals when it is revealed that he is married to a Jewish woman, characterizes Löwenthal as the kind of Jew "other kinds of Jews don't like" (240). As Porter writes,

> Freytag knew the type too well—overfamiliar if you made the mistake of being pleasant to him; loud and insolent if he suspected timidity in you... He's the kind that comes to the door peddling trash; Mary's mother would set the dog on him! He recalled all the queer comic names that Jews made up for each other, names

> of contempt and ridicule, and the worst of them were meant for fellows like this. (240-241)

In the book, moreover, during their meal together Freytag is bitterly criticized by Löwenthal for marrying outside his own ethnic group and thus invading Jewish territory. Banished from the captain's table because of his marriage, and then condemned for marrying outside his ethnic group by Löwenthal, Freytag is caught between the perpetrator's racism and the victim's isolation and resentment.

In Kramer's film, the well-known screenwriter Abby Mann transformed Porter's bitter Jewish-German businessman into a kind, outgoing, liberal, and above all, patriotic character. Proud of his country and a decorated veteran of World War I, Löwenthal in the film cannot be convinced that Germany, with its magnificent cultural heritage, won't overcome this current phase of anti-semitism. He is even homesick for his country. In his dealings with the most vehement anti-Semite on board, the publisher Herr Rieber, with whom he is forced to share a cabin, Löwenthal parries Rieber's virulence not with dread, as in the novel, but with the verbal tools of wit and diplomacy and even manages to gain sympathy points with Rieber. Clearly, Kramer wished the film viewers' sympathies to be on the side of Löwenthal. Here was a German-Jewish character, played by a well-known German actor, who could conceivably garner transnational sympathies.

Another transnational transformation is evident in the casting of the Puerto Rican/American actor José Ferrer as the Nazi publisher, Rieber ("José"). Not casting a German national here was surely also strategy on Kramer's part: Rieber is the most vocal and aggressive Nazi on board the *Vera.*[5] He is loud, arrogant, uncouth, and sexually aggressive. In both the novel and the film, Rieber shares a cabin with Löwenthal, whom he treats with contempt. In the film, however, the cabin scenes demonstrate Löwenthal's perspicacity and humor in vivid contrast to Rieber's rage and vulgarity. For Kramer, Rieber represented "just a common, rich, but thoughtless bigot, the kind who paved the way for Hitler's rise in

Germany and the subsequent mass slaughter" (Kramer w/ Coffey 209). With few exceptions the other characters on the ship don't like him and neither would most viewers.

A third German character, the hunchback Karl Glocken, is also significantly transformed in the film. In Porter's novel, Herr Glocken is an embittered outcast, a man isolated, deformed, unsightly, in physical pain and very self-conscious about his disability. Just as Kramer transformed Löwenthal from a deeply negative to a strongly positive character, Glocken is also transformed into a perceptive and compassionate character. Since he represents the "chorus," he is given the final word at the end, where he reminds the viewer of the transnational significance of the conflicts aboard the ship: "Oh, I can just hear you say, what has all this to do with us? Nothing." Kramer also added very important scenes for Glocken. These include one where he confronts Löwenthal with his naiveté about German attitudes toward Jews, suggesting a liberal and anti-Nazi political persuasion born no doubt, of the National Socialist eugenics policies toward the physically and mentally "compromised." Glocken and Löwenthal are the original outcasts from the captain's table, and their friendship in the film, a friendship that is not created in the novel, privileges their solidarity based upon their status as physical and ethnic outcasts rather than upon their shared nationality. In a typical scene, Glocken and Löwenthal are seated at a table on deck, listening to the ship's orchestra playing German music. This dialogue ensues:

> Löwenthal: Now I ask you honestly, Glocken, when you hear that music, wherever you are, don't you have a special feeling about being a German?
>
> Glocken: Now, I tell you honestly, Löwenthal, when I hear that music wherever I am, I have a special feeling about being a dwarf (*Ship*).

Figure 14. The outcasts aboard the *Vera*, the dwarf Karl Glocken (Michael Dunn) and the Jewish-German salesman Julius Löwenthal (Heinz Rühmann) converse about the meaning of "Germanness" in Stanley Kramer's *Ship of Fools* (1965).

Image courtesy Photofest

Kramer invented the role of chorus for Dunn's character partially, as he stated in his autobiography, because Michael Dunn's talents as an actor could compensate for his small stature (Kramer w/Coffey 205-206). At the same time, on an unconscious level, Dunn's size may have served as a metaphor for conveying the modest role of anti-fascist political elements in Germany in the thirties. In Kramer's adaptation, the dwarf Glocken is transformed into the ideal tourist, a man whose "deterritorialized consciousness" makes him capable of seeing beyond the nationalistic blinders of his fellow passengers on an ocean liner where the rules of nationality are temporarily "displaced" (MacCannell 4). Thus for Kramer, the tourist experience on board a transatlantic ship offered an opportunity to investigate German nationality in a way that spoke to international audiences. By considering the responses of critics and reviewers to this film in both West and East Germany, we can gauge something about just how successful or unsuccessful this strategy was.

The West German response to *Ship of Fools* (1965)

How did West German critics respond to these German characters in *Ship of Fools* in 1965? Did they accept Kramer's transnationalization of the German question by aligning a German Jew and a German dwarf against a virulent Nazi? Basically, they did not. According to one critic, Löwenthal's unproblematic ability to combine Germanness, Jewishness, and patriotism was considered "psychologisch reichlich schief" (psychologically distorted); it demonstrated an "unclear sentimentalism that also occasionally dominated the 'Woche der Brüderlichkeit'" (Brotherhood Week), an annual week officially dedicated to German-Jewish reconciliation that was first established in West Germany in 1952 (Wagner; cf. also "WdB Aktuell"). Commentators who were very critical of the transformation Löwenthal had undergone in the transition from novel to film emphasized the character's aggressiveness and bitterness (in the novel) as a result of his ostracism and victimization in the face of "racialist hysteria" (Kriewitz). Several argued that in their view, in 1933 a German Jew returning to Germany would have been historically unrealistic ("WB"). According to one reviewer, the fact that he is happily greeted by his family at the film's conclusion was functioning (in Germany) to lull the conscience of the (German) viewer (Kriewitz).

Kramer's characterization of the virulent Nazi Herr Rieber was also rejected. West German critics tended to criticize this character for functioning as a Nazi bogeyman against whom it was now easy to take a clear stand. Here was the stereotypical cliché of the bad German so common to Hollywood productions (Kesch, Kriewitz). Rieber's flirtation with Lizzie

Spöckenkieker (Christiane Schmidtmer), a young, ostentatiously blonde woman with clear National Socialist sympathies, was not discussed at all by West German critics, suggesting an unwillingness to thematize questions of German history in relation to female characters.

The character of the dwarf Glocken was mentioned but not discussed as a German type in West German reviews. Despite the importance of his role in the film, German critics seemed incapable of thinking of a dwarf as a "German" type, even if he was the politically correct type. Dunn's size and his role were almost always collapsed in the descriptions of his role in the film[6], though some critics did praise his performance and thought Kramer's utilization of his character as a chorus figure (which he does not play in the novel) to be a good move (see Kesch, Agoston, Engels, "kg", "H.W.K." and Wagner). When Löwenthal and Glocken were depicted together in the German press, it was Löwenthal's (Rühmann's) role that was the focus. For example, in the *Stuttgarter Zeitung* the caption to a film still depicting Löwenthal and Glocken at their separate table stated:

> *Ship of Fools* gives Heinz Rühmann the opportunity to make a name for himself in Hollywood as well. The Americans have entrusted him with the important role of the Jewish passenger Löwenthal, who is en route to Germany on a ship in 1931 together with the cripple Glocken. Both are ostracized to a separate table in the state room. ("Das Narrenschiff")

Thus, in many West German reviews, the film version of *Ship of Fools* was perceived as sentimental, historically inaccurate, and filled with U.S. stereotypes of Germans. These viewers were not impressed by Kramer's efforts to effect a transnational transformation of the German question.

THE EAST GERMAN RESPONSE TO *SHIP OF FOOLS* (1969)

Ship of Fools was not released in East Germany until 1969. Since the construction of the Berlin Wall in 1961, the East German government had followed a "zig-zag" course vis-à-vis U.S. and Western cultural products, allowing some leniency with regard to foreign imports and then cracking down again when such imports seemed to pose a challenge to social and political stability. By the mid-sixties, U.S. cultural products appeared to be less innovative—and therefore less threatening—than were those of other western countries. Thus, when Kramer's film, with its superb acting and moderately left-of-center political message, was allowed to be shown in East German movie theaters a full four years after its original release, critics had two goals: to justify the importation of a film from the "capitalist enemy" (Stott 82) and to demonstrate how this film might reinforce the political agendas of the East (Berghahn, *Hollywood* 23; "Forbidden" 40-51). Yet despite their ideological blinders, East German critics responded to Kramer's film with very different insights than did the West German critics. If Kramer had failed in his transnational transformation of the German characters in the West, in the East he enjoyed some success.

Fascism was a key political theme in *Ship of Fools*, and East German critics focused upon this topic closely, highlighting the contrast between the German-Jew Löwenthal and the Nazi Rieber. In *Neue Zeit, Berlin Ost*, the article was accompanied by a photo of Rieber and Löwenthal with the caption: "a rageful Antisemite... shares a cabin with a Jewish businessman." One reviewer argued that Kramer's film was worth seeing because it dealt with politics: the "inhumane absurdity of fascism is directly shown in the aggressive Antisemite and the Jew who cannot accept that he no longer counts as German" ("H.U"). Another noted that Kramer criticized what East German writers called "anti-humanism" in the confrontation with Fascism shown in the encounter between the German publisher and the Jew Löwenthal ("ak"). The critic in the *Sächsisches Tagblatt, Dresden* wrote: "José Ferrer portrays the anti-semitic publisher Rieber with a brutal totality and a seam-splitting loud mouthed vitality; Heinz Rühmann plays his usual 'Kleinbürger' [petty bourgeois] but on a newer, higher level that embodies his character's foolish but innocent denial of reality" ("E.M."). According to Dr. Manfred Jelenski, writing for the *Berliner Zeitung Ost*, the figure of the naïve German Jew who believes his war medals from World War I make him different from other Jews "raised this film over other American films dealing with the fateful aspects of German history" (Jelenski).

Several East German reviewers including Jelenski, but no West German reviewers, explicitly compared Kramer's characterization of Löwenthal with another literary character: "Professor Mamlock." This character first appeared in a play by the same name written by the physician and author Friedrich Wolf, who wrote it in French exile in 1933 shortly after the Nazis took power in Germany. It tells the story of a Jewish physician who cannot accept the changed political climate in Germany and still hopes for change. After experiencing a series of severe repressive measures, his last hope rests in a new law that would allow him to continue his work due to his status as a veteran of World War I. When his Nazi colleague announces that this clause does not count for "non-Aryans," Professor Mamlock loses all hope and shoots himself with his weapon from World War I. This story was adapted by the Soviets into a film in 1938. It later was remade as a critically acclaimed film by the DEFA, the East German film production company, in 1961, and is considered one of the first German films to deal critically with the theme of the Holocaust. In contrast to the Soviet adaptation, which also emphasized social themes such as poverty and class distinctions, the East German production concentrated upon the individual fate of the lead character more closely (Berghahn, "Forbidden" 40-51; Morozov). [7]

The parallels to the character Löwenthal in Kramer's film are clear and raise the question of whether Kramer or his screenwriter Abby Mann had perhaps seen or were aware of *Professor Mamlock*. On the other hand, Kramer's Löwenthal remains optimistic to the end and does not experience the fate of Professor Mamlock; he is not a figure who ultimately confronts the viewer with the hopelessness of the situation of Jews in Germany in 1933. East German critics who drew the parallel to Mamlock generally did not note this point.

Another issue addressed by East German reviewers concerned the German female character, Lizzi Spöckenkieker. *Der Neue Weg* defined "fascism" as the film portrayed it in terms of the relationship between Rieber and his blonde female counterpart, a dynamic that was not discussed in any West German reviews:

> The dreadful Teutonic state of affairs pollutes the air, even as it attempts to sublimate itself into a staunch coziness. José Ferrer plays this Nazi type with a terrible realism, and Christiane Schmidtmer typifies as his travel companion exactly that blue eyed staunchness, which the SS would soon attempt to cultivate at "Lebensborn." The foolishness of crime, here it is depicted! (G.A. "Der Neue Film...")

Thus, this East German critic connected this character to the Lebensborn program, an eugenic effort during the Third Reich to increase the birthrate of "Aryan" children.

Whereas West German critics had more or less dismissed Rieber as a "cliched" Nazi, had taken an ambivalent stance towards Löwenthal and ignored Spoekenkieker, for East German critics these portraited types appeared to be all too real. Yet like the West German reviewers, the East German critics did not choose to deal with the character of the dwarf Karl Glocken as a German type.

The most frequent general criticism of *Ship of Fools* in East Germany was its tendency to focus upon the personal rather than the political, the "private destinies" of its passengers rather than on their social context. Even the fascist Rieber, wrote the *Thüringer Tageblatt*, was shown as a "Kleinbürger" (petty bourgeois); he did not really embody the inhumanity of the entire system of fascism ("Ein Film"). As Kramer had limited his depictions to the upper deck, his individual stories don't add up to a "big historical picture"; they remain in the private realm and do not achieve a portrayal that is "socially convincing." Viewers who expected a "problem film" like *Judgment at Nuremburg* or *Inherit the Wind* would be disappointed. *Ship of Fools* "told individual stories of psychological troubles; only occasionally do social or political aspects of the unhealthy year 1933 come through..." (Tok).

Stanley Kramer had insisted that the German characterizations he and Mann had created for *Ship of Fools* were real people and not stereotypes (Kramer w/Coffey 205). Interestingly, it was East Germans who agreed with him on this point rather than West Germans. East German critics, with few exceptions, read the character of the Nazi publisher Rieber as an actual type, as did Kramer, while West Germans defined this character as a cliché. His oppositional function vis-à-vis the Jewish character of Löwenthal was seen as progressive in the East; in the West it tended to "lull the conscience of the viewer" (Kriewitz) by localizing the evils of fascism in one character alone. For West Germans, the opposition between Rieber and Löwenthal was, among other things, historically inaccurate, for in their eyes by 1933, that contest had been clearly decided in favor of Rieber. Thus Löwenthal's characterization was "psychologically distorted." For East Germans, he recalled the image of a Jewish doctor incapable of accepting the new political realities of fascist Germany.

In conclusion, Stanley Kramer's adaptation of *Ship of Fools* modified some of Katherine Anne Porter's more negative depictions of Germans because, as a Jewish-American and influential Hollywood filmmaker with a reformist agenda, Kramer wanted his films to appeal to the "mass audience overseas" (Spoto 17) as well as at home. Therefore, he wished to make the German passengers aboard the *Vera* into vehicles of transnational identification "across cultural boundaries" (Färber). As the West and East German reception of Kramer's film reveals, however, he had made his case in Germany only modestly. For West Germans, Kramer had not succeeded in transnationalizing "the German problem." Rather, he had relied on German stereotypes and gotten Germany history wrong. For East Germans, Kramer had indeed shown some aspects of the "great inhumanity of Fascism" ("Ein Film") through the German characters, but because he tended to privilege "individual stories" (Tok), he failed to achieve a "big historical picture" that was "socially convincing" (Schroeder). In the end, Kramer's efforts to use a transatlantic voyage to negotiate a transnational answer to the German question could not transcend German national borders.

NOTES

1. * I would like to thank the Universitätsverlag Winter for permission to reprint a modified version of this essay, which appeared in Udo Hebel, ed. *Transnational American Studies* (Heidelberg, 2012). I also wish to thank Professor Leila Zenderland at CSU Fullerton for her excellent editorial advice. Newspaper articles, reviews and publicity from West and East German newspapers are taken from the file "Das Narrenschiff" from the Deutsches Institut für Filmkunde (DIF) in Frankfurt. All translations from the German are my own. The materials in the file were often cut out of the larger paper and thus do not contain page numbers. Additional primary documents are taken from the Special Collections on Ship of Fools at the Academy of Motion Picture Arts and Sciences, Margaret Herrick Library, in Los Angeles. A further resource of English-language responses to the movie adaptation of *Ship of Fools* is located in the Katherine Anne Porter Papers, Special Collections and University Archives, University of Maryland (*Ship of Fools* [Movie], 1962-1969 and undated, Series 6, Box 2, Folder 26.)
2. Kramer's perception of a negative reaction to *Judgment at Nuremberg* colored most of his comments upon the film. While Muñoz Conde and Muñoz Aunión pretty much confirm that impression, their evidence is rather thin. Etheridge raises questions about the uniformly negative reception when he argues that the American journalists during the Berlin premiere were impressed with the German audiences' response during that event. Etheridge, however, concentrates primarily upon what he terms the "anti-German wave" in the United States and upon U.S. perceptions of Germany.
3. In the U.S. publicity for the film, Rühmann's German film awards (The Bambi) as "Germany's favorite actor" were emphasized. See the Jack Atlas Papers, File 11.f-403, Academy of Motion Picture Arts and Sciences, Margaret Herrick Library, Special Collections, *Ship of Fools*.
4. The film was nominated for the Golden Globe Award for "Best Foreign Language Film" in 1962 and won the Silver Globe in the same category.
5. This was in contrast to *Judgment at Nuremberg*, where the "bad" German judges are all depicted by German nationals and the one thoughtful judge among them is portrayed by the American actor Burt Lancaster.

6. The critics Armand Kesch and Gerty Agoston came the closest to speaking of Dunn as more than just a dwarf character. However, they did not link his character to the question of German identity.
7. Ironically, immediately following the construction of the wall, the East German government felt more confident that it would now be possible to keep "capitalist aggression" at bay; hence, playwrights and filmmakers were given more creative leeway at this time.

WORKS CITED

Agoston, Gerty. (New York), "Einen Oscar für Oskar!" *National Zeitung* Basel, 18 Oct. 1965.

ak. "Der neue Film: Das Narrenschiff." *Mitteldeutsche Neueste Nachrichten* Leipzig, 10 Oct. 1969.

Berghahn, Daniela. *Hollywood Behind the Wall.* Manchester: Manchester University Press, 2005.

———. "The Forbidden Films: Film Censorship in the Wake of the Eleventh Plenum." In Diana Holmes and Alison Smith, eds., *100 Years of European Cinema:Entertainment or Ideology?* Manchester and New York: Manchester University Press, 2000. 40-51.

Caption to Photo. *Stuttgarter Zeitung*. 24 Aug.1965.

"Der Brave Soldat Schwejk"/ Wiki/ URL: http://de.wikipedia.org/wiki/Der brave_Soldat_Schwejk.

"Ein Film der Prominenten," *Thüringer Tageblatt* Weimar 24 Oct. 1969.

"E.M." "Das Narrenschiff," *Sächsisches Tageblatt Dresden* 29 Oct. 1969.

Engels, Dr. Günther. "Weißes Narrenschiff schwamm auf der Seine..." *Kölnische Rundschau* 3 Oct. 1965.

Etheridge, Brian C. "Die Anti-Deutsche Welle: The Anti-German Wave, Public Diplomacy, and Intercultural Relations in Cold War America." In Jessica Gienow-Hecht, ed., *Decentering America.* New York and Oxford: Berghahn Books, 2008.

Färber, Helmut. "Das Narrenschiff" *Film-Kritik* (11/1965): 631-32.

G. A. "Der Neue Film: Das Narrenschiff." *Der Neue Weg*, Halle 9 Oct. 1969.

"Heinz Rühmann und das Narrenschiff", Publicity Essay, Press info. Columbia-Bavaria Filmgesellschaft, 1965.

"Heinz Rühmann"/Wikipedia, URL: http://de.wikipedia.org/wiki/Heinz_R %C3%BChmann

Hitlers nützliche Idole: Heinz Rühmann. (Documentary). Dir. Michael Strauven, 2007.

H. U. "Konflikte einer Reise über den Ozean" *Neue Zeit-Berlin-Ost* 23 Oct. 1969.

H.W. K. "Das Narrenschiff" *General Anzeiger Wuppertal* 6 Nov. 1965.

Jelenski, Dr. Manfred. "Das Narrenschiff" *Berliner Zeitung* (Ost) 29 Oct. 1969.

"José Ferrer"/Wikipedia URL: http://en.wikipedia.org/wiki/Jos%C3%A9_Ferrer

Kesch, Armand. "Panorama menschlicher Leidenschaften." *Die Welt* 14 Aug. 1965.

kg. "Die Menschen werden demaskiert" *Duisburger General Anzeiger* 20 Oct. 1965.

Kramer, Stanley, with Thomas Coffey. *A Mad, Mad, Mad, Mad World: A Life in Hollywood.* New York: Harcourt Brace and Company, 1997.

Kriewitz, Günther. "Vom Narrenschiff zum Showboat." *Stuttgarter Zeitung* 2 Aug 1965.

"Lebensborn/Wikipedia, URL: http://de.wikipedia.org/wiki/Lebensborn.

MacCannell, Dean. *Empty Meeting Grounds: The Tourist Papers.* London and New York: Routledge, 1992.

Morozov, Mikhail. "Der schreckliche Georgier." *Der Spiegel* 14 Jan. 1980. http://www.spiegel.de/spiegel/print/d-14317495.html

Muñoz Conde, Francisco and Marta Muñoz Aunión. *Das Urteil von Nürnberg: Juristischer und Filmwissenschaftlicher Kommentar zum Film von Stanley Kramer* (1961). BWV: Berliner Wissenschaftsverlag, 2006.

"Panorama menschlicher Charaktere" *Sächsisches Tageblatt* Dresden 30 Sept 1969.

Poiger, Uta G. *Jazz, Rock and Rebels: Cold War Politics and American Culture in a Divided Germany.* Berkeley: University of California Press, 2000.

Porter, Katherine Anne. *Ship of Fools.* London: Secker and Warburg, 1962.

"Professor Mamlock," Wikipedia, URL: http://de.wikipedia.org/wiki/Professor Mamlock.

rpm. "Die Deutsche Frage: Stanley Kramer, *Das Urteil von Nürnberg*, und *Das Narrenschiff.* Film Publicity Essay, Ring Press, July 1965.

Ship of Fools. Dir. Stanley Kramer. Columbia Pictures, 1965. Sony Pictures Home Entertainment Inc., 2006 (DVD Release).

Spoto, Donald. *Stanley Kramer: Film-Maker.* New York: Putnam's, 1978.

Stott, Rosemary. "Entertained by the Class Enemy: Cinema Programming Policy in the GDR." In Diana Holmes and Alison Smith, eds., *100 Years of European Cinema: Entertainment or Ideology?* Manchester University Press, 2000: 27-39.

Tok, Hans-Dieter. "Das Narrenschiff." *Leipziger Volkszeitung.* [no date]

Wagner, Friedrich A. "Neue Klischees." *Frankfurter Allgemeine Zeitung* 30 Nov 1965.

"WdB Aktuell." *Deutscher Koordinierungsrat.* Deutscher Koordinierungsrat der Gesellschaften für christlich-jüdische Zusammenarbeit e.V. 2010 Web. 04.02.2012. < http://www.deutscher-koordinierungsrat.de/02_01.php>.

Wronkow, L. "Wenn jeder Narr eine Krone trüge, wären wir alle Könige." *Aufbau* (30 July 1965).

Ship of Fools

A Severe Blow to Faith

Alexandra Subramanian

When *Ship of Fools* was published on April Fool's Day, 1962, Porter knew that her honeymoon with the critics was over. "[L]et it [come]," she had told her publisher, Seymour Lawrence.[1] Indeed, since its publication *Ship of Fools* has invited admiration but also biting criticism from friends, critics, and biographers alike. Some of the criticism, moreover, has been highly personal, highlighting Porter's own faults, prejudices, and shortcomings, at times disregarding her complex humanity, which included a capacity for kindness that cannot be easily dismissed. Theodore Solotaroff, writing a review of *Ship of Fools* in *Commentary* in 1962, summed up the prevailing feeling against the novel. He virtually decimates it from almost every angle, claiming that the "soul of humanity is lacking."[2]

This paper argues against those who have judged *Ship of Fools* as marred by cynicism, prejudice, and the author's darkened view of humanity. The novel will be analyzed, rather, in light of Porter's debilitating sensitivity, deep understanding of human behavior and motives, and acute awareness of the consequences of casual or calculated cruelty, misogyny, and violence. Porter was attuned to the suffering of the vulnerable, whether afflicted by poverty, parental cruelty and neglect, or disability. To Porter's mind, acts of unkindness, insensitivity, and a failure to take responsibility, especially regarding the weak and vulnerable, created a tragic and unnecessary cycle of violence, alienation, and despair.

In the pages of her novel, Porter chronicles brilliantly the interiority of her characters. Many readers and critics, however, have rejected the novel in part because entering into the uncensored, disturbing mental worlds of the men and women aboard the *Vera* can be unpleasant as well as uncomfortable. Her depiction of relentlessly vicious individuals, however, easily blinds one to Porter's repeated attempts to account for their insensitivity and brutality. Porter frequently affords glimpses into the histories of her characters, shedding light upon the darkness of their inner lives and putting their dysfunctional behavior into context. The textual readings that follow thus illustrate the complexity and subtlety of some of the characters aboard Porter's *Ship of Fools.*

In 1941, Porter ventured to explain to her then husband, Albert Erskine, the theme of her novel and her purpose in writing it: "Think about all the evil I know, and have seen, and all the baseness I cannot help but remember. That I still have any gentleness is a wonder," she wrote, "but still I have, and that is something to be grateful for. I want to tell the truth, and I want to tell it so far as I am able to discover it." In an attempt, perhaps, to prepare Erskine for a novel quite distant in spirit from her short fiction, she warned that the novel is "bitter as gall, with the most awful persons and the most hideous situations."

"It is this, my dear," she continues:

> I am the sum of my experience, and that experience has been in the main painful, and I know terrible things, and I can only write about what I know. I am not disillusioned, because I had very few illusions. But I always had a kind of instinctive faith, and this

> apparently cannot die altogether. But I think it part of my work to record some of the severer blows that [my] faith has endured, and so I do. (Katherine Anne Porter to Albert Erskine, August 29, 1941)

Porter understood well that when she chose to reveal human nature unvarnished, as she had observed it in life, she would encounter hostility and resistance mingled with curiosity.

"You know Seymour," Porter wrote to her publisher in response to a critic from *The Sunday Times* who had gotten mad and "busted forth," "I hate to admit this but I think it's true, it makes a certain kind of man furious for a women [*sic*] to take such a tone as I do about politics, personal conduct, and sex. Some very good men, old friends and I think first rate minds, even they have shown a little resentment, and one of them asked me—at a dinner party, 'Just where did you learn so much about men?' and I said, simply, 'From men,' which sort of toned down that topic. Never mind." (KAP to SL, July 2, 1962).

Why, her old friend and dinner party companion might have wished to know, had Porter ventured to present the interior thoughts of her characters without censorship, no matter how disturbing? Men aboard the *Vera* want their women hot, dirty, and often bought, and look upon them more as "live meat" than romantic partners. "Bitch trouble" about sums it up (Porter, *Ship* 438). La Condesa is in the process of being shipped like cargo from one island to another, while the zarzuela women openly traffic their bodies. The respectable Elsa is in the market for a good Swiss husband, who will specialize, no doubt, as Professor Hutten does, in regarding women as no more than hysterical vessels, "merely children of a larger growth . . . [who] needed a taste of the rod now and then to keep them in order" (298). Herr Rieber publishes articles about "the extermination of all the unfit," while Mrs. Treadwell tires of "moral bookkeeping" (428, 415). Circe-like, Porter has merely to let us into the minds of her characters for a few seconds before she turns them into swine.

Not surprisingly, Porter caused a stir behind the scenes at her publishing house, the Atlantic Monthly Press. At the time that *Ship of Fools* was published, Seymour Lawrence, Porter's devoted editor, had been director of the Atlantic Monthly Press for nine years and was "responsible to a very rich and conservative board of directors."[3] The principal owners of the Atlantic were a mother and a daughter, Mrs. Barbara Deering Danielson and Mrs. Marion Campbell. At a board meeting, Mrs. Danielson declared: "I wouldn't want those people in my house," referring to the passengers aboard the *Vera* (ibid). Porter's bestselling novel, although a financial triumph, thus did not reflect well upon Lawrence within the confines of his workplace, where he had shocked the owners of the press with his celebration of an author whose characters were regarded as sordid, crude, and quite outside the bounds of social acceptability.

A few years later, after Lawrence published the "immoral" J. P. Donleavy, Lawrence's resignation was "politely forced" (ibid.). Had Porter been privy to the judgments of Mrs. Barbara Deering Danielson and her daughter, she might have dismissed their complaints as worthy of any one of her unsavory passengers.

Mrs. Campbell and Mrs. Danielson surely had no interest in contemplating the inner lives of the *Vera* passengers they found distasteful, passengers who, if dissected, can be seen, not as merely objectionable or as lacking humanity, but as sadly, metaphorically, wailing. Beneath their swinish exteriors, often twisted beyond recognition, can be found human beings worthy of our interest, even compassion. To my mind, it was not Porter's intent to leave her readers suspended, frustrated, and defeated, wandering around in the nowhere-land of one writer's misanthropy. It was her intention instead to combat easy optimism, which was soon to burgeon into the cult of positive thinking.

In her book *Silences*, Tillie Olsen uncovers a quotation in which Porter states that she rejects "this dreadful idea that whatever you have in you has to come out, that you can't suppress true talent. People can be destroyed," Porter declared. "[T]hey can be bent, distorted and completely crippled. . . . In spite of all the poetry, all the philosophy to the contrary, we are not really masters of our fate. We don't really direct our lives unaided and unobstructed. Our being is subject to all the chances of life" (166).

To be sure, the challenges Porter faced, beginning in childhood, encouraged her belief that individuals cannot entirely control their destinies. In letters, usually to her sister Gay, Porter recalled the pains of her childhood in an effort to make sense of the difficulties both she and her sister had faced in their adult lives. She might have taken responsibility for some of the mistakes that she had made, but she never grew tired of reflecting upon the ways that she and her siblings had been forever marked by their father's inability to provide for his children, emotionally or materially, after their mother's death when Porter was two. "And what he did to his children's lives—it won't bear thinking about," she wrote to Gay when she was in her late sixties.[4] The "bitter melancholy" she felt as a child, the "gloom" that "darkened the very air around" her and her siblings, contributed to a lifelong notion that all "life of feeling" was "tragic."[5]

Notwithstanding, she felt that good character could "survive and give meaning to horrors of life":

> But that does not make the horrors good, nor even necessary. And the suffering of children is not their fault. For everything that has happened to me since I was able to reason, and was thrown on my own resources, I take responsibility and have no comment to make except that if I had a decent, civilized childhood, I might have been better equipped for the ungodly struggle I had to make. But I have no rosy views at all, Honey. I look quite a lot at the world, and it is not a pretty sight on the whole. But there are pretty things in it.[6]

An artist, Porter was extremely sensitive to her surroundings, particularly the people around her. Far from speeding through life in an ambitious, unconscious haze, she felt her way through life, absorbing her surroundings, as she once said in an interview, "through her pores" (Day).

As an example, when Porter was living in Berlin in 1931 and 1932 she was isolated and could speak very little German, yet this dark time was an important one for her, as Porter biographers and critics have detailed.[7] Describing her mode of absorbing the emotional truth of her surroundings, Porter said in an interview: "I don't peep. I don't pry. I don't listen. It comes through my pores. It's like being dipped into something. It's not a thing I do on purpose" (Day).

For most of the time Porter was in Berlin, for example, she felt as if she was wasting the precious money she had been awarded through her Guggenheim fellowship, and she felt guilty about the money she owed to friends and publishers at home. In her letters to her then lover, Eugene Pressly, she frequently described the sensation of not being able to live close to others because she did not have the proper defenses and often felt as if she had "lost at least one layer of skin." Her state of mind was one of an "appalling failure of courage," "sheer cowardice": "I am frightened of something now, and I don't quite know what. . . . horrified, would be a better word . . . It is more like horror than fear. It is beyond fear. . . . It is like a substance in the air here."[8] Not long after she had written this letter, on Christmas Day 1931, she made this assessment of life in Berlin: "This must be the most unhappy time," she told Pressly,

> the most hopeless and lost time the world has known for many centuries? . . . blight on human life, a doom, people go around as if they were expecting the earth to crash under their feet . . . There is something frightening in this country. Something terrible is going on here.[9]

Porter's sensitivities were heightened, for she was experiencing her own internal crises and health problems, and these were magnified by her prescient foreboding that Germany was edging toward something horrific and deeply frightening. She cried inconsolably and often during her time in Berlin. It was this lonely, desperate, and anxious time in the author's life—combined with her devastation years later after the fall of Paris —that set the tone for *Ship of Fools.*

Porter aimed to set aside her Mrs. Treadwell-like love of Paris and other aspects of life that she might have chosen to celebrate. She set about the bleak, at times comic, task of putting the thoughts and actions of her cast of characters under the microscope while setting them in times of duress, rootlessness, and dislocation.

Her passengers frequently inspire disgust and revulsion, yet a closer look reveals that many of them have been traumatized in some way, not unlike the Germans themselves in the aftermath of World War I. We are predisposed to dislike and condemn them, perhaps, as it is easy to do with Porter herself, but not without acknowledging their humanity and the degree to which they are damaged and have been shaped and molded by painful experiences, often from childhood. On the surface, the passengers are able-bodied and perhaps good-looking and well-dressed, but internally they are maimed and broken, vulnerable, and all too often willing to turn against others, especially during difficult times.

The aristocratic men of Veracruz set the tone for the novel, as they do not see the emaciated Indian in the square with his "ragged toenails and cracked heels." Neither do they acknowledge the beggar, "intricately maimed and deformed" as a child "in preparation for his calling," crawling upon "the stumps of his four limbs" and "wagging his hideous shock head from side to side slowly in unbearable suffering," beyond thinking of him as they might "a piece of rubbish rolling before the wind" (Porter, *Ship* 4, 5).

The heart of an Indian nurse, who spends her entire life caring for Señora Ortega and her family, will remain unknown, even by those she serves day and night. The only voice of love the nurse will know is that of her dead mother, who will tenderly, while she is sleeping, call her name, "Nicolasa," "as if she were a child again." In her loneliness, the nurse weeps often in her sleep, for she lives among strangers who don't know her language and "who never once asked her how she felt" (131). We are haunted by the ghostlike tenderness of Nicolasa's mother's voice, because the presence of pure devotion and unconditional love has no place on the ship. The hearts of the passengers are blighted by a cold, judgmental reserve embodied in the person of Mrs. Treadwell, whose heart contracts forever once she marries a man who betrays her trust with violence and cheating.

Herr Professor Hutten and Frau Professor Hutten, a "respectable" German couple, have devoted their lives to running a German school in Mexico but have left their home of exile in order to return to their German fatherland. Not surprisingly, they feel uprooted and apprehensive about returning home. Herr Hutten's insecurities about place and belonging are magnified by how he has constructed his identity and purpose, which depend upon the collusion of everyone in his midst, beginning with his wife and continuing to each and every one of his students, who will submit to his order or be shown severe discipline. Herr Hutten has the luxury of believing, unshakably, "in the fundamental goodness of human nature as a principle." "Men who do evil," he believes, "are afflicted, abnormal—they are perverted from the Divine Plan," though redeemable "in God's good time." If shown the right path, men will eagerly embrace "the good, the true, the beautiful."

As for children, Herr Hutten espouses that "they respond most remarkably to the steady hand, the unwavering point of view, the firm but reasonable methods of dedicated teachers, who can nevertheless, when discipline demands it, wield the rod without mercy, for true justice is stern and must be administered sternly" (289-291).

Frau Hutten, however, while listening to her husband's philosophy, cannot discipline her train of thought and finds herself recalling that she has spent her entire marriage interposing herself, "literally, bodily, between her husband and the seamy, grimy, mean, sordid, tiresome side of life that he simply could not endure." Her husband had never so much as been seen carrying "even the smallest parcel in hand" in his walk to and from school; it had been her bounden duty at all times and in all places to ensure that the "superiority of his mind" and the dignity of his profession be preserved. Her payment had been that she was thought of as "The Ideal German Wife."

For that honor, she is in turn entrusted to the task of disciplining "the younger students, embittered, tenacious, rebellious beyond their years." She would never have "beaten, starved, or terrorized" a child of her own had she been blessed with one. Yet, when it came to the students, "she never failed to subdue even the most recalcitrant spirit" (291, 292).

For her sacrifices, her husband lives in a world of his own imagining, one in which he has the perfect marriage: "If he had forgotten their first five years of marriage," Frau Hutten muses, "well and good, let him. For herself, she could never forget, for the many lessons taught her then had gone into her blood and bones, and changed her almost beyond her own recognition" (292). So bent, distorted, and transformed was Frau Hutten after these first years of marriage, she could no longer have any idea of who she was beyond her training, which had conditioned her to become terrified each time her thoughts strayed disloyally. It was not acceptable for her to think—let alone speak—thoughts about her husband that might in any way undermine his absolute authority.

How many spirits had been broken, violently, to preserve the sanctity of Herr Professor Hutten's superiority? His wife and countless students had been terrorized and finally subdued, all so that Herr Professor Hutten might maintain his naïve, unblemished view of mankind's unshakable goodness.

While readers may easily dismiss Frau Hutten completely as another one of Porter's dislikable, comic creations, we are wise to note that Porter asks us to acknowledge that we can never know her, just as she will never know herself. Frau Hutten's guilty musings serve to show us that the purpose of her traumatic early years of marriage was to dissolve all traces of her autonomous self.

Even what Mrs. Treadwell describes as "good wholesome German family life" does not escape the microscope. Frau Baumgartner, for instance, lives under the rule of her husband, who demands the customary obedience and approval from his wife, Gretel. It is her job to support and love him unconditionally, despite his weaknesses, which include drinking himself to death. With no outlet for her frustrations, Frau Baumgartner smothers and humiliates her son. When Hans, dressed for the cold mountain country, begs to remove his garments, she rebukes and threatens the boy, who writhes in his scratchy, sweat-stained garments. Finally conceding to let him remove his jacket, she calls her son a baby and suggests that he needs a bottle to nurse— "a bottle with a rubber nipple, with milk and sugar." She tells him he shall have nothing for his supper and begins to enjoy her cruelty, "the pleasant feeling that she could hurt his pride even if he had won in the matter of the jacket" (32). The boy keeps losing the mother he loves to the abyss of her frustrations and resentments, which center upon a husband she despises for having ruined their lives with his drinking.

Finally, the Baumgartners argue bitterly on deck and later bring their feud into the cabin where their darling Hans sleeps. Their son is awakened by their violence, but after hurling insults the parents soften toward one another, realizing that they must stop for their son's sake. Discovering their repressed passion, they begin to fondle Hans instead of each other; finally, they let the boy go and settle him into bed. Promptly, they undress and begin their moaning and lovemaking. Hans, bewildered by the sounds, finally falls into a deep sleep.

Hans is humiliated and smothered by parents imprisoned within a stifling code of patriarchy that keeps women subservient and bitter and the men feeling inadequate and shamed. Frau Baumgartner has no power, so she unloads her frustrations on those closest to her. She specializes in the humiliation and emasculation of her men; it is the only pleasure and relief she knows. Porter thus gives a biting critique of patriarchal marriage, illustrating from numerous angles that mindless adherence to conventional codes creates a domestic atmosphere that stifles healthy growth.

The novel tells us of passengers on the upper decks who are warped by painful experiences, and they in turn commit cruelties, consciously or unconsciously, with heartbreaking consequences. Cruelty mattered to Porter, especially when it was directed toward the vulnerable, including children and disabled persons. It was the theme she treated with delicacy and empathy in her short stories "He," "Holiday," and "The Downward Path to Wisdom."

Porter wrote frequently and sensitively about children who suffer at the hands of adults, for she believed the suffering of children to have lifelong consequences. In "The Downward Path to Wisdom," she shows how a four-year-old boy reacts when his father rejects him as stupid and is repelled by his presence. The boy's reaction to his father's words is visceral and instinctual, and he turns this pain in on himself and rejects the world, a pattern we see developed as the story progresses, and the child learns that he cannot love or be loved.

Porter continued her exploration of this topic in *Ship of Fools* through the mild-mannered Hans Baumgartner whose passivity contrasts sharply with a pair of twins so destructive and unlikable that even the calm, gentle-spirited Dr. Schumann can only admit their humanity with great reluctance. Ric and Rac, who name themselves after comic strip characters, belong to Lola and Tito but are collectively raised by the zarzuela company, a band of entertainers who are also swindlers, prostitutes, and thieves. Not surprisingly, the children mirror the behavior of their elders, mimicking gleefully their base sexuality and criminality and thumbing their noses at all respectable types who dare to foil their rampages. They are never supervised and amuse themselves with throwing an animal overboard and harassing adults at every turn. Passengers hope for their demise and consider them inherently evil and beyond redemption. As readers, it is easy to collude with the passengers aboard the *Vera*, to refuse them compassion or allowance for their tender age or the viciousness of their guardians.

When the twins steal La Condesa's pearl necklace and throw it overboard, their parents descend upon them violently, and what follows is a hair-raising scene of child abuse. Lola wraps her legs around her son and presses down his fingernails, one at a time, until he writhes and howls. She threatens to turn them backward, stick pins under them, and pull out his teeth. She then turns his eyelids back with her thumbs, ignoring his screams of terror, and threatens to tear them out. The other dancers want a confession and urge Lola and Tito on. Finally, the boy collapses between her knees, tears flowing, and admits that he thought his mother had said the necklace was only beads. Rising up and slapping him, she declares that he is an idiot and threatens to leave him in Vigo where he can starve. His sister, wishing to be left in Vigo along with her brother, tries to free herself from her father's grasp, but he flails her head and shoulders with his fist. Setting her free, he seizes his son's arm and twists it slowly until the shoulder nearly turns in its socket. The boy falls to his knees with a whimper and huddles with his sister; both wail and nurse their bruises. When finally deserted, the children crawl "into the upper berth looking for safety; they lay there half naked, entangled like some afflicted, misbegotten little monster in a cave, exhausted, mindless, soon asleep" (360). Cruelty and inhumanity are all the twins know.

While the dancers are flagrant and shameless about their wrongdoing, others like the Baumgartners abuse discreetly and within the bounds of convention. These cruelties are no less damaging and life changing, for the ripple effects that result from neglect and a poverty of love and compassion, Porter implies, are devastating and interfere with normal human development.

Jenny Brown, for example, cannot receive love from her man because David Scott, damaged like the little boy in "The Downward Path to Wisdom," is incapable of making a meaningful human connection. He has embraced misogyny, disrespect, and drinking because it is a convenient hiding place for a man who fears abandonment and emotional exposure.

David remembers his relatives as "tight-mouthed, tight-handed, tight-souled old gaffers" who had poisoned his blood and prevented him from being able to enjoy his life. When David's father left the family once and for all, claiming he had finally found a higher, more spiritual love that no one else could fathom, David felt a sense of freedom and relief. His mother, too, put up a brave front, until she broke down completely, cradling her nine-year-old son in her arms like a baby and sobbing uncontrollably. David threw up his dinner from disgust and slept "but woke in the night with the most terrifying feeling of pure desolation. Quietly, secretly, he cried bitterly too, cried himself to sleep again in his dampened pillow smelling of old feathers."

As a grown man, David is self-destructive and toxic to all who approach with intentions of intimacy. He is incapable of embracing his life's work or "loves" with passion. Jenny will never find satisfaction in a man who is threatened by her sociability and has withdrawn into himself, having perfected his "terrible trick of not-being" (130, 327).

Cruelty and insensitivity, whether indulged by a middle-class father, a band of thieves, or parents from respectable German stock, maim the vulnerable and perpetuate a cycle of violence, alienation, and suffering.

This cycle of suffering extends to the disabled through Porter's treatment of Herr Glocken, a character Porter uses to address directly her disgust with the notion that humans can entirely control their destinies. Herr Glocken corrects William Denny sharply when Denny proudly tells Herr Glocken, who is severely misshapen, that "It's not the shape of your body but your mind that shapes your life . . . I'll bet no matter what, you'd have wound up with a newsstand." "I'll tell you something," he continues, "I believe we get what we want!" Herr Glocken releases a deep groan, for what he calls "one of the great lies of this life!" and goes on to tell Denny that he had wanted one thing in the world, "to be a violinist!" When David asks why this is impossible, Herr Glocken, dismayed, asks how David could ask him this question after looking at him, declaring that "it is impossible to make one understand. But I had the soul . . . and I have it yet, and that consoles me a little" (276, 277).

The passengers aboard the *Vera* gaze at Herr Glocken's physical body and shudder. They do so, perhaps, because, while they are blind to it, they are as internally maimed and as severely disabled as he. They suffer from more than the ailments ascribed to them at the outset of the novel when we first meet them, discouraged and disheveled after doing battle with the Veracruzanos, who are delighted to extract from the travelers "every possible toll, fee, extortion, and bribe" (3). These passengers, physically whole and fairly well dressed, suffer from internal ailments mirrored in the visible suffering of the Indian, the beggar, Herr Glocken, and the woodcarver.

Porter vividly shows the human tendency to don masks and block out or reject what is too painful to contemplate, just as the passengers in the steerage ignore the woodcarver, Etchegaray, who grieves when his knife is confiscated. It is taken away for nothing the carver has done, so that now he cannot carve animal figures. He cannot be an artist, the vocation that gives his life purpose and meaning: "A man, very bony and ragged and worn, but perhaps young . . . was sitting, back to the rail, his knees drawn up and his bare toes curling and uncurling with sorrow; he was crying openly and loudly like a child" (175). The faces of those around him are stony, indifferent. They walk over and past him as if he did not exist, an act of hostility and a denial of the man's humanity.

Finally, in the concluding paragraph of the novel, we see the musicians preparing to disembark, including "a gangling young boy, who looked as if he had never had enough to eat in his life, nor a kind word from anybody." Yet the boy stares with blind eyes toward Bremerhaven, "as if the town were a human being, a good and dear trusted friend who had come a long way to welcome him" (497). As foolishly hopeful as the gangly boy, Jenny Brown snuggles up to David Scott, who shivers with delight when she gives any sign of "weakness and defeat." The passengers likewise draw into their immediate families, reminding themselves of their separateness and superiority. Like the gangly, starved boy who whispers "Grüss Gott" to the town in a voice just above a whisper, readers and passengers alike, Porter seems to tell us, are starved, wounded creatures who lack tolerance, self-acceptance, empathy, and community.

Porter once said in an interview: "I've known some marvelous people. We all have good and evil—and there is such a thing—they're real—we have it—the whole life is a challenge to not be as evil as you want to be sometimes" (Day). She then looked the interviewer straight in the eye, as if to say, "isn't it so, don't you know that it's true?" Who among us, she challenged silently, doesn't think thoughts that, if dissected, might be described as crude, damaging, treacherous, or mean-spirited?

In "A Prologue to the Ship of Fools," Sebastian Brant—whose 1494 bestselling *Das Narrenschiff* gave Katherine Anne Porter the title for her own novel—describes his book as a "looking glass": "Both rich and poor these fools will be; / Each ass his very kind will see." Like Sebastian Brant, Porter invites her readers, however unwilling, to see themselves in the pages of her novel.

It is deeply embedded in our natures to attempt to distance ourselves completely from the wretched personalities we meet aboard the *Vera*, to say that we would never succumb, as Frau Schmitt does, when she weakens her resolve to be good and joins in with her cohorts at the Captain's table, feeling a sensual pleasure come over her as she gives up the fight to stand up for what is just and right. Yet, Sebastian Brant reminds us that we are all passengers: "The dunces all shall hear the truth / Though it displease them all, forsooth" (4, 5).

Like Sebastian Brant, Porter holds a mirror up to each one of her readers, whether or not we wish to gaze into it, with the hope that we might see that every moment is a struggle to "try to be a little less evil than we want to be." For although humans are capable of goodness and purity, as we see in the figure of the woodcarver and in the person of Nicolasa, who only wishes to be known and loved, more often than not we confront the daily challenge to resist cruelty and collusion.

Owing to our fractured selves and internal disabilities, lurking beneath the masks we don, we can all too easily crush the spirit of a child or participate, like Frau Schmitt, in small horrors. It is the theme Porter illustrated over and over again in a series of subplots in the novel. It is a theme, I believe, that illuminates her vision of humanity as indeed dark but never without hope. *Ship of Fools* enables and invites us to stop and to look unflinchingly into the mirror of our foolishness and capacity for cruelty, to see ourselves as deeply flawed, as perhaps able-bodied, but internally maimed, well-practiced in the arts of collusion, just like Katherine Anne Porter, the artist and architect aboard.

Notes

1. Porter told Lawrence that the "long years of praise and appreciation from colleagues and fellow writers and critics must I don't doubt come to an end. But let it . . . I was in danger of getting spoiled." KAP to Seymour Lawrence, November 1, 1961, KAP Papers.
2. See Theodore Solotaroff's "*Ship of Fools* and the Critics" in Robert Penn Warren, ed., *Katherine Anne Porter: A Collection of Critical Essays* (Englewood Cliffs, NJ: Prentice-Hall, Inc.) 134-149.
3. Seymour Lawrence to Glenway Wescott, January 27, 1967, Seymour Lawrence Papers, Special Collections, University of Maryland Libraries.
4. Katherine Anne Porter to Gay Porter Holloway, January 18, 1958, Katherine Anne Porter Papers, Special Collections, University of Maryland Libraries.
5. Katherine Anne Porter to Miss Cora, October 21, 1952, Katherine Anne Porter Papers, Special Collections, University of Maryland Libraries. Cora Posey was a close friend of Porter's mother.
6. Katherine Anne Porter to Gay Porter Holloway, October 10, 1930, Katherine Anne Porter Papers, Special Collections, University of Maryland Libraries.
7. For in-depth discussions about Porter's time in Berlin, see Austenfeld, Unrue's "The German Interval," Stout, and Givner.
8. Katherine Anne Porter to Eugene Pressly, November 23, 1931, Katherine Anne Porter Papers, Special Collections, University of Maryland Libraries.
9. Katherine Anne Porter to Eugene Pressly, December 25, 1931, Katherine Anne Porter Papers, Special Collections, University of Maryland Libraries.

WORKS CITED

Austenfeld, Thomas, "Winter in Berlin" in *American Women Writers and The Nazis: Ethics and Politics in Boyle, Porter, Stafford, and Hellman.* Charlottesville: University Press of Virginia, 2001. 31-43.

Brant, Sebastian Brant. *The Ship of Fools,* trans. William Gillis. London: Folio, 1971.

Day, James. Interview with Katherine Anne Porter, "Day at Night: Katherine Anne Porter, Novelist and Short Story Writer." December 1, 2012. http://www.youtube.com/watch?v=k6SUfHOn3W0.

Givner, Joan. "The German Experience" in *Katherine Anne Porter: A Life.* New York: Simon and Schuster, 1982. 243-268.

Olsen, Tillie. *Silences.* New York: The Feminist Press, 2003.

Porter, Katherine Anne. *The Collected Stories of Katherine Anne Porter.* New York: Harcourt, Brace, Jovanovich, 1965.

---. "Letter to Albert Erskine." August 29, 1941. Katherine Anne Porter Papers, Special Collections, University of Maryland Libraries.

---. "Letter to Seymour Lawrence," November 1, 1961. Katherine Anne Porter Papers, Special Collections, University of Maryland Libraries.

---. "Letter to Seymour Lawrence." July 2, 1962. Katherine Anne Porter Papers, Special Collections, University of Maryland Libraries.

---. *Ship of Fools.* Boston: Little, Brown, 1962.

Solotaroff, Theodore. "*Ship of Fools* and the Critics" in Robert Penn Warren, ed., *Katherine Anne Porter: A Collection of Critical Essays.* Englewood Cliffs, NJ: Prentice-Hall, 1979. 134-149.

Stout, Janis P. "Between Two Worlds in a Falling World" in *Katherine Anne Porter: A Sense of the Times.* Charlottesville: University Press of Virginia, 1995. 92-114.

Unrue, Darlene Harbour. "The German Interval" in *Katherine Anne Porter: The Life of an Artist.* Jackson: University Press of Mississippi, 2005. 132-141.

---, ed., *Katherine Anne Porter Remembered.* Tuscaloosa: University of Alabama Press, 2010.

The Weimar Moment in Katherine Anne Porter's *Ship of Fools*

Joseph Kuhn

Katherine Anne Porter's statement, made in a letter to her editor in 1956, that she planned to write "a parable of political action" in *Ship of Fools* (1962) has not received the attention it deserves (Porter, *Letters* 501). From the first, commentators have observed what is obvious, that the novel depicts the approach of the Third Reich, but they have perhaps not appreciated enough that this approach had to be through the political system of the Weimar republic and that Porter's "parable" is set during this stage of transition. Porter intended that the German passengers on the *Vera* be seen as citizens of the Weimar state and, since she gives the voyage of the ship the time frame of August to September 1931, this makes them citizens during the unstable government of Chancellor Heinrich Brüning (1930-1932). Some interpreters treat the German passengers as though they are virtually National Socialists already, but the Captain, the ship's doctor and middle-class passengers such as the Huttens have the monarchist allegiances appropriate to supporters of the traditionalist right (which was in power in Brüning's government and that of his successor Franz von Papen). What Porter presents in parable-like form in *Ship of Fools* are the "political action[s]" whereby this nationalist right was outflanked by the radical right. The deliberateness of Porter's setting her novel in Brüning's Germany is also shown in a comment Porter made in a slightly later letter to her editor in which she said that her novel should try to bring out "the political and economic cross currents" of the crisis years of 1931-1932 (Porter, *Letters* 504).

Biographers and critics of Porter have long recognized that *Ship of Fools* was based upon Porter's voyage from Mexico to Germany in the late summer of 1931 and her stay in Berlin between October 1931 and January 1932. But Porter has frequently been seen as a political *naïf* who was not well-prepared to understand what she saw in Germany. Her critics often say that Porter's two works that are set in Germany in 1931, *Ship of Fools* and "The Leaning Tower" (1941), are marred as representations of a historical period by the anti-German stereotypes in which Porter sometimes seemed to indulge (she once called the Germans "the most naturally unattractive people in the world") and by an ahistorical tendency to shift anti-Semitic attitudes amongst Germans back from the Hitler period to the Weimar republic (Porter, *Selected* 193).[1] Porter's one-time friend, the novelist Josephine Herbst, complained that "this is 1931 ... and there is only one question—the Jewish question .... The issues that even Hitler had to hurdle before he could get around to the Jewish question are not present" (Herbst).[2] Readers of the novel from Herbst to Northrop Frye have a tainted word for what they see as this retrospective shuffling of events: "allegory" (Herbst; Frye 341). The frequent negative criticism of *Ship of Fools* tends to see it as an allegorical waxworks rather than as a novel as such.

Part of Herbst's denigration of Porter's novel is the claim that "Her Germans have never heard of the Weimar republic" (Herbst). But this statement is not very plausible, at least not if one considers what Porter herself seems to have intended. She refuted a similar assertion made by a critic about her Weimar story "The Leaning Tower," insisting that she was not "politically unconscious" in her stay in Germany (Porter, *Selected* 171). As soon as she arrived in Berlin, she observed in a recollection from 1975, she understood the threat of National Socialism to the republic and tried to tell major American journals about it: "I stood there and I knew—I went through five revolutions in Mexico—what was happening" (Dolan 178).[3] Given that Porter during her Mexico years in the 1920s and early 1930s was quite microscopically attuned to the intricacies of that nation's political affairs, it seems likely that she took some of this awareness to a country which, together with the Soviet Union, she saw in 1931 as the most "promising and hard-driven" in post-war Europe (Porter, *Selected* 85).

It is therefore a probable hypothesis that Porter knew exactly what she was doing in making the ancient figure of the ship of state, which goes back to Plato's *Republic* (Book VII), specific to the late summer of 1931. The vertical structure of the *Vera* from Captain Thiele on the bridge down to the unemployed workers in the steerage reproduces the quasi-monarchical hierarchy of the Weimar republic, particularly that of the last three presidential governments (those of Brüning, Franz von Papen, and General Schleicher), which more or less dispensed with the Reichstag. The bridge, the table, and the steerage hold are instances of *kosmoi* in Angus Fletcher's term: of ornamental elements of space so disposed as to lay out a hierarchical order (108-109). In this ship of state what comes to the fore is the dense moment of possibilities evident in 1931—what George F. Will has called "the Weimar moment"—prior to the foreclosure of these possibilities in the silence of the Nazi state.[4] But it is this concrete historical flow that is primary in the novel and it is out of this flow that what Wilhelm Freytag calls "signs and portents" of the future emerge (Porter, *Ship* 141). These undoubtedly do refer to future events in the Third Reich but they do so on the model of what Erich Auerbach called figural realism, a model that "permits both its poles—the figure and its fulfilment—to retain the characteristics of concrete historical reality" (195).[5] For example, when Frau Rittersdorf, after seeing Herr Glocken the hunchback, writes a query in her notebook about the advisability of euthanasia for "all defective children" she is, of course, predicting the T-4 program of 1939-1941 in which the mentally and physically handicapped in Germany were killed (352). But Frau Rittersdorf's query taps into a dangerous latency in the Weimar period:

there was already in the 1920s a widespread eugenic discourse that wished to "improve" the racial stock, for example in lawyer Karl Binding and psychiatrist Alfred Hoche's tract *Permission for the Destruction of Life Unworthy of Life* (1920). Frau Rittersdorf appears to have some knowledge of this type of discourse when she proposes to "read all the arguments in favor" of what she calls "the blessings of euthanasia" (352). The only difference between these Weimar proposals and those of the Nazi state was that the latter had the determination to carry such deadly thoughts into action. One senses the direction in which Frau Rittersdorf's biopolitical musings are heading in some analogous remarks of Herr Rieber when he starkly advises putting the sugar workers "in a big oven and turn[ing] on the gas" (59).[6]

Porter's technique of picking out ideational and metaphorical prefigurations of the Third Reich in the Weimar moment of 1931 means that her novel is not primarily focused on the psychological or plot-like development of character (a frequent complaint of critics). *Ship of Fools* can be seen as belonging to a modernist prose genre that Robert Penn Warren called the "philosophical" novel, the novel that dramatizes the political and the theological idea (58). Like the other pre-eminent southern variant of the philosophical novel, Warren's *All the King's Men* (1946), *Ship of Fools* examines the question of a crisis of sovereignty in the liberal state and of the creation of a biopolitics. Porter, however, was very critical of Warren's novel, regarding its portrait of the Huey Long figure Willie Stark as a "sentimental apology" for a "Fascist demagogue" (Porter, *Selected* 205). She took particular exception to Warren's narrator, Jack Burden, whom she regarded as a "man without a center" and one whose impressionability before the mere power of Stark meant that Warren was not able to clarify "the important thing in any book," "[t]he attitude of the author toward his theme and his characters" (Porter, *Selected* 195). Perhaps *Ship of Fools* can be regarded as a delayed answer to Warren's novel, one that treats analogous subject matter but with a more severe ethical attitude toward the dictatorial possibilities of the modern *polis* and with a perspective that ties the deviations of the characters to a vertical, late-medieval pole of judgment. The latter gives rise to the organizing schema of the book in which the community on the *Vera* becomes an exemplification of disparate fooleries in the manner of Sebastian Brant's *Das Narrenschiff* (1494).

In Brant's work the fools are in transit on their ship to the land of Narragon and it would seem that Brant saw this as a rendering in satire of the Christian notion of life as pilgrimage. The great historical-existential exposition of this notion is Saint Augustine's description in *The City of God* of the soul in pilgrimage from the earthly city to the heavenly city. That Porter probably had this Augustinian exposition in mind in planning her novel is seen in the prefatory note when she says that the voyage of the *Vera* illustrates a "simple almost universal image of the ship of this world on its voyage to eternity" and she cites as the epigraph to the final section of her novel part of the quintessentially Augustinian line from the *Epistle to the Hebrews* chapter 13, verse 15: "For here have we no continuing city ..." (361). The unquoted part of the line from the epistle continues, "but we seek the one to come." This "one to come" was read by Saint Augustine as the heavenly Jerusalem. [7] A major aesthetic resonance of Porter's novel derives from the way the impermanence of transit is blended with the individual longings of the passengers, longings which are perhaps articulated best in the maneuverings around one another of the mutually tormenting equilibrists, Jenny and David.

It is not surprising that Porter should make reference to Saint Augustine. She was baptized into the Roman Catholic church just before she reached the age of twenty (even though she became a caustic critic of most Church dogma) and she claimed in her essay "St. Augustine and the Bullfight" (1955) that she had been a constant reader of *The Confessions* since first being able to read. [8] The notion of a "city" of the human *communitas*, is essential to the conception of *Ship of Fools* because Porter sees individuals as inherently belonging to a collective body (the ship figure well serves this purpose). The passengers might feel that they can keep their "pride and separateness" within their private selves but, despite what they want, they belong willy-nilly to a common entity (11). It is therefore a romantic delusion, for example, that Jenny can hope that she and David will have "a wonderful private life," cut off from all others (54).

Porter's insistence on the community-in-history brings her fiction close to the work of the Nashville Agrarians. Although Porter was not a contributor to *I'll Take My Stand* she was bound to the group by her friendship with Robert Penn Warren, Allen Tate, Caroline Gordon, and Andrew Lytle (and she did call the Agrarians' manifesto "a very seriously good book") (Porter, *Selected* 76). Most importantly, perhaps, her anti-romantic aesthetic had affinities with the hard, dry, neo-classical style of John Crowe Ransom, Henry James, T. S. Eliot, and T. E. Hulme. Tate had described the Agrarians as being "the last Europeans" and Porter's work also belongs to a regional need in the modernist period to relate the southern literary sensibility to the historic, ecumenical body that Eliot in 1919 called "the mind of Europe" (Davidson and Tate 230); (Eliot 16). When the arc of this return was described in such Eliot-like works as Tate's "Fragment of a Meditation" or Warren's "Terror," however, it became apparent that the imaginative positing of Europe as a restorative Latinate order was, in the conditions of the 1920s and 1930s, simultaneously an acknowledgment of the disintegration of that order, a disintegration lent outward shape by the post-Versailles fragmenting of the *jus publicum Europaeum*. *Ship of Fools* heightens this strategy by taking its point of focus into the very political center of this disintegration, late Weimar Germany. It is evident that on the *Vera* "the mind of Europe" has been grievously wounded by war. The latter day professional representatives of intellect on board the ship, notably Professor Hutten, tend to reduce this mind to a form of nationalistic ideology, thereby exemplifying what Julian Benda called in 1927 *la trahison des clercs*. The Professor, for example, believes that all "greatness" of thought is animated by "the old Germanic spirit" (342).

As well as being a meditation on the crisis of the European mind in the fifteen years after World War I, Porter's novel is more directly a dramatization of the instabilities that undermined the Brüning chancellorship.[9] These instabilities went beyond the fluctuations of the international market that cause the unemployment of the sugar workers on the *Vera.* They were rather structurally inherent in the government of a republic that did not want to be a republic and one whose conservative leaders, Brüning and then von Papen, worked for a return to the monarchy. Porter's middle- and upper-class Germans have the same Wilhelmine longings. Frau Hutten recalls how "the whole German colony" in Mexico City went to the newsreel of the funeral of the ex-Kaiser's wife in 1921 and how they all wept for their lost "homeland" (81-82). The *Vera,* "ruled" as it is by two members of the old aristocratic caste, the Lutheran Captain Thiele and the Catholic Dr. Schumann, represents the Weimar ship of state in that this state was a nominal republic that was governed by members of the upper order of society. Porter takes care to specify that both the Captain and the Doctor are of "the good old Junker class" and that they belong by hereditary privilege to "the great old society" in which they were born—which is to say, Wilhelmine Germany (346). Captain Thiele, who in many respects is a similar figure to the last president of the republic, Paul von Hindenburg, has "never ceased to mourn the Kaiser," broods constantly on "his vanished Germany ... that fatherland of order, harmony, simplicity, propriety," and loathes "the debased pseudo-republicanism of defeated Germany" (429, 427). The republicanism and parliamentary nature of the Weimar state was perceived by many conservatives as an imposition by the Western powers on Germany of the French principles of 1789 and as such alien to the older medieval origins of the Reich. But the office of the president in the Weimar constitution retained something of the old monarchical idea and was called by Max Weber, one of the framers of the constitution, "the bearer of the principle of the unity of the Reich" (qtd in Kennedy, location 163). This was especially evident in the executive powers of the president, under the powers granted in Article 48 of the constitution, which allowed for presidential government by emergency decree without the support of the legislature. It was through Article 48 that Chancellor Brüning, with the support of President Hindenburg, was forced to govern in 1931 because the Reichstag would not support his austerity measures. This "state of emergency" was a dangerous empowerment of the executive in the last three presidential chancellorships and one that prepared the way for Hitler's dictatorial transformation of the office of Chancellor after January 1933.

It might be thought that Porter could not have this degree of familiarity with Weimar politics but the Captain specifically uses the phrase "a state of emergency" to explain his early retreat to the heights of the bridge in order to deal with the "thousand difficulties" consequent upon leaving port (104).[10] Captain Thiele's sovereignty comes into force during "the Freytag crisis," the expelling of Wilhelm Freytag from the Captain's table because he is married to a Jew (244). It is noteworthy that this is a decision that meets with the academic acclamation of Professor Hutten who, in common with other authoritarian Weimar thinkers such as Carl Schmitt and Martin Heidegger, has a hunger for decisionism. As Professor Hutten sees it, the "Freytag crisis" had to be resolved by "sudden, decisive, and, naturally, successful action" against "the enemy" (245). Schmitt even felt that the decision of the sovereign in an emergency constituted its own legitimacy and could give foundation to law in a situation where normal constitutional procedure broke down. In his classic work *Political Theology* (1922) he came up with the lapidary equation: "Sovereign is he who decides on the exception" (5). He found an analogue for the decision in the divine intervention that breaks up the dead positivistic repetition of events, and it is notable that the much put-upon widow, Frau Schmitt, thinks of the Captain as "a visible present incarnation" of "the mystical male force which rules not only the earth and all its creatures but indeed, as God the Father, the universe" (248).

Porter's novel makes use of the imaginative architecture of a system of thought that was invented in the Weimar period, political theology, and its core insight that political forms are secularizations and reworkings of theological ideas.[11] But, even though she accepts for imaginative purposes this architecture, she is also a debunker of the presumptions of this "mystical male force," calling the Captain "a pompous minor god" and allowing him to parade on deck in "a monumental ornate cap, white as plaster" (94-95). The whole language of sovereignty and crisis is seen from a critical angle when Porter reveals that the Captain has a "riotous, violent imagination" and longs for a "cinematic crisis full of darkness" in which he overcomes bloody disorder from the bridge: the Captain's traditionalist monarchism is suddenly seen in fantasized alliance with cinema, the essential medium of Weimar modernity (173). Porter sees that in the early 1930s such traditionalism was under pressure to recompose itself in more reactionary forms, forms that paradoxically incorporated such modernistic elements as the movies and their dream life. A similar perspective is shown when the Captain is said to be fascinated by "American gangster films," although he imagines himself as a gangster who works for "established government" (426).[12] This is Porter's profane translation of Schmitt's notion that the sovereign lies outside of the law and yet founds the law. In addition, Porter intuitively anticipated the more recent Schmittian insights of Giorgio Agamben, who argues that the Weimar implementation of a decisionistic sovereignty brings into the modern *polis* a complementary figure of *homo sacer* or of a bare life that is utterly subject to executive power (55). Herr Glocken, a "hunchback" and a "dwarf," and Herr Löwenthal, the Jewish passenger, are two such figures (17). They are examples of the helpless exposure of biological being that arises concomitantly with the state of exception: the hunchback is labelled a "symbol of every kind of degeneration" by some of the passengers and Herr Löwenthal feels pushed back into "the dark and airless ghetto of his soul" (351, 95).

If the *Vera* is the Weimar ship of state, then the unemployed Spanish sugar workers in the hold are a reminder of this state's shaky foundations in the international economic market, especially that following the October 1929 crash. Chancellor Brüning, despite his severe deflationary measures, was not able to halt the economic slide and by February 1932 there were over seven million unemployed in Germany, about a third of the work force. The Captain's reactionary rhetoric, which sees the sugar workers as "scum" and "filthy cattle," is essentially uncomprehending of the intrusion of economic forces into his model of a traditional society: for him the workers only represent the rising up of "the elemental forces of darkness and disorder against the very spirit of civilization—that great Germanic force of life" (345, 216). But the unemployed workers, and the fat labor agitator who tries to stir them up, indicate a fundamental structural problem in a state that cannot contain the economic disorder within it. The *Vera* embodies a state that, unlike its nineteenth-century counterpart in a *jus publicum Europaeum*, no longer stands above society as a distinct entity. Instead state and society permeate one another in an unstable ensemble.

This interpenetration particularly became evident in the Weimar republic after the September 1930 elections when the Nazis dramatically moved in from the nationalist margins to capture 107 seats in the Reichstag. From September 1930 the National Socialists, a mass participatory movement that went beyond being a parliamentary party, were able to infiltrate the state structure and threaten to become the largest party in the legislature (they did so in July 1932, almost a year after the novel is set). All the last three presidential Chancellors tried to lean toward the Nazi party between 1930 and 1933: they attempted to accommodate the state to society. The bending of the nationalist or traditional right toward the radical right in the last years of the Weimar republic is reflected in the incident when Herr Rieber and Fräulein Lizzi Spöckenkieker invade the bridge and prevail upon the Captain to expel from his table Herr Freytag, whom they have learnt is married to a Jew. There is no question that there is a large difference of class between the Captain and his two lower-middle-class visitors, both of whom are in the ladies' garment trade. Indeed the snobbish Captain finds Lizzi "positively repellent" in the clucking vulgarity of her manner (232). Nevertheless, the Captain's response to their appeal shows that the anti-Semitism of the conservative right can make common cause with the radical right version of this prejudice. He accedes to the request of the proto-Nazi couple and even repeats their biological rhetoric of race in conversation at the next meeting at the Captain's table. This meeting is indeed significant with regard to the larger political meaning of the book. The closing in of a "ring" on the part of the members of the table and their discovery of "special intimate bonds of blood and sympathy" rehearses a lateral process by which society merges with state around a *völkisch* principle (247). Porter shows how traditionalist, monarchist forms of authority can no longer legitimate themselves in the face of the dispersive secular forces of political modernity. These hierarchical forms are undermined by "strange senseless states of mind" in the guests at the table, who are no longer capable of rational expression of the political idea and hence succumb to biological fantasy and communal sentiment (227).

One of the next episodes at the Captain's table reflects a further loss of its symbolic authority. This occurs when the table is invaded by the zarzuela company during the party in supposed honor of the Captain. The Spaniards embody pure lawlessness and their various orations hover between panegyric, insolence, and pastiche. The Captain realizes to his mortification that the "political trend of their words" is intended to undermine his own Wilhelmine monarchism (and it befits the Weimar scheme of the novel that the Spaniards view the Captain as a surrogate of the "great leaders" of the conservative right "who are restoring order and government" to Germany) (429, 431). In her toast Lola speaks in orotund language of "the eternal friendship of our two great nations, the Kingdom of Spain and the Empire of Germany" (431). Neither of these two imperial monarchies existed any longer in September 1931—part of Lola's sly dig is that Alfonso XII, the last king of Spain to reign until the death of Franco, abdicated in June 1931, two months prior to the embarking of the *Vera*—and putting them together in this way is a mocking reproduction of the Weimar conservative rhetoric of Reich, which frequently evoked the Holy Roman Empire as a *sacrum imperium.*[13] The Spaniards' tribute to the Captain becomes so overbearing that he is forced to flee the party. At the heart of the Captain's humiliation is his feeling that fixed hierarchies have been turned on their head and that this "ragtag bobtailed lot" have desecrated the "high glorious cause" of the monarchy by calling themselves "royalists" (429). The zarzuela company then cap their subversion of nostalgic sentiment toward the Germanic past—this time for the Second Reich—by dancing an "insulting parody" of the German waltz (433). But another dance has come to the fore at the Spaniards' party. It is that of paper-hatted Herr Baumgartner, a lawyer making a mockery of the law, who plays pied piper to the future children of the Nazi state as they goose-step after him in "shrieking disorder" (408).

It is in keeping with the spirit of this dance that the *Vera* arrives in a Bremerhaven that is seen as the "holy earth" of the "Fatherland" (494). The "Fatherland" has become the *völkisch* equivalent of the heavenly Jerusalem, a profane counterpart of the Augustinian notion of pilgrimage.[14] It is this Germany that appears in an ecstatically naive form to the boy trumpeter in the last scene of the novel as he stares at the town with "blinded eyes" (497). Such a vision is an offspring of the political idea of the Reich, which originated in Weimar conservatism but which Hitler was able to make electoral use of in the early 1930s. At the very first dinner at the Captain's table the Mexican Germans already feel that that they have entered into a "mystic Fatherland"—they are members of a diaspora that is being gathered up within an idea of a Greater Germany (40). Such feelings have a sharp contemporary point because it was in the middle of 1931, in the second year of his government, that Brüning adopted an increasingly nationalistic foreign policy in order to compensate for a desperate economic situation at home. [15] What Porter pinpoints in these passengers are the emotional correlations to this idea of the Reich, especially the lazy, diffuse sensuousness of the "belonging" sentiment. Frau Schmitt, for example, feels after the Freytag incident "the warm wave of blood kinship with her great and glorious race" (248). Freytag himself refers such feelings to "the drooling German soul," an exclamation prompted by his witnessing the lachrymose reaction of Frau Hutten to the near drowning of her bulldog (315). In this stinging phrase Porter is responding with a Hulme-like antipathy to all forms of political romanticism as "spilt religion" and together with Hulme she thinks of romanticism as moist in contrast with the hardness and dryness of the classical (Hulme 118). Her antipathy is brilliantly tactile: the pulpy wet mass of the bulldog is offset by the sculptural dignity of the corpse of the unmourned Basque, the rescuer of the animal. However, at this point in 1931 neither Frau Schmitt nor the Captain nor the Huttens "are" Nazis (in fact it is notable that the word Nazi is never used in the novel); it is rather that their sentiments for the Reich have a vulnerable overlap with the Nazi aspiration for a Third Reich. Throughout the novel the emphasis is not so much on the proto-Nazis, Lizzi and Herr Rieber, who in themselves are ridiculous, as it is on the characters who are representatives of the traditional right such as the Captain or the Huttens.[16] The political situation was theirs to throw away and throw it away they did. When she looked back on this period Porter spoke of Hitler as a "dreadful and psychopathic clown," yet a "clown" who somehow managed to have a strong grip on the middle-class (Letter to Pogue). Her point in the "Freytag crisis" is that this very clownishness in the persons of Herr Rieber and Lizzi could become a mask behind which an unconscious tendency to evil in the more upright characters could hide itself. This is Porter's sharpest contemporary use of Brant's motif of the fool.

What, then, is there to set against the condition of what might be called Weimar helplessness? The principal counterweight is Dr. Schumann. Essential to the Doctor's character is a sense of measure, which, in the Weimar context, can be traced back to his Bavarian Catholicism, a "whole great structure built upon the twin pillars of justice and love" (373). The Doctor's beliefs make him wary of the neo-paganism inherent in the *völkisch* principle and in this he is only following the Catholic attitude to Hitler's anti-Semitic policies made explicit by Pope Pius XI when he said in 1938 that "Spiritually, we are all Semites" (qtd in "We Remember"). So when the Captain tries to question the Doctor about rumors of Freytag's Jewishness, the Doctor is "not in the least concerned whether Freytag was a Jew or not" and he regards the question as "beneath contempt" (227). Later at the Captain's table the Doctor is asked his opinion of "the Jews" by Frau Rittersdorf and answers, "I have nothing to say against them. I believe we worship the same God" (230). He thereby rebukes the opinion that has just been offered by Professor Hutten that the God of the Jews is "Old Jahweh," "a most primitive kind of God" (229). Here once again Porter shows her instinct for Weimar discriminations. For the Professor is following the arguments of many German liberal Protestants of the 1920s in saying that the "primitive" Old Testament was inconsistent in its legalism and supposed vindictiveness with the purity of Jesus' gospel. Such arguments went beyond the varieties of Protestantism that Porter knew from her native Texas. For surely no Texas Baptist or Methodist, no matter how much they said that the grace of Christ superseded the Jewish law, could accept that "old Jahweh" was a different kind of God from that of the New Testament.[17] That this liberal Protestantism might be translated into something more poisonous is indicated by the bigoted turn that Herr Rieber gives the theological discussion when he talks about preserving "the bloodstream of our race" (230).

The Doctor is, however, not to be over-idealized and he perhaps can represent a certain Catholic quietism or alliance with the radical right that was to become more evident after the caving in of the Catholic Centre Party to Nazi leadership shortly after Hitler became Chancellor in January 1933 (it even voted for Hitler's Enabling Act) and after the Concordat between the Vatican and the Third Reich later in the year. In keeping with these tendencies the Doctor does seem often to be oddly disengaged. For example, he simply joins the Captain's table after the "Freytag crisis" and, although he doesn't say anything in support of what has happened, he seems by default to belong to the tightening "ring" of nationalist sentiment that celebrates the expulsion of Freytag. On the earlier occasion of the discussion of the Jewish God the Doctor quickly leaves the table after his curt remarks, giving the impression that somehow his mere embodiment of principle frees him from having to argue the case for his beliefs in antipathetic company (and the Catholic Church in Germany showed much moral evasion with regard to the criminality of the Nazi state). Freytag on this occasion understandably sees the Doctor as an "old hypocrite, who had got out without committing himself" (232). Even the Captain observes a "dangerous moral inertia" in his companion, a drifting off into some inner sanctum of the apolitical (346).

But this is not all that can be said about the Doctor's "benevolent detachment" (228). For the Doctor does have the capacity for self-examination; in him one can see how the Augustinian faculty of the will can be the bridge that brings the mind into engagement with the world. The most important scene that illustrates this process in the Doctor occurs after La Condesa leaves the ship for exile on Tenerife and the Doctor has a sudden insight into his "moral collapse." He realizes that he has imposed a medicalized imprisonment on La Condesa by giving her sedatives and that he has tormented her with his "guilty love" without allowing either of them "any human joy" in his attachment. But he has a crucial reflection: he sees that he is "not altogether ... a coward," not altogether "if he did not choose to be!" (373). It is the narrow space of choosing not to be a coward that saves Porter's characters from being the closed bleak fates that so many readers take them to be. The Doctor subsequently tries to make contact with La Condesa, offering her future medical and personal help, but she spurns his attempt.

For the tough Augustinian moralist of the will that Porter shows herself to be in *Ship of Fools* these choices are hard won and subject to backsliding. The will after all begins in the earthly city and that it has begun there from earliest childhood seems to be the point of Porter's extended portrayal of Ric and Rac, the unspeakable Spanish twins who get pleasure from such activities as throwing bulldogs overboard. To describe the sheer malice that is in the twins the Doctor uses a term that Augustine invented, "Original Sin" (200). For the Doctor this sin is an inner warp within the will—and by the will he understands it is ultimately his own will that is in question. In a discussion at the dinner table the Doctor attempts to give a theological definition of evil and what he says is a revealing comment on his own sense of "collusion." He first agrees with the Captain's statement that "it requires a certain force of character to be really evil" (288). He then adds that for most of us "[o]ur collusion with evil is only negative, consent by default, you might say. I suppose that in our hearts our sympathies are with the criminal because he really commits the deeds we only dream of doing!" (294).

One can read this statement in two ways. It is apparent that the Doctor's description of the cowardice of the "good" is only too apposite to the reaction in late Weimar to the arrival of the "criminal" in politics.[18] But there is something else in this harsh statement. For the Doctor also points to a structural contradiction in the will that enables it to be a human will at all and that prevents "the human race" from being divided into a Manichean opposition of what the Doctor calls "embattled angels and invading devils" (294). The Doctor is saying that even when the will affirms the good or the bad it at the same time creates a counter will for that which is its opposite. Hannah Arendt comments that because the will in Augustine is a will rather than a compulsion and because it is not entire but always inwardly riven, the faculty of will divides up into two: the will to do and the will not to do, the will of the heavenly city and that of the earthly (location 5345-5465). Both the Doctor and Augustine in *The Confessions* are unstrung by this division but without it they would not be pilgrims. For Saint Augustine the will needs the complement of grace to bring to an end its self-contradiction. It is noteworthy here that the Doctor experiences his insight into his mistreatment of La Condesa as an "instantaneous miracle" or the "psychic equivalent of a lightning stroke" (373).

The larger ground plan of *Ship of Fools* positions the characters between the earthly city and the continuing city of Saint Augustine. At one pole the characters are subject to the impermanence of transit on a sea vessel. This passing temporal moment is critical to the book's conception and it fits this sense of time as passage that Porter should have a very concrete historical sense of the late summer of 1931 in Weimar Germany. On the other pole the characters are seen in the light of a standard of permanence and as though they are *sub specie aeternitatis.* This is probably why Porter turned to the late medieval universalism of Sebastian Brant in conceiving her book because his poem offers "the world's whole course in one brief look" (Brant 59). It is this desire to see the characters from a perspective of permanence that gives Porter's novel its aesthetic aspect of the finished. The characters are seen externally as members of a *communitas.* On a number of occasions they are either compared to a "gargoyle" (Herr Glocken) or are seen lying in the "habitual posture of early medieval effigies" (Dr. Schumann) (Porter *Ship* 51, 420, 374). It is as though Porter was here indicating how in her novel individuality yields to a universal, external form and takes the shape of figures of a medieval cathedral. The novel is balanced between the poles of the historical moment of summer 1931 and the fixing judgment of a final value.

NOTES

1. In answer to the claim that Porter shifts anti-Semitic attitudes backwards into the Weimar period (found, for example, in Zacharasiewicz [133]) it might said that the ostracization of the Freytags reflects prejudices that were already strong in the Germany of the late 1920s. Heinrich Winkler even calls anti-Semitism "a quotidian affair" in this decade (416).
2. I should like to thank Beth Alvarez for providing uncollected letters by Josephine Herbst and Katherine Anne Porter.
3. Admittedly, in the light of Porter's published correspondence from her stay in Germany in 1931-1932, this claim made in 1975 about knowledge of late Weimar politics might seem an exaggerated assertion. But at the very least, this remark shows that after the twenty-five years that elapsed between her visit and her final work on the novel, Porter felt that she had to provide evidence that she "knew ... what was happening" in 1931-1932 and that now she had to the retrospective opportunity to demonstrate this. The differences between the diary-letter that she wrote on the *Werra* and the much increased role of the German characters in the novel indicate that it was this German part of *Ship of Fools* that was especially expanded in retrospect. In this letter the originals for Spanish characters such as La Condesa and the Cuban students are easily identifiable, but the German passengers only merit general description (there are models in the letter for two of the crew, the Captain and Dr. Schumann, but the Captain is only skimpily outlined in the letter and in the novel receives a much expanded political profile) (Porter, *Letters* 49).
4. Will first used this phrase in a *Washington Post* article in August 2007. It has subsequently assumed a life of its own, usually without acknowledgment being given to the source.
5. Figural realism is the patristic and medieval schema whereby a certain historical event in the Old Testament was said to prefigure and to find its fulfillment in a later historical event in the New Testament. Abraham's near sacrifice of Isaac, for example, both actually happened and was a prefiguring of the Crucifixion. However, any such fulfillments that eventuate from Porter's "signs and portents" belong not to the coming of an order of grace that fulfills the Old Testament but to a profane mockery of any such order. Paweł Stachura's article on *Ship of Fools* discusses the place of figural realism in the novel (97-100).

6. Herr Rieber does later push Frau Rittersdorf's comments nearer to the T-4 program when, making pointed reference to Herr Glocken, he says that he is going to publish a "very learned, very scientific" article by "a doctor," "advocating the extermination of the unfit" (420). Frau Rittersdorf's speculations are best seen in the context of the proposals by scientists and politicians in most European nations of the 1920s in support of a gardening state, which would be cultivated through such eugenic measures as sterilization. Such proposals had been mooted since the beginning of the century but World War I led to a radicalization of them. (Frau Rittersdorf, the war widow, says bitterly that the conflict destroyed "the sound in body" and left only "the defectives to carry on the race" [156].) The National Socialists proceeded to sweep aside any lingering humanistic doubts about enacting these schemes. Porter must surely have been aware of the T-4 program, which resulted in the "Doctors' Trial" at Nuremberg between 1946-1947. She owned a copy of Peter Calvocoressi's *Nuremberg: The Facts, the Law and the Consequences* (1948) and some of her annotations to this book and others in her library refer to the Holocaust and to "gas-ovens" (for examples, see Bloemendaal 133).
7. In fact Saint Augustine was one of the first Christian writers to envisage the pilgrimage of the believer as that of a wayfarer on an ocean voyage (Skrine 581). It was Augustine's immense contribution to the metaphor of the Christian life as a journey that helped to make the metaphor of the voyage and of the ship already "very old and durable" by Brant's time (in the words of Porter's note)(vii).
8. Porter's library contains a copy of *The Confessions of St. Augustine* (London: JM Dent 1932) that is annotated in her hand and signed "K.A.P. Boston, February 1936 7th copy". She also possessed a 1945 translation of *The City of God* and wrote in this copy: "Katherine Anne Porter/5 December 1947/Santa Monica" (Katherine Anne Porter Library). Even if Porter had only read *The Confessions* a strong case can be made that this work is a forerunner of *The City of God* because it conceives of the individual pilgrim's moves toward or away from the Godhead through the figure of spatial journey and even ocean voyage. Augustine's word for pilgrim (*peregrinus*) was derived from the legal term in ancient Rome that was used for those foreigners who lived outside their native land within the Empire and did not have the full rights of citizens (Claussen 35-36). This is apposite to Porter's understanding that her characters have "no continuing city" and to the ironic interplay in the novel between the Augustinian *peregrini* of the "voyage to eternity" and the secular concept

of *peregrinus* held by the Mexican Germans, who are returning to their Fatherland.

9. This is a controversial claim, particularly since it presumes a knowledge of Weimar politics and culture on Porter's part that is not reflected in her published correspondence from the Berlin period. But quite apart from the fact that in the novel itself there are a number of references to Weimar society—from gender inversion in Marlene Dietrich to Oswald Spengler's reactionary understanding of the color red (it is the "childish" colour favoured by Jenny and Herr Glocken)—there is also Porter's art of transposition to consider (140, 76-77; Porter, *Selected* 95). For it could be argued that what Porter partly does with historical events from the Weimar period is to internalize them in the text as "parable." An analogy can be made between the structure of the power relations in the novel —that is to say, the shifting balances between the representatives of the traditional right, the radical right, and the middle class—and that in the final stages of the Weimar republic. This analogy pertains even if, as Porter put it, "no party or system is named" (Porter, *Letters* 501).
10. "A state of emergency" usually refers to a government decree (its equivalent in German—*Ausnahmezustand*—was used by Carl Schmitt to refer to Article 48). In this instance from the novel it refers to difficulties of navigation, but navigation of the ship of state is also implied.
11. Essays such as "On a Criticism of Thomas Hardy" (1940) show that Porter had a native sense of the political implications of theology. Naturally these implications are not specific to the Weimar republic and go back at least to Eusebius's support of the Constantine church. But since Frau Schmitt is thinking of the theological attributes of the ruler as these apply in the Captain's case, and the Captain is a surrogate for state authority in 1931, it is an arguable thesis to say that Porter was thinking about the political implications of theology in the case of the Weimar ship of state. In her Hardy essay Porter saw that there could be a political theology from above, which in her opinion often "harnessed" the idea of God to "the worst evils in secular government" (it is this authoritarian usage that the Captain embodies), or there could be a political theology from below, as in "the great tradition of dissent" in which she placed herself and Hardy (Porter, *Collected* 598-600). In the fictional embodiment of the novel, however, both versions are virtually identical in that they grasp that the ship of state is a hierarchical space.
12. The American gangster film, which was enthused over by Weimar cinemagoers such as Bertolt Brecht, was in its definitive phase in the early

1930s. Porter shows an exact knowledge of the types of fantasy encoded in Weimar cinema, as is seen in Elsa Lutz's extensive retelling of the plots of two romantic comedies ("German, and so sweet") that she has viewed on board the ship (187). Both films involve aristocrats, one of whom is an Austrian Archduke, dressing up in disguise out of love for a lower-class woman. Such films were popular with German cinemagoers in the mid-twenties (those Siegfried Kracauer designated "the little shop girls"): they capitalized on longings for the vanished Austro-Hungarian Empire and for plots about the modern Haroun al Raschid (Kracauer 300-302, 309). Elsa's enthusiasm is Porter's way of cross-referencing the personal and the political, the wish fulfilment of a lovelorn teenager with that of the Weimar nostalgia for conservative forms of the Reich (187-189).

13. Although it could be said that there was an "eternal friendship" of the monarchies in this First Reich because the Hapsburg monarch Charles V, grandson of Maximilian I (whom Sebastian Brant venerated as Emperor), had ruled over both Spain and the Holy Roman Empire, any such invocation of "friendship" in 1931 can be no more than an anachronism. This is not to say that Lola is aware of this connection, only that Porter, who read widely in the history of Renaissance Europe, most probably was.
14. Sebastian Brant in *Das Narrenschiff*, section 99 "Of the Decline of Faith," is a passionate advocate of the Holy Roman Empire and of the revival of the German people under the leadership of his patron, Maximilian I. The echoes of these hopes in Porter's novel can only be ironic, given the drastic economic depression and street violence of the early 1930s, which made Germany utterly unlike any integrated medieval polity.
15. Brüning tried to revive the idea of a greater Germany through a customs union with Austria in the summer of 1931.
16. Porter later commented of her stay in Berlin in 1931 that "oddly there was then very little talk of Hitler. There was only the infection of his ideas" (Porter, *Selected* 171).
17. Porter seems to be reflecting the Marcionite arguments of such liberal theologians as Adolf von Harnack, who published a book in 1924 stating that the Old Testament should be dropped from the Bible (this is not to say that Porter had read von Harnack, only that she was aware of the drift of the liberal Protestantism of Professor Hutten toward the Aryan Christianity of the 1930s).
18. It is true that the Doctor's notion of "collusion" is the central moral principle in Porter's work and therefore not restricted to *Ship of Fools.* It is found, for example, in the short stories "Theft" (1929), "Flowering

Judas" (1930) and "Noon Wine" (1937). But, as Porter said in a 1961 interview on her forthcoming novel, in *Ship of Fools* such collusion is given the specific historical focus of 1931. In that period, Porter explained, the principle was demonstrated by the "tacit consent" of "good worthy people" in Hitler's rise and even their vicarious participation in his "crimes" (Ruoff and Smith 397).

Works Cited

Agamben, Giorgio. *Homo Sacer: Sovereign Power and Bare Life*, trans. Daniel Heller-Roazen. Stanford: Stanford University Press, 1998.

Arendt, Hannah. *The Life of the Mind.* San Diego: Harcourt, 1977. *Kindle* ebook file.

Auerbach, Erich. *Mimesis: The Representation of Reality in Western Literature*, trans. Willard R. Trask. Princeton: Princeton University Press, 2003.

Bloemendaal, Jan. "Constructing Identities: Ethnicity and Race in Katherine Anne Porter." Ph.D. thesis, University of Leiden, 2005.

Brant, Sebastian. *The Ship of Fools*, trans. Edwin H. Zeydel. New York: Dover Publications, 1962.

Claussen, M.A. "'Peregrinatio' and 'Peregrini' in Augustine's 'City of God.' *Traditio* 46 (1991), 33-75.

Davidson, Donald, and Allen Tate. *The Literary Correspondence of Donald Davidson and Allen Tate*, eds. John Tyree Fain and Thomas Daniel Young. Athens: University of Georgia Press, 1974.

Dolan, Mary Anne. "Almost Since Chaucer with Miss Porter." *Katherine Anne Porter: Conversations*, ed. Joan Givner. Jackson: University Press of Mississippi, 1987. 177-183.

Eliot, T. S. *Selected Essays.* London: Faber and Faber, 1951.

Fletcher, Angus. *Allegory: The Theory of a Symbolic Mode.* Ithaca: Cornell University Press, 1964.

Frye, Northrop. The "Third Book." *Notebooks of Northrop Frye, 1964-1972: The Critical Comedy*, ed. Michael Dolzani. Toronto: University of Toronto Press, 2002.

Givner, Joan. Katherine *Anne Porter: A Life.* New York: Simon & Schuster, 1982.

Herbst, Josephine. Letter to Daniel Curley. 26 April 1962. Josephine Herbst Papers. Series 1, Box 21, Porter, Katherine Anne, 1940-1962. Yale Collection of American Literature. Beinecke Rare Book and Manuscript Library.

Hulme, T. E. *Speculations: Essays on Humanism and the Philosophy of Art*, ed. Herbert Read. London: Routledge and Kegan Paul, 1924.

Katherine Anne Porter Library. Special Collections and University Archives, University of Maryland Libraries.

Kennedy, Ellen. *Constitutional Failure: Carl Schmitt in Weimar*. Durham: Duke University Press, 2004. *Kindle* ebook file.

Kracauer, Siegfried. *The Mass Ornament: Weimar Essays*, trans. and ed. Thomas Y. Levin. Cambridge, Mass.: Harvard University Press, 1995.

Porter, Katherine Anne. *Collected Stories and Other Writings*, ed. Darlene Harbour Unrue. New York: Library of America, 2008.

---. Letter to Samuel Pogue. 17 March 1942. Series 1, Box 35. Katherine Anne Porter Papers. Special Collections and University Archives, University of Maryland Libraries.

---. *Letters of Katherine Anne Porter*, ed. Isabel Bayley. New York: Atlantic Monthly Press, 1990.

---. *Selected Letters of Katherine Anne Porter: Chronicles of a Modern Woman*, ed. Darlene Harbour Unrue. Jackson: University Press of Mississippi, 2012.

---. *Ship of Fools*. Boston: Little, Brown, 1962.

Ruoff, James and Del Smith. "Katherine Anne Porter on *Ship of Fools*." *College English* 24 (Feb. 1963), 396-397.

Schmitt, Carl. *Political Theology: Four Chapters on the Concept of Sovereignty*, trans. George Schwab. Cambridge, Mass.: MIT Press, 1985.

Skrine, Peter. "The Destination of the Ship of Fools: Religious Allegory in Brant's 'Narrenschiff.'" *Modern Language Review* 64 (July 1969), 576-596.

Stachura, Paweł. "The American Sybils. Prophecy as a Mode of Fiction Writing" in *American Experience—The Experience of America*, eds. Andrzej Ceynowa and Marek Wilczyński. Frankfurt am Main: Peter Lang, 2013.

Warren, Robert Penn. *Selected Essays*. New York: Vintage, 1958.

"We Remember: A Reflection on the Shoah," 16 March 1998. *Vatican: The Holy See*. Web. 25 Nov 2012.

Winkler, Heinrich August. *Germany: The Long Road West. Volume 1: 1989-1933*, trans. Alexander J. Sager. Oxford: Oxford University Press, 2006.

Zacharasiewicz, Waldemar. *Images of Germany in American Literature.* Iowa City: University of Iowa Press, 2007.

Katherine Anne Porter's *Ship of Fools*

Failed Novel, Classic Satire, or Private Joke?

Darlene Harbour Unrue

In the summer of 1962, after Katherine Anne Porter's *Ship of Fools* had been published the previous April to enthusiastic reviews and for many weeks had sat comfortably on the bestseller list of the *New York Times Book Review*, the influential American critic Wayne Booth posed the question others had indirectly raised: Is *Ship of Fools* really a novel? Investigating Booth's question and some answers proffered by Booth and other critics—and even by Porter herself—helps us classify and subclassify *Ship of Fools* and by extension reach a better understanding of it. In the process we discover that Porter's only long novel encapsulates her artistic canon and much of her life, marked in the novel not only by obvious autobiographical elements but also by private reprisals and jokes.

By implicitly asking the question "How can we tell what a work means, let alone whether it's good or bad, if we don't know what it is to begin with?" Booth took for granted the formalist assumptions that all of literature can be first divided into kinds and then into sub-kinds and that every work can be evaluated according to the degree to which it incorporates genre requirements. Booth answered his own question of whether *Ship of Fools* is really a novel by invoking F. R. Leavis's *The Great Tradition* and rather tepidly concluding that *Ship of Fools* is "not quite Leavis's idea. . . of what the novel ought to be" (637). Because it also ran afoul of Booth's own narrow definition of "novel" and his bias for a tightly woven plot, *Ship of Fools* was not quite Booth's idea of a novel either.

Other reviewers and critics waded in with additional suggestions for categorizing Porter's *Ship of Fools*. M. M. Liberman argued that instead of "novel" *Ship of Fools* should be called an "apologue" (385), an allegorical tale in which the moral is more important than narrative minutiae. Others wanted to call it an epic, a comedy, a moral allegory, a parody, a parable, or a satire. Porter, aware of Booth's question and various answers to it, provided her own rejoinder a decade later. "Most of the critics have made all their guesses and almost everyone is wrong," she told Carl Griffin. "The book is a novel and I have no doubt this will be discovered and cleared up in the next fifty years" (*Selected Letters* 326–27).

Now, fifty years after the publication of *Ship of Fools*, its classification as a novel is unchallenged, and its place among twentieth-century modernist novels is fixed.[1] From the vantage of historical hindsight we can see that had Porter completed it in the early 1930s, when it was first evolving from its embryonic stage as the third part of a novel she had conceived in the late 1920s,[2] it would have found a more welcoming reception by reviewers and critics who embraced such novels as Joyce's *Ulysses* and Faulkner's *Absalom, Absalom!*—re-writings, as it were, of classic works and bold illustrations of Ezra Pound's injunction to "Make it New!" and of Eliot's point in "Tradition and the Individual Talent" that the past and the present collaborate in the mind of the artist.[3]

Porter thought of herself as a modernist well before her mature fiction began to appear in the early 1920s, nearly a decade after she had discovered Joyce's *Dubliners* in a little bookshop in Texas ("It was a great day," she said). She recalled that from that point on she "had gone like a house afire through everything 'new'—that word meant something peculiar to the times—absolutely everything 'new' that was being published; also in music; also in painting" ("Reflections on Willa Cather," *Collected Essays* 33).

The "it" in Pound's mandate to "make it new" was the "older" literature modernists were transforming into something new. Porter, who professed to have a taste for "older" art at least equal to her appreciation for the contemporary, was satisfied with the conflation. Indeed, reviewers and early critics who proposed such a range of classifications for *Ship of Fools* were illuminating Porter's choices for fulfilling the modern aesthetic.

It would seem to be logical to explore first the classification "moral allegory" as a means of identifying the "old" that Porter had transformed. Porter herself pointed readers in that direction when in a prefatory note on the verso of the Contents page she attributed her inspiration to Sebastian Brant's fifteenth-century *Das Narrenschiff*, which she called a "moral allegory" that fit her "purpose exactly" and which she appropriated for her own the English translation of his title. A case also can be made for Porter's reliance on other moral allegories, such as Erasmus' *The Praise of Folly*, Prudentius's *Psychomachiae*, Dante's *The Divine Comedy*, Bunyan's *Pilgrim's Progress*, Swift's *Gulliver's Travels*, and Johnson's *Rasselas*. But Porter was not completely comfortable labeling her twentieth-century novel in precisely the same way. When Barbara Thompson in an interview for *The Paris Review* in 1963 suggested that the title itself as a "medieval emblem" seemed to identify her novel as an allegory, Porter responded, "It's just exactly what it seems to be. It's an allegory if you like, though I don't think much of the allegorical as a standard" (Givner, *Conversations* 97). More tellingly, two years later, in an interview with Roy Newquist, instead of calling it a "moral allegory" Porter referred to *Das Narrenschiff* as a "satiric poem" (Givner, *Conversations* 118). In fact, analyses of all the suggested categories confirm that it is an investigation of the satiric, within Porter's *Ship of Fools,* not the moral allegory, that best illuminates her aims, methods, and themes and underscores her modernist vision.

Most of the questions about the quality of the satire in *Ship of Fools* have centered on whether Porter juxtaposes the actual and the ideal, whether she clearly indicates the desired alternatives to her fools' behavior or whether her view is only pessimistic and misanthropic, that is, whether the satire exists only in an ironic discrepancy between her fools' self-delusions and an appalling reality. The reactions of some reviewers and critics suggest that Porter's satire is Juvenalian, only invective, closer to the imagination and style of Jonathan Swift, whom Porter venerated.[4] Lodwick Hartley called *Ship of Fools* "a floating hell" (92) with characters "contemptible and loathesome" (86). Alfred Kazin called it "a harsh personal statement" (73) with Porter contending that "life is a voyage to nowhere, and time makes monkeys, dwarfs, and dupes of us all" (171). Theodore Solotaroff in *Commentary* judged it "little more than misanthropy and technique" without "the soul of humanity" (286). John Thompson, in *The Partisan Review,* called the novel "a curse, a cold, joking, remorseless, unpitying curse" (610). Herbert von Borch in a review in *Die Welt* called the novel a "Dokument des Hasses [a document of hatred]."

More than one critic, however, warned that if Porter's *Ship of Fools* were not read with care, if every scene and character were not taken into consideration, it could easily be *mis*read.[5] Some critics and reviewers have insisted that readers who saw only horror, disillusionment, cruelty, misery, and misanthropy in this novel overlooked or ignored the dominant theme of love woven throughout the narrative and consequently misread the whole work. In fact, it can be argued convincingly that reviewers such as Granville Hicks who did not see what Ray B. West called the "sense of human possibility" (43) in *Ship of Fools* did not read the *satire* accurately.

An analysis of the satire in the novel necessarily begins with an identification of implied desirable alternatives to folly to which Porter directs the reader, alternatives frequently designated by the names she gave her characters. Most often she selected her allusive names from the world of art—whether literary, musical, or visual. In one instance, however, she found her moral standard in events contemporary to her composition of her novel and to a name very much in the news while she was writing the third segment, published as "The Strangers" in 1946.

In the first two published excerpts from *Ship of Fools*, the captain of the *Vera* is not named. But sometime in 1945 or early 1946 Porter assigned the ship's captain the name "Thiele," an almost certain allusion to General Fritz Thiele. The *Vera*'s Captain Thiele, who exemplifies the foundations of Nazism, believes he belongs "to a larger plan. . . [and fulfills] his destiny in his appointed place" (174). He also displays his low regard for human life: "Gazing downward" into the steerage at the passengers whom he earlier has seen as "heaps of refuse," he despises "these filthy cattle" (216). The Captain cannot imagine himself "on any side except that of established government" (426), and he often revels "secretly in the notion of lawless murderous fury breaking out again and again at any time, anywhere—in some place he could not even fix on the map, but always among people whom it was lawful to kill, with himself at the center, always in command and control" (427).

General Fritz Thiele, in marked contrast to the ship's captain, served in the German Army in both World War I and World War II before becoming part of the German resistance and participating in the assassination attempt against Adolf Hitler on July 20, 1944. After the attempt failed, he was arrested August 11, condemned to death August 21, and hanged on September 4.[6] General Thiele, the anti-Nazi martyr, illustrates the human possibility that the *de facto* Nazi Captain Thiele cannot imagine.

Porter's selecting names from the world of art to represent an ideal she juxtaposes to folly is not surprising. She long before had staked out her position on art, and like many modernists, exalted it to the level of religion: "I agree with Mr. E. M. Forster," she said, "that there are only two possibilities for any real order: in art and in religion" ("1942: Transplanted

Writers," *Collected Essays* 459). A decade later, in her opening speech at the Congress for Cultural Freedom, she described the artist as one who speaks "to all of us" and "interprets for all of us." She called the artist a "sacred madman" (*Collected Essays* 217).

Herr Professor Hutten is the literary namesake of Ulrich von Hutten, a Renaissance German satirist and humanist poet Porter greatly admired, reading his *Letters of Obscure Men* in Basel the summer of 1932. Porter's Herr Professor Hutten, holding forth in lengthy, blathering discourse at every opportunity, represents the arrogance and dryness of the worst of academics, whom Porter had grown to dislike during her stints as writer-in-residence on college campuses in the 1940s and 1950s. Indeed, the professor's condescending treatment of his wife, Frau Professor Hutten, represents the attitude Porter perceived in her temporary colleagues at Stanford and the University of Michigan who thought her inferior because she had no academic degrees. To make sure the personal satire would not be missed, Porter gave Frau Professor Hutten the name "Käthe."

Herr Siegfried Rieber's given name provides a clue to a noble standard he fails to meet. Porter probably had in mind both the character Siegfried in Richard Wagner's opera *Der Ring des Nibelungen*, which she saw several times, and also Wagner's source for the hero in his opera, the valiant dragon-slayer Siegfried of the German medieval poem *Das Nibelungenlied.* Porter loathed Wagner, whom she described as "a loud and noisy charlatan, a shell-game man, a rotter" (*Letters* 207). She said he became for her, "with Nietzsche and Schopenhauer, a part of Hitler's Germany" (*Letters* 208). That description applies equally to Porter's portrayal of Siegfried Rieber, no less offensive for his antic buffoonery, but she also provides a glimpse into the degree of Rieber's failure by simultaneously reminding the reader of the brave, martyred slayer of dragons in an heroic age.

Dr. Schumann's name, which Porter changed from "Sacher" during the course of her novel's composition, is a reference to the German composer Robert Schumann (1810-1856). In some ways the doctor's alignment with the Romantic German composer is perfectly logical, for he is part of that Romanticized past, his dueling scar a symbol of what Porter quoted a young poet in Germany describing to her as the "old soft-headed Germany." Porter obviously preferred the past poets to the "new race of poets, tough and quick, like . . . prize fighters" ("Notes on Writing," *Collected Essays* 443). Dr. Schumann is the most moral character in Porter's novel, despite his failings, because he has more insight into the human condition than the others and because, as he develops increasing self-awareness, he learns the meaning of love, the sources of evil, and the limits of a Romantic view of life.

Herr Wilibald Graf, the frail dying man who is a sexually repressed sadist and a religious fanatic convinced he has the power of healing, finally abandons his prayer to be enfolded in the arms of God and replaces it with a prayer for oblivion. His name is an allusion to one of Porter's favorite artists, the Swiss Renaissance painter and printmaker Urs Graf, whose works she also studied in Basel in 1932. Graf's sincere religious beliefs and humility in the face of his human failings made him a natural choice for representing a moral ideal juxtaposed to the perverted piety of the messianic Wilibald Graf.

Two other characters bear names of highly celebrated artists, but the names in these instances are used to draw a satiric parallel instead of a satiric contrast. The name of Wilhelm Freytag, one of the most complex characters in the novel, is very likely an allusion to the German novelist and playwright Gustav Freytag (1816-1895), said to be repelled by both the democratic radicalism of the *Jungdeutschen* and the escapism of the Romantics. His fame was established with his 1854 comedy *Die Journalisten*, and he achieved international renown with his widely translated 1855 novel *Soll und Haben* and with *Die Technik des Dramas* (1863), a critical textbook in which he explained a system for dramatic structure later named "Freytag's Pyramid." *Soll und Haben*, however, also anticipated the Nazi state of the next century by depicting Poles and Jews as inferior "colonists" whose land should be seized and whose language and culture should be eradicated by the German master race.

Gustav Freytag's literary representative, Wilhelm Freytag in *Ship of Fools*, is devoted to a paternalistic social hierarchy. In a scene in which Jenny Brown is dancing with one of the Cuban students, Freytag smiles at her condescendingly and asks, "Tell me, you should know this, do all women prefer thugs and *maquereaux*, and guttersnipes at heart? What is this strange feminine taste for lowness? *La nostalgie de la boue*?" (436). But his chauvinism goes beyond gender to nation. "He knew he was altogether German, a legitimate son of that powerful German strain able to destroy all foreign blood in its own veins and make all pure and German once more; and the whole world had been for him merely a hunting ground, a foraging place, a territory of profitable sojourn until the day should come when he would go home for good, having never been away in his soul. Wherever he had been, he had felt German ground under his feet and German sky over his head; there was no other country for him" (134). And, ironically, among many others on board the *Vera*, he is anti-Semitic, despite the fact that he himself is the object of anti-Semitic hatred and cruelty when his wife's Jewishness is revealed. Below the love he professes for his wife lies a racial hatred comparable to that revealed in Gustav Freytag's *Soll und Haben*.

Etchegaray, the Basque woodcarver who loses his life saving the bulldog Bébé, is the namesake of José Etchegaray, one of the leading Spanish dramatists of the last part of the nineteenth century. Although José Etchegaray's early work was heavily Romantic, under the influence of Henrik Ibsen he turned to social realism and problem plays. With the Provençal poet Frédéric Mistral, he was awarded the Nobel Prize for literature in 1904. Porter's Etchegaray is a true artist, frustrated and depressed beyond imagination when his carving knife is confiscated and he no longer can fulfill his artistic impulse. His jumping overboard to save the drowning dog costs him his life, which has become meaningless to him as a stifled artist. In this instance, Porter is drawing a parallel between two artists equal in their adherence to the artistic spirit, one a simple primitive woodcarver unrecognized by the world and the other a playwright celebrated by the world.

Many reviewers of *Ship of Fools* remarked on the microcosmic quality of Porter's ship and its passengers and its mirror reflection of humanity. Mark Schorer's review in *The New York Times Book Review*—"We're All on the Passenger List"—established the thesis. Although Porter had written in her prefatory note in the novel, "I am a passenger on that ship," neither Schorer nor anyone else at the time knew just how much she was in fact present or how much of her life was integrated in it. Four years after the publication of the novel, in a letter to Dayton Kohler, Porter expanded on her statement: "The question most often asked me by students and random readers is. . . 'Where are you in the book? Which character do you represent?' My answer is considered either flippant and evasive or just downright deception: I tell them that I am everybody on board ship from the sea-sick bull dog to the Captain on the bridge, the fat man in the cherry-colored shirt who sang and made mischief, the deported sugar workers in the steerage—in fact, I am the ship, too, and I suspect, even the ocean and the islands in the sea—for I wrote the book, and all of my living substance is in it—all I had to give at the time" (*Selected Letters* 314). [7]

Scholars have not applied that abstract aesthetic concept to an analysis of *Ship of Fools* beyond illustrating the way the long novel encloses and summarizes Porter's short fiction and identifying Jenny Brown, Mary Treadwell, Frau Rittersdorf, and La Condesa as autobiographical characters of varying degrees. No one recognized the full extent of the Swiftian satire in the characters Porter created as private jokes that also served as revenge on real persons or the fact that Porter was holding herself up to ridicule as well.

The name of Herr Julius Löwenthal clearly suggests Walter Lowenfels, an expatriate poet, playwright, and editor of the *Communist Daily Worker*, whom Porter ridiculed by associating him with her persecuted Jew who cynically sells Christian artifacts to the Christians. "There's money in it" (96), he says. Walter Lowenfels was in the news in 1932 while Porter was in Basel and Paris. In August 1932 he filed a lawsuit against the authors, composers, and producers of the Broadway hit *Of Thee I Sing*, charging they plagiarized several hundred elements in his unproduced play *U.S.A.* and simply added music. Among the defendants in the plagiarism suit were George B. Kaufman, George and Ira Gershwin, and Irving Berlin. In December Judge John Woolsey dismissed the case and ordered Lowenfels to pay costs, including attorney fees, for having brought a frivolous lawsuit.[8]

Porter met Lowenfels in Paris early in 1933. She didn't like him or his poetry, which was heavily political. After Henry Miller presented a thinly disguised Lowenfels as the poet Cronstadt in *Tropic of Cancer*, Porter remarked that she would have thought better of Miller if he hadn't mistaken Lowenfels for a poet. She was also angry with Lowenfels for trying to use her name to gain entrée to her friend and patron, the wealthy heiress Barbara Harrison.[9] Although she had sympathy for Lowenfels when in the 1950s he was among American Communists persecuted by the witch-hunting House Un-American Activities Committee, her sympathy wasn't enough to keep her from using an easily identifiable version of his name for one of her fools. [10] It was also her counter to Miller, a comeuppance to him as well as to Lowenfels.

Other characters represented in the novel are more personal to Porter, in particular former lovers, ex-husbands, and at least one member of her family. Porter always had an adversarial relationship with her younger sister, Mary Alice, named for their dead mother but always called "Baby," even as an adult. Porter envied Baby for her beauty in childhood (and mocked her morbid obesity in adulthood). Convinced that Baby was their father's favorite, as she seemed in fact to be, Porter tried all her life to elicit from their father some expression of love and approval equal to what he lavished on Baby. Her joke on Baby, who bred Boston bulldogs,[11] was to make the dog in the novel a bulldog and name him "Baby," or rather, "Bébé," the French form of the name.

Another member of the Zarzuela troupe, Pancho, bears the common nickname for "Francisco" and points directly to Francisco Aguilera, Porter's 1924 Chilean lover who is generally credited with fathering the child she delivered stillborn in December of that year. When she ran into him in Washington, D. C. in 1942 she told her friend Marcella Winslow she was "madly in love with him once and almost murdered him" (60). The eventual murder was literary, as she made him a very minor character—and a pimp—in *Ship of Fools.*

One other former lover was handled more gently. Felipe Carillo, governor of Yucatán, was briefly Porter's lover in Mexico in 1920 and 1921. Although she seemed always to have a lingering affection for him, she felt betrayed when he became engaged to another American woman, the journalist Alma Reed. Carillo was assassinated, however, before he could marry Alma. Porter told John Dorsey that Carillo was "as civil and gentle a man as I ever saw" (Givner, *Conversations* 148), but she retaliated against him—and Alma—by making him a celibate (and an ineffectual priest) in *Ship of Fools.*

Of Porter's five known husbands, only her fifth husband, Albert Erskine, escaped her satirist knife. Her fourth husband, Eugene Pressly, although not represented by name, is the model for David Scott, described in images of coldness and death throughout *Ship of Fools.* Reminders of her first three husbands, John Henry Koontz, Otto Taskett, and Carl von Pless, abound in the names Johann, Otto, and Karl, either actually aboard the *Vera* as passengers or as former husbands or lovers recalled or imagined by female passengers. Herr Graf's nephew Johann is a cruel, sex-starved youth who feels mostly contempt for his sickly and parsimonious uncle. Karl Baumgartner is a hopeless drunkard, and Karl Glocken is a hunchback. Both Frau Rittersdorf and Frau Schmitt mourn dead husbands named Otto. Porter's most scathing portrayal, however, is reserved for her first husband, John Henry Koontz, although she does not rely on his name to carry the satire. The character William Denny is J. H. Koontz in very thin disguise.

Porter married Koontz when she was barely sixteen years old, and according to the divorce decree nine years later in 1915, the marriage was marked by his serial infidelity, his predilection for prostitutes, and his routine physical abuse of Porter that resulted in her bloody nose, broken bones, and hospitalizations. Mrs. Treadwell, one of the most autobiographical characters in the novel, muses at one point, "Was I really ever married to a man so jealous he beat me until I bled at the nose?" (208). The fictional character William Denny began as a conflation of two men who were actually passengers with Porter on the *Werra*, which sailed from Veracruz, Mexico, to Bremerhaven, Germany, in August of 1931. According to a letter Porter wrote to Caroline Gordon as a kind of log she kept during the voyage, one of the men was a young engineer from Kenedy, Texas, and the other was an oculist from Corpus Christi, Texas. She told Gordon that the engineer was "nice," but she quoted the oculist's angry condemnation of "dirty Bolsheviks" and sarcastically told Gordon, "He represents a great part of whatever enlightenment that place has to offer" (*Letters* 48).

William Denny, the supreme bigot, is much more despicable than the two real-life Texans. Intolerant of every place, belief, or culture that is not his own narrow one, Denny longs for a return to Brownsville, Texas, "where a man knew who was who and what was what, and niggers, crazy Swedes, Jews, greasers, bone-headed micks, polacks, wops, Guineas and damn Yankees knew their place and stayed in it" (333-334). Considered physically disgusting by his cabin mate, David Scott, Denny routinely reads "a fully illustrated clothbound book entitled *Recreational Aspects of Sex as Mental Prophylaxis*, with the subtitle *A Guide to True Happiness in Life*. After becoming roaring drunk and trying to arrange for the services of the dancer-prostitute Pastora for the lowest possible fee, he mistakenly goes to Mrs. Treadwell's cabin instead of Pastora's, seizing her gown and calling her "Whore" while threatening to break every bone in her body. When she pushes him so hard he falls against the wall and slumps to the floor unconscious, she beats him furiously with the stiletto heel of her shoe until his face is a bloody pulp of little horned moons. Stanley

Edgar Hyman, in a review of *Ship of Fools* in *The New Leader*, recognized the satire in the Texan Denny, remarking that "the scene in which Mrs. Treadwell beats the drunken Denny" is her "ghastly valentine to her native state" (24). It actually was her "ghastly valentine" to her abusive first husband, John Henry Koontz.

When Porter described her presence in the novel as "everybody" on board the ship, her statement was not interpreted to include the many ways in which she held herself up to exposure and ridicule. It is easy enough to see that Jenny Brown is very much based on a younger Porter, and Jenny's love affair with David Scott represents the doomed relationship of Porter and Eugene Pressly. But while some critics recognized autobiographical elements in the character Mrs. Treadwell, at the time of the novel's publication no one knew the full extent of the biographical relevance. The identities of Porter's first three husbands had not been revealed, and Mrs. Treadwell's musings about an abusive former husband had not been linked specifically to Porter.[12] Porter's disclosing the savagery under the surface of Mrs. Treadwell's decorum was a deep probe into the violence within herself, a subject Porter had treated in her 1955 essay "Adventure in Living." Frau Rittersdorf, however, conveys Porter's harshest self-ridicule. Although there are significant differences between Porter and Frau Rittersdorf, they share former husbands named Otto, and Frau Rittersdorf sends herself flowers from fictional lovers named Johann and Karl and muses about a Mexican lover not unlike Felipe Carillo. Whether Frau Rittersdorf's meandering thoughts about euthanasia for defective children is Porter's confronting her guilt over a 1921 abortion in Mexico can't be ascertained. But Frau Rittersdorf also keeps a diary in which she records sordid details about her fellow passengers that is another version of the notes posted on the bulletin board by the Zarzuela dancers and perhaps another version of exactly what Porter is doing in *Ship of Fools* by unmasking herself as well as others, even if it is, in her case, under the banner of art.

Many reviewers and critics recognized the presence of satire in Porter's *Ship of Fools*, but no one fully understood its range or the necessity of its function within a modernist frame.[13] In fact, those who faulted the novel, including Booth, commonly cited—as proof of failure—the absence of plot, the rapid movement from one scene to another, and an overabundance of thinly developed characters, unchanged in the course of the voyage and remaining for the most part caricatures. Those traits, however, are precisely what critic Alvin P. Kernan identified as the traditional components of classic satire: a plotless narrative with rapidly shifting and crowded scenes peopled with multiple characters who create "the effect of a disordered world in which there is a limitless amount of depravity" and a pessimistic satirist "dedicated to truth" (273). Instead of plot there is a stasis between satirist and fools. "Fundamentally," Kernan writes, "we are looking at the same world, and the same fools, and the same satirist we met at the opening of the work" (271).

No careful reader of *Ship of Fools* can argue that the novel is based on a tightly woven plot driven by the development of an ordinary number of characters or that the ironic narrative voice is reluctant to point out painful truths and ugly deceptions. The opening of the novel, a prologue set in Veracruz, Mexico, prior to the sailing of the ship, reveals the passengers' alienation from one another despite their shared circumstances:

> This common predicament did not by any means make of them fellow sufferers. On the contrary, each chose to maintain his pride and separateness within himself. After ignoring each other during the first feverish hours, there crept into eyes meeting unwillingly, for the twentieth time, a look of unacknowledged, hostile recognition. "So there you are again, I never saw you before in my life," the eyes said, flickering away and settling stubbornly upon their own matters. The travelers witnessed each other's humiliations, rehearsed their private business in everybody's hearing, answered embarrassing questions again and again for some sticky little clerk to write down once more. They paused in small groups before the same sights, read signs aloud

> in chorus, asked questions of the same passers-by, but no bond was established between them. (11)

Twenty-eight days later, after sexual encounters, cruelties, intrigues, deaths, a few epiphanies, and at least one discovery of love, the passengers arrive at Bremerhaven, their destination: "Eyes met eyes again vaguely, almost without recognition and no further speech. They were becoming strangers again, though not suspicious and hostile as at first. It was a pleasant indifference to everything but the blessed moment of escape to life once more" (494).

Some critics have argued (myself included) that Mrs. Treadwell, Jenny Brown, and Dr. Schumann are among the passengers who take steps toward self-awareness during the voyage. Mrs. Treadwell discovers the violence within herself, Jenny discovers what love is *not*, and Dr. Schumann discovers the irrationality of love and the apathy that underlies evil. But the illuminations are fleeting and do not lead to significant change. Most of the passengers, Porter's fools, refuse to take advantage of the opportunities for acquiring knowledge about themselves or the general human condition.

Porter's shifting and circling focus, moving from one fool to another, requires the characters to be largely caricatures, drawn with the broad incisive strokes of caricaturists such as Albrecht Dürer, whom Porter discovered in her youth, and José Clemente Orozco and Miguel Covarrubias, both of whom she discovered in Mexico in the early 1920s.[14] Porter introduced her 1925 review of a collection of Covarrubias's drawings by explaining the history of caricature in Mexico:

> In Mexico there is a well seasoned tradition of fine caricature: almost every one of the younger painters possessed this lacerating gift. It goes with the Mexican aptitude for deadly discernment of the comic in the other person, together with each man's grave regard for his own proper dignity. In arguments, whether personal or political, they resort early to popular songs and cartoons that carry sharper fangs than any other sort of debate. They have

> a charming habit of disregarding the main point at issue long enough to call attention to some defect or weakness, preferably an irremediable one, in the opponent. ("¡Ay, Que Chamaco!," *"This Strange, Old World"* 39)

Porter called Covarrubias's drawings "keen satirical comment" (40).

It is true that caricature was first associated with exaggeration in the visual arts, but it has expanded to include literary modes, largely due to the influence of Charles Baudelaire, who wrote three essays on the essence of caricature while incorporating the technique in his poetry.[15] Michele Hannoosh argues that Baudelaire "offers the theory of a radically new principle: the status of comic art, and notably caricature, as a 'high' art, one especially well suited to the paradoxes and contradictions of the modern temperament" (11). As Hannoosh interprets Baudelaire's theory, caricature captures the dualism of human existence, embodying simultaneously the incongruity of the ephemeral and eternal, the ugly and beautiful, the particular and universal (253).

Dürer's caricatures emerged from his early anatomical drawings, which provided the beginning point for exaggeration of a physical feature to make a symbolic or allegorical point. Other caricaturists incorporated plants into their drawings of humans, and in Mexico animals became a favorite source for representing dualism and contradictions and revealing the true character behind the mask. Porter appropriately sets up the basis for her caricature in the opening frame in Veracruz, where an anthropomorphized dog, cat, monkey, and parrot fight among themselves and Veracruzanos observe the passengers with condescension, labeling them with such names as "burros" "monkeys," and "quarreling birds." One nameless passenger they describe as a peahen, another as "pig-snouted." The narrative voice picks up the comparisons and sustains them throughout the novel, while many of the passengers apply similar tags to one another.

Porter's employment of caricature perfectly conforms to Baudelaire's definition, and it is no accident that Porter chose for the epigraph to

Part I, "Embarkation," an ironic question drawn from Baudelaire's *Fusées* (1897): "*Quand partons-nous vers le Bonheur*?"—"When do we set sail for Happiness?" Once under sail, the passengers believe they are en route to a place better than the one they left. The German passengers and crewmembers believe they are going "home" to happiness and security. The profound irony lies in the historical hindsight with which the novel is imbued from beginning to end: In 1931 all of them are going to the near collapse of modern civilization. It is as if Porter, in directing the reader to Baudelaire at the outset, wanted to underscore the satire and the concomitant caricature in her modern novel.

*

I would answer then in this way the question posed in the title of this essay: Yes, *Ship of Fools* is really a novel, and not a failed one when it is examined in light of Porter's aim and the requirements of modernism. We also can take issue with Booth, who declared that Porter's novel was "not quite Leavis's idea of what a novel ought to be," by pointing out that Leavis, an early supporter of Pound and Eliot and a proponent of the modernist aesthetic, set the standard for greatness as those novelists who showed an intense "moral interest" in life. Surely Porter and *Ship of Fools* meet that standard. But it is Leavis's further explanation that is especially important here. That "moral interest," he argued throughout *The Great Tradition*, would determine the nature of the fictional form, a concession that becomes in effect a defense of Porter's own position on the indivisible link between form and content and a proof of Porter's alignment with Pound, Baudelaire, and other modernists. The remaining parts of the question are equally easy to answer. Porter's satire is classic, and part of it is indeed Juvenalian, aimed at herself as well as at persons on whom she wants to exact revenge. And, yes, there are private jokes embedded in her satire.

NOTES

1. Janis Stout in Chapter Nine ("*Ship of Fools* and the Problem of Genre") of her book *Katherine Anne Porter: A Sense of the Times* seems to agree with Booth that *Ship of Fools* is not a novel in the conventional sense. "Dangerous as it is to hazard a statement on what a novel should be or do," Stout writes, "one can surely say that in general a novel should develop ideas or characters in such a way that the reader experiences them as evolving or growing. There should be a sense of discovery, both for the reader and within the experiences of the characters as it is presented" (215).
2. For an account of Porter's three-part autobiographical novel with the working title "Many Redeemers" see Unrue, *Katherine Anne Porter: The Life of an Artist* 113, 118, 140, 144, 147, 151, 155, and 162.
3. Although Porter agreed with Eliot on aesthetic matters, she had disagreements with some of his religious views. See Porter, "Notes on a Criticism of Thomas Hardy." Pound's mantra was also the title of his book *Make It New*, a collection of essays on aspects of modernism.
4. Porter told Cleanth Brooks, "I could love Yeats if only because he loved Dean Swift. I am apt to be fond of persons who are fond of (1) St. Augustine. (2) St. Francis. (3) Joan of Arc. (4) Sir Thomas More. (5) Dr. Johnson. (6) Dean Swift" (*Selected Letters*, 166).
5. See, for example, Murphy, 88.
6. See Fest.
7. Nearly a decade earlier, commenting on Willa Cather's relationship to the characters in her short stories, Porter said, "She was not Paul in travesty, nor the opera singer in 'The Diamond Mine,' nor that girl with the clear eyes who became an actress: above all, not the Lost Lady. Of course she was all of them. How not? She made all of them out of herself, where else could they have taken on life?" ("Reflections on Willa Cather," *Collected Essays*, 35-36.)
8. See "Must Pay for Suit on 'Of Thee I Sing'" and "Play 'Of Thee I Sing' In Plagiarism Suit."
9. An unpublished letter from Lowenfels to Porter, 11 June 1933, is essentially a defense of what he regarded as Porter's unfair charge. Katherine Anne Porter Papers, The University of Maryland, College Park.

10. See "Alleged Communist Leaders Are Held in $175,000 Bail," "[Eight] in Philadelphia Indicted as Reds," and "[Nine] Reds Get Jail in Pennsylvania."
11. Not a pure breed; rather a cross between a Boston Terrier and the English Bulldog.
12. Joan Givner (*Life*) discovered the identity of Porter's first husband, John Henry Koontz, but she mistakenly identified Ernest Stock as Porter's second husband and did not discover the third, Carl von Pless.
13. Jon Spence has been the only critic to address specifically the satire in *Ship of Fools.* Primarily a study of the characters in the novel, his essay also focuses on animal imagery and the degree to which Porter's satire, like Swift's, succeeds in holding a mirror up to humans, who discover everyone else in the looking-glass except themselves.
14. Joan Givner was the first Porter scholar to write specifically about Porter's use of caricature as a technique (See "Katherine Anne Porter and the Art of Caricature"). See also Thomas F. Walsh's survey of the Mexican art of caricature in *Katherine Anne Porter and Mexico: The Illusion of Eden.* Walsh writes, "If Porter didn't learn the art of caricature in Mexico, then she sharpened her satiric skills there in several art forms" (66).
15. Baudelaire's three essays on caricature are *De l'essence du rire et généralement du comique dans les arts plastiques* (1855); *Quelques caricaturistes français* (1857); and *Quelques caricaturistes étrangers* (1857). Ainslie Armstrong McLees complements Hannoosh's study by tracing the origin and development of Baudelaire's theory and use of caricature.

WORKS CITED

"Alleged Communist Leaders Are Held in $175,000 Bail." *New York Times*, 31 July 1953, 9.

Booth, Wayne C. "Yes, But Are They Really Novels?" *Yale Review* 51 (Summer 1962): 630-637.

Borch, Herbert von. "'Die Deutschen sind alzumal grausam, böse und fanatisch': Dokument des Hasses: K. A. Porter's 'Narrenschiff.'" *Die Welt*, 9 June 1962. No. 133.

Dorsey, John. "Katherine Anne Porter on. . . ." *Baltimore Sun Magazine*, 26 Oct. 1969, 16. Rpt. in Givner, *Conversations* 139-154.

"[Eight] in Philadelphia Indicted as Reds." *New York Times*, 4 Aug. 1953, 11.

Eliot, T. S. "Tradition and the Individual Talent." *The Sacred Wood: Essays on Poetry and Criticism*. London: Methuen & Co., 1920.

Fest, Joachim. *Plotting Hitler's Death: The Story of the German Resistance*, trans. Bruce Little. New York: Henry Holt, 1996.

Givner, Joan, ed. *Katherine Anne Porter: Conversations*. Jackson: University Press of Mississippi, 1987.

Givner, Joan. *Katherine Anne Porter: A Life*. New York: Simon and Schuster, 1982.

———. "Katherine Anne Porter and the Art of Caricature." *Genre* 5 (1972): 511-560.

Hannoosh, Michele. *Baudelaire and Caricature: From the Comic to an Art of Modernity*. University Park: Pennsylvania State University Press, 1992.

Hartley, Lodwick. "Dark Voyagers: A Study of Katherine Anne Porter's *Ship of Fools*." *University Review* 30 (Winter 1962): 83-94.

Hyman, Stanley Edgar. "Archetypal Woman Archetypal Germans." *New Leader*, 2 April 1962, 23-24.

Kauffmann, Stanley. "Katherine Anne Porter's Crowning Work." *New Republic* 146 (2 April 1962): 23-25.

Kazin, Alfred. *Bright Book of Life: American Novelists and Storytellers from Hemingway to Mailer*. Boston: Little, Brown/Atlantic Monthly, 1973.

Kernan, Alvin P. "A Theory of Satire." *Satire: Modern Essays in Criticism*, ed. Ronald Paulson. Englewood Cliffs, NJ: Prentice-Hall, 1971. 249-78

Leavis, F. R. *The Great Tradition*. London: Chatto & Windus, 1948.

Liberman, M. M. "The Responsibility of the Novelist: The Critical Reception of *Ship of Fools*." *Criticism* 8 (Fall 1966): 377-88.

Lowenfels, Walter, to Katherine Anne Porter, 11 June 1933. Unpublished TLS. The Katherine Anne Porter Papers, University of Maryland, College Park.

McLees, Ainslie Armstrong. *Baudelaire's "argot plastique": Poetic Caricature and Modernism*. Athens: University of Georgia Press, 1989.

"Must Pay for Suit on 'Of Thee I Sing.'" *New York Times*, 29 Dec. 1932, p. 17.

Murphy, Edward. "Book Reviews: [*Ship of Fools*]." *Ramparts* 1 (Nov. 1962): 88-91.

Newquist, Roy. "An Interview with Katherine Anne Porter." *McCall's* 92 (Aug. 1965): 88. Rpt. Givner, *Conversations* 99-119.

"[Nine] Reds Get Jail in Pennsylvania." *New York Times*, 21 June 1955, 12.

"Play 'Of Thee I Sing' in Plagiarism Suit." *New York Times*, 9 Aug. 1932, 20.

Porter, Katherine Anne. "Adventure in Living." *Mademoiselle* 41 (July 1955): 28-34. Rpt. as "St. Augustine and the Bullfight" in *Collected Essays and Occasional Wrtings of Katherine Anne Porter*, 91-101.

———. "Ay, Que Chamaco." *New Republic* 45 (23 Dec. 1925): 141-42; Rpt. in *"This Strange, Old World" and Other Book Reviews by Katherine Anne Porter* 39-41.

———. *The Collected Essays and Occasional Writings of Katherine Anne Porter*. New York: Delacorte, 1970.

———. *Letters of Katherine Anne Porter*, ed. Isabel Bayley. New York: Atlantic Monthly Press, 1990.

———. "Notes on a Criticism of Thomas Hardy." *Southern Review* 6 (Summer 1940): 150-161. Rpt. as "On a Criticism of Thomas Hardy" in *The Collected Essays and Occasional Writings of Katherine Anne Porter* 3-13.

———. "Notes on Writing—From the Journal of Katherine Anne Porter." In *New Directions in Prose and Poetry*, ed. James Laughlin. Norfolk, Conn.:

New Directions, 1940, pp. 195-204. Rpt. in *The Collected Essays and Occasional Writings of Katherine Anne Porter* 442-450.

———. "Reflections on Willa Cather." *Mademoiselle* 35 (July 1953): 62-65, 102-104. Rev. and rpt. in *The Collected Essays and Occasional Writings of Katherine Anne Porter* 29-39.

———. *Selected Letters of Katherine Anne Porter: Chronicles of a Modern Woman*, ed. Darlene Harbour Unrue. Jackson: University Press of Mississippi, 2012.

———. *Ship of Fools.* Boston: Little, Brown, 1962.

———. *"This Strange, Old World" and Other Book Reviews by Katherine Anne Porter*, ed. Darlene Harbour Unrue. Athens: University of Georgia Press, 1991.

———. "Transplanted Writers: A Symposium." *Books Abroad* 16 (July 1942): 274. Rpt. as "1942: Transplanted Writers" in *The Collected Essays and Occasional Writings of Katherine Anne Porter*, 458-459.

———. "Yours, Ezra Pound" [rev. of *The Letters of Ezra Pound, 1907-1941*, ed. D. D. Paige]. *New York Herald Times Book Review*, 29 Oct. 1950, 4, 26. Rpt. as "It Is Hard to Stand in the Middle" in *The Collected Essays and Occasional Writings of Katherine Anne Porter* 40-46.

Pound, Ezra. *Make It New: Essays by Ezra Pound.* London: Faber and Faber, 1934.

Schorer, Mark. "We're All on the Passenger List." *New York Times Book Review*, 1 April 1962, 1, 5.

Solotaroff, Theodore. "*Ship of Fools* and the Critics." *Commentary* 34 (October 1962): 277-86.

Spence, Jon. "Looking-Glass Reflections: Satirical Elements in *Ship of Fools.*" *Sewanee Review* 82 (Spring 1974): 316-30.

Stout, Janis P. *Katherine Anne Porter: A Sense of the Times.* Charlottesville: University Press of Virginia, 1995.

Thompson, Barbara. "The Art of Fiction XXIX—Katherine Anne Porter: An Interview." *Paris Review* 8 (Winter-Spring 1963): 87-114. Rpt. Givner, *Conversations* 78-98.

Thompson, John. "The Figure in the Rose Red Gown." *Partisan Review* 29 (Fall 1962); 608-612.

Unrue, Darlene Harbour. *Katherine Anne Porter: The Life of an Artist.* Jackson: University Press of Mississippi, 2005.

Walsh, Thomas F. *Katherine Anne Porter and Mexico: The Illusion of Eden.* Austin: University of Texas Press, 1992.

West, Ray B. *Katherine Anne Porter.* University of Minnesota Pamphlets on American Writers, No. 28. Minneapolis: University of Minnesota Press, 1963.

Winslow, Marcella Comès. *Brushes with the Literary: Letters of a Washington Artist 1943-1959.* Baton Rouge: Louisiana State University Press, 1993.

Notes on Contributors

Thomas Austenfeld is Professor of American Literature at the University of Fribourg, Switzerland.

Jewel Spears Brooker is Professor of English Literature emerita at Eckerd College, Florida.

Dimiter Daphinoff is Professor of English Literature at the University of Fribourg, Switzerland.

Joachim Knape is Professor of Rhetoric at the University of Tübingen, Germany.

Beth Alvarez is Curator of Literary Manuscripts emerita at the University of Maryland at College Park.

Robert H. Brinkmeyer, Jr. is Emily Brown Jefferies Professor of English and Director of the Institute for Southern Studies at the University of South Carolina in Columbia, S.C.

Christine Hait is Professor of English at Columbia College in Columbia, S.C.

Anne-Marie Scholz is Adjunct Professor of American Studies at the University of Konstanz, Germany.

Alexandra Subramanian is Adjunct Professor of English at California Lutheran University in Thousand Oaks, California.

Joseph Kuhn is Professor of American Literature at the Adam Mickiewicz University in Poznan, Poland.

Darlene Harbour Unrue is Professor of English emerita at the University of Nevada at Las Vegas.

Index

Abels, Cyrilly, 86, 98, 103
Academy Awards, 131–132, 137
Accent, 85, 90
Agamben, Giorgio, 195
Agrarians, 192
Aguilera, Francisco, 223
allegory, 5, 12, 31–33, 40, 46, 59–60, 64, 134, 188, 214–216
Allegory of Intemperance, The (Bosch), 31–33, 40
All the King's Men, 190
anti-Semitism, 35, 119, 154, 196, 204
Arendt, Hannah, 202
Ashley, Elizabeth, 150
Atlantic Monthly, 95–96, 101
Atlantic Monthly Press, 14, 172
Augustine of Hippo, 4–5, 14, 18, 22, 25, 28, 191, 201–202, 205, 230
Austenfeld, Thomas, 1, 5, 20, 49, 136, 145–146, 185

"Baby" (Mary Alice Porter Hillendahl), 222
Barclay, Alexander, 6, 46, 53, 56, 68, 79, 127, 134
Basel, Switzerland, 6, 17, 38, 53, 56, 67, 69, 71–74, 218–219, 222
Baudelaire, Charles, 228–229, 231
Berlin, Porter's sojourn in, 38, 152, 158–159, 164, 174, 185, 188, 206–207, 222
Booth, Wayne, 2, 14, 79, 213–214, 226, 229–230
Bosch, Hieronymus, 8, 31–33, 40, 46
Brace, Donald, 86–88, 100, 102
Brant, Sebastian, 5–8, 20, 31–35, 38, 45–46, 49–50, 53–54, 56–66, 69, 71–74, 79–80, 127, 134, 183, 191, 199, 202–203, 205, 207, 215
Brave Soldat Schwejk, Der, 152
Brinkmeyer, Robert H., 3, 9, 27, 113, 128, 135–136, 140–142
Brown, Jenny, 11, 19, 89, 92–93, 95, 98, 101, 116, 180, 182, 220–221, 225, 227
Brüning, Heinrich, 187

Campbell, Mrs. Marion, 172
caricature, 18–19, 24, 227–229, 231
Carillo, Felipe, 223, 225
Catholicism, 118, 121, 124, 199
children, according to St. Augustine, 22, 25, 28
civil rights movement, 143
Condesa, La, 9–10, 12, 23, 90–91, 94–95, 100, 115–116, 118, 121, 123–124, 138–142, 171, 180, 201–202, 204, 221
Covarrubias, Miguel, 227–228
Cowley, Malcolm, 38

Danielson, Barbara Deering, 172
Denny, William, 88, 93, 181, 223–224
Dietrich, Marlene, 138, 206
"Downward Path to Wisdom, The", 179–180
Dubliners, 215
Dunn, Michael, 151, 156, 158, 165

Dürer, Albrecht, 38, 227–228

East Germany, 150, 157–158, 161
Eco, Umberto, 12
écriture automatique, 51
Eichmann, Adolf, trial of, 130, 145
Eliot, T. S., 12, 27, 192, 214, 229–230
Enchiridion (*Handbook of the Christian Soldier*), 20–21
Encomium Moriae (*The Praise of Folly*), 40
Erasmus, Desiderius, 5, 8, 17–22, 24–25, 28, 32–33, 38, 40–45, 215
Erskine, Albert, 10, 86, 170–171, 223
Etchegaray, José, 182, 220
Eve of Destruction, The, 143
eugenics, 3, 155

fascism, 3, 150, 152, 159, 161–162
Fathers, Sam, 114, 116, 120
Faulkner, William, 9, 113–114, 120–121, 145, 214
Ferrer, José, 150, 154, 159, 161
"Flowering Judas", 21, 207–208
Folly (narrator of *Praise of Folly*), 8, 17–22, 25–26, 28, 32, 35, 38–46, 135, 140, 142, 215–217
Foucault, Michel, 59, 80
Freud, Sigmund, 20, 25, 27
Freytag, Gustav, 219–220
Freytag, Wilhelm (character in novel), 89, 153, 189, 194, 219–220

"Gay" (Anna Gay Porter Holloway), 173, 185
Genette, Gérard, 55, 63, 80
Givner, Joan, 20, 146, 185, 215–216, 223, 231
Glocken, Karl, 161, 223
as chorus, 141, 151, 155–156, 158
Go Down, Moses, 113–114
Golden Bough (Frazer), 27
Gordon, Caroline, 2, 192, 224
Graf, Urs, 219
Graf, Wilibald (character in novel), 38–40, 219
Greco, José, 150

Hansen, Arne, 90, 92
Harper's, 85, 92–95, 97–98
Heidegger, Martin, 11, 194
Herbst, Josephine, 86, 188, 204
Hillendahl, Mary Alice (Baby) Porter, 89, 178, 181, 222
Hitler, Adolf, 2, 127–128, 131, 134, 154, 188, 194, 198–200, 207, 217–218
Holocaust, 5, 10, 128, 130, 132, 143, 145, 160, 205
Holy Roman Empire, 197, 207
Holloway, Anna Gay Porter, 173, 185
Husserl, Edmund, 52, 79
Hutten, Frau, 18, 39, 176–177, 193, 198
Hutten, Professor, 39, 171, 176–177, 192, 194, 200, 207, 218
Hutten, Ulrich von, 218

Judgment at Nuremberg, 128, 130, 137–140, 151–153, 164

Kael, Pauline, 133–135
Kjellin, Alf, 150
Koontz, John Henry, 223, 225, 231
Kramer, Stanley, 2–3, 127, 133, 149–150, 156, 162

Lawrence, Seymour, 2, 11, 27, 86, 101, 169, 172, 185
"Leaning Tower, The", 188
Leavis, F. R., 214, 229
Leigh, Vivien, 131, 150
Little, Brown (publishers), 11, 95, 98, 101
Locher, Jakob, 53, 67, 79–80
Lowenfels, Walter, 221–222, 230
Löwenthal, Herr Julius (character in novel), 221
Luther, Martin, 5, 18, 34
Lutz family, 62, 89–90, 92–93, 207
Lytle, Andrew, 18, 192

Mad Men, 13
Mademoiselle, 85–86, 92, 98–99, 101
"Man in the Tree" , 86
Mann, Abby, 3, 10, 128, 130, 133–134, 137–138, 141, 146, 154, 160, 162
"Marriage Is Belonging", 22, 26
Marvin, Lee, 132, 150
Maryland, University of, Libraries, 85, 164, 185, 230
McCaslin, Ike, 9, 113–114, 117, 120
Mexico, KAP and, 1–2, 27, 65, 91, 149, 188–189, 193, 223–225, 227–228, 231
Mintz, Alan, 130, 145
modernism, 21, 25, 51, 144, 229–230
More, Thomas, 8, 32, 42–45, 55, 92, 100, 215–216, 230
Moria (narrator of *Praise of Folly*), 40–44, 46

Narrenschiff, Das (Brant), 5, 149, 183, 191, 207, 215
Nazi Party (National Socialist Party), 196
"Necessary Enemy, The", 26, 28
Never-Ending Wrong, The, 4–5
Nicolasa, 175, 183
"Noon Wine", 86, 208

"Old Mortality", 21, 86
Olsen, Tillie, 172
Orozco, José Clemente, 227

"Pale Horse, Pale Rider" (short story), 21, 86
Pale Horse, Pale Rider (book), 86
Papen, Franz von, 187, 189, 193
paratexts, 8, 49, 51–55, 64–65, 80
Partisan Review, 85, 89, 97, 216
Patterson, James T., 143–144
Pawnbroker, The, 10, 131–133, 143
peritexts, 51, 55
Peter, Saint, 34
Porter, Katherine Anne, 5–6, 8, 14, 17, 31–32, 35, 38, 40, 45–46, 49–50, 53–54, 58, 64, 95, 113, 127, 141, 146, 152, 164, 171, 183–185, 187, 204–205, 213
- and Catholicism, 199–200
- and education, 2, 18, 21, 23
- and Mexico, 1–2, 27, 65, 91, 149, 188–189, 193, 223–225, 227–228, 231
- and short fiction, 1–3, 7, 11, 18–21, 24, 27–28, 60, 86–88, 129, 134–135, 137–138, 162, 170, 179, 207, 221, 230
- as Southern writer, 7, 9, 144, 190, 192

Pound, Ezra, 214–215, 229–230
Praise of Folly, The, 17–19, 21, 28, 38, 40, 42, 44, 215
Pressly, Eugene, 174, 185, 223, 225
Professor Mamlock, 160

"Promised Land", 86

Republic (Plato), 145, 189
rhetorical analysis, 8, 49, 51–52
Ric and Rac, 8, 23–24, 39, 61–62, 88, 95, 122, 179, 201
Rieber, Herr Siegfried, 218
Rittersdorf, Frau, 12, 23, 88, 93, 99, 118, 189–190, 199, 205, 221, 223, 225
Roney, Lisa, 3, 142
"Rope", 4
Rühmann, Heinz, 151–153, 156, 158–159, 164

Sacco and Vanzetti, 4
satire, 4, 8, 12, 17–19, 35, 45, 134, 149, 191, 213–214, 216, 218, 221, 223, 225–226, 229, 231
Schmidtmer, Christiane, 150, 158, 161
Schmitt, Carl, 11, 194, 206
Schmitt, Frau, 40–41, 89–90, 93, 122, 183–184, 194, 198–199, 206, 223
Schorer, Mark, 137, 145–146, 221
Schumann, Dr., 9, 11, 18, 23–24, 39, 62, 98, 113–119, 121–125, 138–142, 179, 193, 199, 203–204, 218–219, 227
Scott, David, 88, 90, 93, 97, 180, 182, 223–225
Segal, George, 150
Sewanee Review, 85, 88, 91
Siegfried (German hero), 207, 218
Ship of Fools (film), 2–3, 127–130, 133–135, 137–140, 143, 149–152, 156–159, 161–162
Ship of Fools (novel)
  and allegory, 5, 12, 31–33, 40, 46,

Ship of Fools (novel)
  and allegory (*continued*), 59–60, 64, 134, 188, 214–216
  and publication history. See Alvarez chapter
  and portrayal of Jews, 99, 133, 157, 159
  and portrayal of marriage, 22, 26, 178
  and portrayal of religion, 4, 7–8, 17–19, 45, 134, 149, 214, 216, 221, 223, 225–226, 229, 231
  and satire, 4, 8, 12, 17–19, 35, 45, 134, 149, 191, 213–214, 216, 218, 221, 223, 225–226, 229, 231
  and Texas, 4, 24, 98–101, 200, 215, 224
  and transnational theme, 10, 149–151, 154–155, 158–159, 162–164
Signoret, Simone, 131, 141, 150
Solotaroff, Theodore, 2, 133, 145, 169, 185, 216
Sound of Music, The, 10, 131–133, 145
Spöckenkieker, Lizzi, 11, 90, 95, 99, 118, 161, 196
Spruchgedichte, 57, 60
St. Augustine (Augustine of Hippo), 4, 22, 28, 191, 205, 230
"St. Augustine and the Bullfight", 4, 22, 191
Stout, Janis, 4, 19–20, 129, 145, 185, 230
Swift, Jonathan, 216

T-4 Program, 189, 205
Taylor, Peter, 7
Texas, and Porter, 4, 24, 98–101,

Texas, and Porter (*continued*), 200, 215, 224
Texas Quarterly, 86, 98–101
Thiele, Captain (character in novel), 11, 189, 193–194, 217
Thiele, General Fritz, 217
Third Reich, 153, 161, 187, 189–190, 199–200
Titus, Mary, 27, 141–142, 146
totalitarianism, 136
Treadwell, Mrs., 39, 89, 93, 97, 99, 122–123, 150, 171, 175–177, 224–225, 227

Unrue, Darlene Harbour, 4, 12, 21, 131, 136, 141–142, 146, 185, 213, 230
Utopia (More), 42–43

Vera, 5, 11, 23, 35, 61–63, 65–66, 95, 149, 151, 154, 156, 162, 170–172, 179, 182–183, 187, 189, 191–193, 195–198, 217, 220, 223
Veracruz, 2, 6, 89, 91–92, 100, 149, 175, 224, 226, 228
Vietnam, war in, 143

Walsh, Thomas, 18–19, 21, 24, 231
Warren, Robert Penn, 7, 21, 185, 190, 192
Weber, Max, 193
Weimar republic, 187–189, 196, 206
Werner, Oskar, 131, 141, 150
West Germany, 10, 157
"Why I Write About Mexico", 1–2
Wolf, Friedrich, 160

CPSIA information can be obtained at www.ICGtesting.com
Printed in the USA
LVOW09*0350090415

433695LV00009B/51/P

9 781574 415933